BEGINNING COMAL

THE ELLIS HORWOOD SERIES IN
COMPUTERS AND THEIR APPLICATIONS

Series Editor: BRIAN MEEK
Director of the Computer Unit, Queen Elizabeth College, University of London

The series aims to provide up-to-date and readable texts on the theory and practice of computing, with particular though not exclusive emphasis on computer applications. Preference is given in planning the series to new or developing areas, or to new approaches in established areas.

The books will usually be at the level of introductory or advanced undergraduate courses. In most cases they will be suitable as course texts, with their use in industrial and commercial fields always kept in mind. Together they will provide a valuable nucleus for a computing science library.

BEGINNING COMAL

BORGE CHRISTENSEN
Principal Lecturer, Mathematics and Computing
College of Higher Education
Tonder, Denmark

ELLIS HORWOOD LIMITED
Publishers · Chichester

First published in 1982 by
ELLIS HORWOOD LIMITED
Market Cross House, Cooper Street, Chichester,
West Sussex, PO19 1EB, England

*The publisher's colophon is reproduced from
James Gillison's drawing of the ancient Market
Cross, Chichester*

© 1982 B. Christensen/Ellis Horwood Limited

British Library Cataloguing in Publication Data
Christensen, Borge
Beginning COMAL. – (The Ellis Horwood series in
computers and their applications)
1. COMAL (Computer program language)
I. Title
001.64'24   QA76.73.C26

ISBN 0-85312-435-3 (Ellis Horwood Ltd. – Library Edition)

Typeset in Press Roman by Ellis Horwood Ltd.
Printed in Great Britain by R. J. Acford Chichester.

Table of Contents

Foreword

"It is practically impossible to teach good programming to students that have had a prior exposure to BASIC: as potential programmers they are mentally mutilated beyond hope of regeneration."

E. W. Dijkstra.

Programs for computers are of increasing importance and more and more are being written every day. Most of these programs are written to be used in areas where they will influence human life in such matters as economy, health, and culture. The computer extends our linguistic potential; man has always been able to use language to trigger off movements and changes in his environment. But it is only recently that we are now able to leave the traces of our language in tools which, perhaps far away from the place where they were written, then translate the message into action. The consequence may be new knowledge, new potentials, new wealth, but also disasters that may live long in our history. That is why good programming languages are of vital importance.

Furthermore, we must not overlook the fact that programming languages are not only used to control computing machinery but also for the communication of ideas. Programs are of course code for computers, but they are also texts meant to be read by people. This aspect of programming is of growing importance. A program is most likely to be evaluated, adapted, and maintained by persons other than those who wrote it. It is therefore a matter of great concern that programs are easy to read and understand.

The programming language COMAL (COMmon Algorithmic Language) was designed in 1973 by Benedict Loefstedt and myself in order to make life easier and safer for non-computer people who wanted to use computers. We did this by combining the simplicity of BASIC with the power of Pascal.

If you take a close look at BASIC you will see that its simplicity stems mainly from its operative environment, and not from the language itself. In BASIC a beginner can type in one or two statements and have his small program executed immediately by means of one simple command. Line numbers are used to insert, delete, and sequence statements.

You do not need a sophisticated Text Editor or an ambitious Operative System Command Language. Input and output take place in a straightforward way at the terminal.

On the other hand there is no doubt that as a programming language BASIC is hopelessly obsolete. It was never a very good one, but seen from a modern point of view it is a disaster. People who start to learn programming using BASIC may easily be led astray and after some time, find themselves fighting with problems that could be solved with almost no effort if they used a programming language more suited to guiding human thinking.

COMAL includes the gentle operative environment of BASIC and its usual simple statements, such as INPUT, PRINT, LET etc., but it adds to all that a set of statements modelled on Pascal that makes it natural to write well structured programs. Instead of leading people away from the modern, effective way of professional programming, COMAL offers an introduction to this new art.

Several years of experience with COMAL in its homeland, Denmark, has proved that it is easy to learn and yet powerful to use. People get their programming jobs done in a neat and clean way, and those who need to go on to even more powerful languages such as Pascal or Ada, find it natural to do so.

Therefore this book is not only about COMAL; it is also an introduction to structured programming in general.

Borge R. Christensen.

Tonder, Denmark, May 1982

Big deal! What does that mean?

Acknowledgements

To my many friends in Denmark and England who have helped me by participating in discussions or sending me letters about COMAL and structured programming.

In particular I wish to thank Roy Atherton, Bulmershe College, who started COMAL in England, Max Bramer, the Open University, who made some invaluable analysis of the ideas behind COMAL, and Len Lindsay, COMAL Users Group, USA, whose work on a COMAL handbook helped to sort out some dangerous ambiguities in the original definition of the language. My sincere thanks also goes to John Burne, Colleen Kitchen, and Kevin Ryan at Trinity College, Dublin, for encouragement and generous support in having the final definition of the COMAL Kernal set up.

A programming language only comes to life when implemented. Nobody would be able to run the programs in this book without the works of those brilliant young Danes Arne Christensen, Mogens Kjaer, Lars Laursen, and Jens Erik Jensen, who made the implementations of the latest versions of COMAL.

I also thank Mogens Pelle, the manager and owner of Metanic, who had COMAL implemented to be running on all CP/M computers, and to Richard Pawson, then at Commodore, who had COMAL implemented on the CBM computers and made it possible to use the language on a larger scale worldwide, and that ever enthusiastic Nick Green, Commodore UK, who never ceased to back that effort.

My thanks to Brian Meek for adjusting my english and weeding out "Scandinavisms" and for much good advice leading to substantial improvement of both the contents and the style of the book.

1

The computer writes a message

Let us take a look at this line:

25 PRINT "HI, THERE."

The line consists of a **line number** (25) followed by a **statement**, namely

PRINT "HI, THERE."

The statement begins with the **keyword** PRINT and continues with the **string constant**

HI, THERE.

A string constant is a string of characters contained between quotation marks. If you enter the line by typing it in and then press the RETURN key, the COMAL system will **read** it. If it is a legal COMAL statement, it is **stored** in the workspace, and the system is ready to take in another line. If the line for some reason or other is not legal, the system displays an error message, and the line is not stored in the workspace. You first have to correct the error and then press the RETURN key once more.

Exercise 1.1 □
Type in this line

25 PRINT "HI, THERE."

Press the RETURN key when you have finished typing the line. Now type RUN and press the RETURN key. Your COMAL system answers by printing out a text on the screen.
★

When you want the system to **execute** a line which is stored in the workspace, you must type in the **command** RUN.

□ This is a special symbol which means that you will need a computer to complete this exercise

> THE RUN COMMAND CAUSES THE SYSTEM TO EXECUTE LINES IN THE
> WORKSPACE.

When a PRINT statement containing a string constant is executed, the string surrounded by quotes is printed.

> A PRINT STATEMENT IS USED WHEN YOU WANT THE SYSTEM TO PRINT
> OUT STRINGS OF CHARACTERS.

The quote characters are said to **delimit** the string constant and are known as **delimiters**. Note that the quote characters themselves are not displayed by the PRINT statement, and they are not considered to be part of the string constant.

Exercise 1.2
Look at this COMAL line:

        25 PRINT "DEAR PETER,"

What is the number of the line? .... Which keyword does the statement begin

with? .... What will be printed out when the line is executed?

....
★

Exercise 1.3 □
Type in the line from Exercise 1.2 (do not forget to press the RETURN key), and type RUN (and press RETURN). Compare the output with the answer given in 1.2.
★

Exercise 1.4 □
Enter a line numbered 25 that will make the system display the following text on the screen:

        THIS IS A TEXT WRITTEN BY A LINE.

Have your system execute the line and check that the printout is correct.
★

As seen from the exercises you can have the system print out anything you may wish. That means you are the one responsible for whatever results from running the program!

So far we have only allowed the system to execute one line at a time. Of course it can do better than that, but before we go on to see how, we shall learn about yet another command, namely

> NEW

(followed by the usual pressing of the RETURN key). This command clears the workspace of all its contents, returning it to its original state, as if you had just turned the computer on. It should be used each time you start working on a new program in order to avoid getting mixed up with lines already entered.

THE NEW COMMAND CLEARS THE WORKSPACE OF ITS PRESENT CONTENTS.

Exercise 1.5 □

Type NEW (and press RETURN). Then enter these lines

> 20 PRINT "I AM THE FIRST ONE,"
> 30 PRINT "AND I AM THE SECOND ONE."

(don't forget to press RETURN after each line). Now type RUN and watch the printout. Type in the following two lines

> 30 PRINT "WHO IS FIRST NOW,"
> 20 PRINT "ME OR THE OTHER ONE?"

Let your system execute the two lines (RUN) and watch the printout. Which line is

executed first? . . . . Type LIST and depress the RETURN key. Watch the printout from the program and copy it on the lines below.

. . . .

. . . .

★

As seen from the exercise the command

> LIST

causes the system to display the statement lines present in the workspace. The entire collection of these statements is referred to as a **program**. Thus the command RUN causes the program in the workspace to be **executed**, whereas the command LIST **displays** it on the screen.

THE **LIST** COMMAND DISPLAYS THE PROGRAM IN THE WORKSPACE ON THE SCREEN.

Exercise 1.6

Mr. Murphy enters the following program

```
30 PRINT "MADE ME"
10 PRINT "BACON, BEEF,"
40 PRINT "WHAT I AM."
20 PRINT "AND HAM."
```

What message is displayed by the program whenever it is executed? Write your answer on the lines below.

. . . .

. . . .

. . . .

. . . .

The system of itself arranges the lines of a program in the workspace in accordance with the line numbers.
★

Exercise 1.7 □

Type LOAD "EXE17" and press the RETURN key. Wait until the system has loaded the program and then type LIST (RETURN). A listing of the program in the workspace is now displayed. Compare this listing with the one below.

```
10 PRINT "XXXXXXXXXXXXXXXXXXXXXXXXXXXXXXXXXXXX"
20 PRINT "X                                  X"
30 PRINT "X                                  X"
40 PRINT "XXXXXXXXXXXXXXXXXXXXXXXXXXXXXXXXXXXX"
```

Now type in a line like the following

```
25 PRINT "X          PAUL MURPHY          X"
```

but perhaps insert a name other than PAUL MURPHY. Try to arrange for the name to be printed nicely around the centre of its line. As usual spaces are introduced by pressing the spacebar. Type the command LIST and notice where the system has placed line 25. Type RUN and watch the output.
★

Very often we shall want to copy a selected program from the diskette (or cassette) into the workspace. This is done by using the LOAD command. The keyword LOAD must be followed by the name of the program as in

```
LOAD "EXE17"
```

from the last exercise. The contents of the diskette are not affected by the LOAD command, but any previous program in the workspace will be erased. Therefore no explicit NEW command is needed when a new program is entered into the workspace in that way.

THE **LOAD** COMMAND IS USED TO COPY A PROGRAM FROM THE DISKETTE (CASSETTE) INTO THE WORKSPACE.

The LOAD command has the general form

LOAD "⟨name of program to be copied⟩"

In Exercise 1.7 spaces are used to force a name to be printed near the centre of a line. In this line

30 PRINT "   YOURS TRULY"

the string constant begins with 11 **blanks** (spaces). The blank " " is of course a character just as much as, for instance, "A" or "9" or "?". If a string constant is to begin with spaces, then do not forget to enter the double quote *before* you press the spacebar.

Exercise 1.8 □
Type LOAD "EXE18" and depress the RETURN key. Type LIST and compare the displayed program listing with the listing in the textbook to check that the correct program has been loaded. Now type in the following

DEL 20

and press the RETURN key. Have the system display a new program listing (LIST). What

has happened to the original program? . . . .
★

Exercise 1.9 □
Type LOAD "EXE19" and press the RETURN key. Type LIST and check the program listing displayed by the system with the listing in the textbook. Now type in

DEL 20-50

and press the RETURN key. Make the system display a new program listing and compare it with the previous one. What has happened to the original program?

. . . .
★

If you enter the keyword DEL followed by the number of a line at present in the workspace, then the line in question is erased. Thus the command

DEL 110

causes the line numbered 110 to be erased. The DEL command may also be used to remove a whole range of lines from the workspace. The following command

>   DEL 140–300

will cause all lines from 140 to 300 inclusive to be deleted. Of course, the DEL command is not executed until you press the RETURN key.

THE **DEL** COMMAND IS USED TO DELETE LINES FROM THE WORKSPACE.

Exercise 1.10 □
Type LOAD "EXE110" and check the program that has been copied from the disk against the listing in the textbook. Then type in the following

>   20 PRINT "HEAVE A HEAVY SIGH."

(RETURN). Enter the LIST command and compare the listing now displayed with the

previous one. What has happened to the original line 20? . . . .

. . . .

★

If you enter further lines with the *same line number* as previous ones only the *last one* remains in the workspace. This means that it is very easy to *replace* a given line by another one. Just enter the new line with the same line number as the one it is to replace.

IF MORE THAN ONE LINE WITH THE **SAME LINE NUMBER** IS TYPED IN, ONLY **THE LAST ONE ENTERED** REMAINS IN THE WORKSPACE.

Exercise 1.11
Write a program to produce this text

```
XXXXXXXXXXXXXXXXXXXXXXXXXXXXXXXXXXXXXXXXXXXX
X                                          X
X   IT IS HEREBY ANNOUNCED THAT FOURTH FORM X
X   PUPILS ARE NO LONGER PERMITTED TO EAT   X
X   CARROTS IN MY GARDEN DURING LUNCH HOUR. X
X                                          X
X                       HEADMASTER.        X
X                                          X
XXXXXXXXXXXXXXXXXXXXXXXXXXXXXXXXXXXXXXXXXXXX
```

★

Exercise 1.12 ☐
Type in the program written in Exercise 1.11 and run it.

Note. If you have a line-printer connected to your system, you may use the command

    SELECT "LP"

to direct the printout from the program to the printer instead of the screen. To switch back to screen mode use the command

    SELECT "DS"

If you find it hard to keep the many characters and especially the many blanks in check, use a piece of squared paper to write on and give each individual character its own square.

2
The computer writes a reminder

Here is another program line

      10 INPUT AMOUNT

As usual the line consists of a line number (10) and a statement. In this case the statement begins with the keyworld INPUT followed by the **variable name** AMOUNT.

Exercise 2.1 □
Type NEW and press RETURN. Then type in the following program:

      10 INPUT AMOUNT
      20 PRINT AMOUNT

Now type RUN and press the RETURN key. The system reacts by displaying the "?" sign on the screen, and then nothing more happens. The system is, however, *waiting* for you to *enter a number* which it may use as a *value* of the variable AMOUNT. You should now type 87.25 and then press the RETURN key. When that has been done, the rest of the program is executed immediately. What is printed out?. . . . .
★

We have already seen that PRINT statements may be used to display strings of characters on the screen. Exercise 2.1 shows that PRINT statements may also be used to print out numeric quantities.

> A **PRINT** STATEMENT MAY BE USED TO DISPLAY NUMERIC VALUES ON THE SCREEN.

It is often useful to enter data from the keyboard during program execution. Exercise 2.1 demonstrated how this can be done. To obtain a clear understanding of both the INPUT statement and the concept of a variable, we shall take a closer look at the small program from Exercise 2.1. When the line

> 10 INPUT AMOUNT

is typed in, it is stored in the workspace to be ready for later use. But another thing happens, too. In the statement a variable name AMOUNT is present. When the COMAL system encounters a specific variable for the first time, it *reserves a location* in the workspace with enough room to hold a number, and at the same time it notes that this location is to go by the name specified in the program. Using the variable AMOUNT as an example, we may picture that it looks like this:

> AMOUNT: [   ]

As line 20 with the PRINT statement is typed in, it will also be stored in the workspace. Since the variable AMOUNT has already been noted, nothing more happens right now. When the program is executed and the system encounters the statement in line 10, it pauses, as we have seen, and waits for us to type in a number to store in the location that has already been reserved. If we enter the number from Exercise 2.1 we may picture that it looks like this in the workspace afterwards:

> AMOUNT: [87.25]

The next statement to be executed is the one in line 20:

> PRINT AMOUNT

The system now prints out the **number** that has been stored under the name of AMOUNT. To the system the statement PRINT AMOUNT means something like "print-out the number that is referred to by the name AMOUNT". It is *very important* that you note the difference between a **string constant** and a **variable name**. String constants are always surrounded by quotes, variable names never are! Try to compare this statement

> PRINT AMOUNT

with the following one

> PRINT "AMOUNT"

When the former is executed, the system prints out the **number** referred to by AMOUNT (e.g. 87.25); when the latter is executed, it outputs the word

> AMOUNT

The five characters that have been brought together in both cases, have two very different meanings! One might compare the system's use of variable with the way in which we use a printed form. Let us imagine that we have filled in a form like this

> QUANTITY:.. 2 ...   SIZE: .. 80 ..   TOTAL PRICE:. 23.85

Any form of this kind looks the same, and has little significance if it has not been filled in, which is to say that *numbers have been written* in the individual spaces.

After a program has been typed in, the locations reserved for such variables, are retained until the program is deleted by a NEW or a LOAD command. On the other hand, the numbers, that have been stored in the locations, may be changed as often as you like. A number that has been stored in a location named by a variable is said to be the **value** of the variable.

Exercise 2.2 □
Type LOAD "EXE22" (do not forget to press RETURN). Type LIST and check that the displayed program listing matches the one in the textbook. There are two variables in the

program. Their names are . . . . and . . . .
Type RUN and watch the system display the "?" sign. Now type in the number 7 and press the RETURN key. Another "?" sign will be displayed, and you then type 12.85 followed by RETURN. Note the print out from the program. RUN the program a few more times, and enter values of your own choice for the two variables.
★

A VARIABLE KEEPS ITS **NAME**, BUT ITS **VALUE** MAY BE CHANGED WHENEVER WISHED.

Exercise 2.3 □
Type LOAD "EXE23". RUN the program and enter values for the variables when the program asks for them. Now type this **command**

        PRINT QUANT

(note: **no line number**) and press the RETURN key. What does the system print out?

. . . . Then key in the command

        PRINT AMOUNT

and press the RETURN key. What does the system display now? . . . .
RUN the program a few more times and use the PRINT command each time it has been executed to check the values of the variables.

★

If you want to know the present value of a variable, you can use the PRINT command which may be considered a kind of a "peephole" into the values of variables.

THE **PRINT COMMAND** MAY BE USED WHEN YOU WANT TO KNOW THE PRESENT **VALUE** OF A VARIABLE.

As mentioned before, variables may change values whenever you want them to. But do not forget that at the same time as a variable assumes a new value, its earlier value is deleted. We also say that the present value is *overwritten* by the new value.

WHEN A VARIABLE GETS A NEW VALUE, ITS PREVIOUS VALUE IS OVERWRITTEN.

Exercise 2.4 □
Type NEW. Then enter the following program:

```
0010 INPUT AMOUNT
0020 PRINT "PLEASE PAY ",AMOUNT
```

In the statement of line 20 a **string constant** as well as a **variable** is found. Copy the string

constant here: .... What is the name of the variable?

.... Type RUN and enter the number 35.95 when the system

has displayed the "?" sign. What does the program then print out?...................

....

Now type in this line

```
0020 PRINT "PLEASE PAY ",AMOUNT," POUNDS TO COVER EXPENSES."
```

(Be *very careful* with each character). The statement now holds two *string constants* and

one *variable*. The string constants are:...

and .... The name of the variable is........................
RUN the program and enter the value 34.55 for the variable. What does the program

print out now? ....

★

The list of items or **elements** which follow the keyword PRINT is referred to as the **output list**. The individual elements of the list are separated by **commas**. So far we have seen that elements of an output list may be variables or string constants. Strings and numbers are also called **data**, and an output list may be considered as a special case of a **data list**, the individual elements of which indicate data to be printed out. The output listing which follows PRINT in the line

```
0020 PRINT "THERE IS A TOTAL OF ",TOTNUM," ITEMS."
```

holds three elements, viz. the string constant "THERE IS A TOTAL OF ", the variable TOTNUM, and the string constant " ITEMS.". It is now easy to see that string constants must be put in quotation marks in order that they may not be confused with variables.

> A **PRINT** STATEMENT CONSISTS OF THE KEYWORD **PRINT** FOLLOWED BY AN **OUTPUT LIST**.

Exercise 2.5
The following program is given:

```
0020 PRINT "YOU MUST PAY ",AMT," POUNDS INTO OUR ACCOUNT"
0030 PRINT "BEFORE ",DATE
```

What printout does the program produce if DATE has a value of 800301 and AMT has a value of 14.25?

. . . .

. . . .

★

Exercise 2.6 □
Write a program to produce letters like this:

```
        PLEASE PAY 145.35 POUNDS BEFORE
        THE DATE 801105. FAILURE TO DO SO
        WILL MEAN THAT YOUR BARROW WILL BE
        REMOVED WITHOUT FURTHER NOTICE.

                A. MEANY,
                BARROW FACTORY, LTD.
                WHEELEY.
```

The program must be designed and written such that the **amount** and the **date** are both variables, the values of which are entered at the beginning of the program. Type in the program, RUN it and check that it is in order.

★

The computer writes a bill

Here is another line that may be executed by the COMAL-system:

20 QUANTITY:=20; PRICE:=12.85

The line consists of the line number (20) followed by two **assignments**, QUANTITY:=20 and PRICE:=12.85. The assignments are separated by a **semicolon** (;). The token ":=" means "is assigned the value", such that for example "QUANTITY:=20" can be expressed as "the variable QUANTITY is assigned the value 20". When the line above has been executed, QUANTITY holds the value 20 and PRICE holds the value 12.85.

Exercise 3.1
Look in the program booklet to find the program for this exerise. What printout will it give if executed?

. . . .
★

In executing an assignment, COMAL may also *compute a numeric expression.* Let us look at this program:

```
0050 QUANTITY:=20; PRICE:=15.25
0060 SELLINGPRICE:=QUANTITY*PRICE
0070 PRINT "A TOTAL OF ",SELLINGPRICE," POUNDS."
```

The assignment:

SELLINGPRICE:=QUANTITY*PRICE

causes two events to happen: First the value of the *numeric expression is computed*, i.e. the *value* of QUANTITY is *multiplied* by the *value* of PRICE; then the *result of this computation is assigned to the numeric variable* SELLINGPRICE. When line 70 is executed the following message is printed out:

A TOTAL OF 305 POUNDS.

THE ":=" MEANS "IS ASSIGNED THE VALUE" AND IS USED WHEN YOU WANT TO **ASSIGN VALUES** TO VARIABLES.

Exercise 3.2

Look in the program booklet to find the program for this exercise. What printout will it give when executed?

. . . .

★

Any expression which, when evaluated, produces a numeric result is said to be a numeric expression. Some examples are:

QUANTITY*PRICE,   LENGTH*WIDTH,   A+B, Q/(B+C)

In numeric expressions you may use the following **operators**: *addition* (+), *subtraction* (−), *multiplication* (*), and *division* (/). The "−" may also be used as a *unary minus*. In numeric expressions values may be given by *numeric constants* or *numeric variables*. You may also use *parentheses* according to the usual rules of mathematics.

THE GENERAL FORM OF AN **ASSIGNMENT** IS:
⟨numeric variable⟩ := ⟨numeric expression⟩

Note that the "/" signifies division. Also note that in COMAL the multiplication operator "*" must always be used when multiplication is to be done, whereas in algebra it often may be left out.

IN NUMERIC EXPRESSIONS YOU MAY USE **NUMERIC CONSTANTS**, **NUMERIC VARIABLES**, THE **OPERATORS**: +, −, *, AND /, ALONG WITH **PARENTHESES** ACCORDING TO THE USUAL RULES OF ALGEBRA.

Numeric expressions are also called **arithmetic expressions**. We shall have more to say about such expressions later in this book.

Exercise 3.3
Suppose that the following lines have been executed by the COMAL system:

```
0010 QUANT:=20; PRICE:=45; VATPCT:=25
0020 L:=20; B:=10; H:=40
```

Imagine that each of the following expressions are computed later in the program. Write down the values that would result from this computation:

QUANT * PRICE: .... , QUANT*PRICE*VATPCT/100:.........

QUANT * PRICE * (1+VATPCT/100): ...., L*B*H/4: ....

QUANT * PRICE/100 * VATPCT:............., L+B/H+B: ....

QUANT * PRICE/(100+VATPCT) * 100: ....

L+H/(L+B): ...., H/L/B: ....

If you want to, you can have the computer check your results. To do this key in the lines 10 and 20 above. Then type RUN. The COMAL system now knows the variables and their values. The values of the individual expressions are displayed by using the PRINT command as in: PRINT QUANT*PRICE (and press RETURN).

★

Exercise 3.4
Look in the program booklet to find the program for this exercise and answer the following questions:

What is the value of AMOUNT after line 30 has been executed? .... What is the

value of VAT, when line 40 has been executed? .... What value has been assigned

to TOTAL, when line 50 has been completed? ....
★

Exercise 3.5 ☐
Check your answers to the questions in Exercise 3.4 by typing LOAD "EXE34" ⟨RETURN⟩, RUN ⟨RETURN⟩, and then use the PRINT command to get the system to display the values of the variables (PRINT AMOUNT, etc.).
★

Whenever you write a program you must be very careful to enter the *correct characters* and see that the variable names are *spelled correctly*. Take a look at line 30 in the program from Exercise 3.4 and imagine that someone has typed AMUONT instead of AMOUNT.

The value of the expression QUANTITY*PRICE is then stored in the workspace under the name of AMUONT, and you cannot expect the system to find that value if you later ask for it using the name AMOUNT. Therefore it is important to use variable names that are *easy to remember and recognize.* A variable name may consist of as many as *16 letters or digits*; it must *start with a letter,* and all letters and digits are significant. Thus:

QUANTITY, AGENT007, NUMBEROFUNITS, OLSEN, A234567B

are all legal variable names, whereas attempts to use for example

ANTON++B, 2KB8, TOOMANYCHARACTERSINTHISNAME, PR$45

causes the system to display an error message.

A **VARIABLE NAME** MAY CONSIST OF AS MANY AS 16 CHARACTERS, ALL OF WHICH ARE SIGNIFICANT. THE FIRST CHARACTER MUST BE A LETTER, THE FOLLOWING MAY BE **LETTERS** OR **DIGITS**.

Exercise 3.6

Look in the program booklet to find the program for this exercise. Then answer the following:

What value is assigned to AMOUNT, if a value of 20 has been input to QUANTITY and a

value of 2 to PRICE? .... What value will VAT have ...., and TOTAL?

.... What printout does the program produce?

....

....

....

....

★

Exercise 3.7 □
Write, run and test a program to produce letters like this:

```
WE CAN OFFER YOU 10 MOUSTACHE CUPS
MADE OF COPENHAGEN PORCELAIN AT 10
POUNDS EACH.
THE TOTAL PRICE IS THUS 100 POUNDS,
EXCLUDING VAT.
IF VAT AT 15 PCT. IS ADDED, YOU GET
A GRAND TOTAL OF 115 POUNDS.

                    SINCERELY,
                    B. RITTLE,
                    MERCHANT.
```

The program must be designed to accept the *number of cups* and the *price per cup* as input from the keyboard. The *VAT rate* should be given as a program specified constant, since it only changes occasionally. The program written for Exercise 3.6 may give you a hint on how to design the program. You might start like this:

```
0010 VATPCT:=15
0020 PRINT "NUMBER OF CUPS: ",
0030 INPUT QUANTITY
```

★

In the program to be written in Exercise 3.7, the number of cups, and the price per cup must be *typed in* during execution of the program. A set of data thus entered to a program as part of running it, is called the **input of the program**. The value of the VAT rate is not entered through the keyboard or otherwise but is assigned in the statement

VATPCT:=15

Each time the program is run, the variable VATPCT has *the same value* independent of the input. A variable, the value of which is thus defined and not altered later in the program, will be called a **program specified constant**. When the program has been run, some text and numbers are printed out. Such a set of data, displayed by the program as a result of the processes done by it, is called the **output of the program**.

4

The computer discriminates

When the COMAL system encounters the statement

INPUT QUANTITY

a "?" is displayed as a signal to the user to enter data. The system pauses until the user types a number and presses the RETURN key. The variable QUANTITY is assigned the value which is entered and the system then executes the next statement in the program. The "?" is referred to as a **prompt**. If you have not written the program yourself or if it is a long time since you designed it and typed it in, you may not remember what the value that is keyed in is going to be used for. And the prompt "?" does not say anything about that. This problem can be solved by telling the program to submit a **prompt message** to support or replace the "?". In the first case the INPUT statement can be preceded by a PRINT statement displaying a message, as in

10 PRINT "NUMBER OF UNITS",
20 INPUT QUANTITY

When these lines are executed the message

NUMBER OF UNITS?

appears on the screen, and the system then pauses to let the user enter a value for QUANTITY.

Note the **comma** terminating the PRINT statement. It has been put there to prevent the COMAL system from starting on a new line, which it would normally do after finishing a PRINT statement. Had it not been present, the prompt would have looked like this:

NUMBER OF UNITS
?

which is not nearly as nice and does not communicate the message as clearly as in the original case.

IF THE OUTPUT LIST IN A **PRINT** STATEMENT **ENDS WITH A COMMA,**
THE **LINE IS NOT SHIFTED** AFTER THE STATEMENT IS FINISHED.

Exercise 4.1 ☐
LOAD the program EXE41 (LOAD "EXE41"). List it and compare it with the listing in
the program booklet. Try to find out how the program works. Then add the following
two lines to it:

        5 PRINT "NUMBER OF UNITS",
        15 PRINT "PRICE PER UNIT",

and RUN the program to test that it works correctly. What must line 5 look like if the
following:

        NUMBER OF LOOSE SCREWS?

is to appear on the screen when line 5 and 10 are executed?

. . . .

★

Exercise 4.2 ☐
LOAD the program EXE42 from the disk. List it and compare this with the listing in the

program booklet. What is the output when the following is the input: 34? . . . .

45? . . . ., 100? . . . . Execute the program five more times and use an input of

your own. Write down your input as well as the program output for each run: . . . .,

. . . .; . . . ., ...; . . . ., ...; . . . ., ...; . . . .,

. . . . What happens to the value of NUMBER when line 20 is executed?. . . . .

. . . .

★

Exercise 4.2 demonstrates clearly that the ":=" is something very different from the
sign "=". Let us take a look at the statement

        NUMBER:=NUMBER+1

In this statement it is not asked whether NUMBER *is equal to* NUMBER+1, but the
system is instructed to assign the value of the expression NUMBER+1 to the variable
NUMBER. How can this be done? How can a variable appear on both sides of the assignment? Imagine that it looks like this in the workspace:

        NUMBER: | 45 |

When the assignment is executed, the value of the numeric expression NUMBER+1 is first computed. The result, 46, is then assigned to the variable NUMBER as its *new value*. The present value of NUMBER is of course *overwritten* during this process. As the calculations and the assignment is over, we can imagine this state of affairs in workspace:

NUMBER: 46

The whole chain of events may be illustrated by this small diagram:

$$45 + 1 \quad = \quad 46$$
$$\uparrow \qquad\qquad \downarrow$$
$$\text{NUMBER:} \qquad 45 \qquad\qquad 46$$

You should note that the value of NUMBER is not altered during the first step of the process. It is not until the new value is assigned that the present value is overwritten.

Exercise 4.3

Take a look at this statement (assignment):

SELLINGPRICE:=SELLINGPRICE * 80/100

What value has SELLINGPRICE assumed *after* the statement has been executed, if it has the following value *before* the statement is encountered:

100? . . . ., 500? . . . ., 5? . . . ., 1000? . . . ., 50? . . . .
★

Exercise 4.4 □

A mail order company has the following problem: If a very small number of articles is ordered, the dispatch costs rise out of proportion to the total price of the goods. To encourage the customers to buy in larger quantities, the company decides that from now on a discount of 5% of the normal selling price should be given if more than 20 units are ordered at a time. The house programmer writes a small program which computes the final price of a delivery, taking the discount into consideration. This program is stored on the disk under the name of DISCOUNT. LOAD it (check it by looking at the program listing in the program booklet) and RUN it. Input values at your own choice to be assigned to NUMBER and PRICE. Inspect the output of each run to check that the program deducts the discount correctly each time a customer orders more than 20 units of an article.
★

Take a closer look at the program DISCOUNT from Exercise 4.4. It may be split up in three parts: First values to become assigned to NUMBER and PRICE are entered (line 10–40). Then the total price, with discount deduction, if any, is calculated (line 50–80), and finally the result is displayed on the screen (line 90). This may be represented as follows:

INPUT number of units and price per unit
COMPUTE the total with discount, if any
PRINT the final result

The first and last part of the process is easy. The problems are hidden in the central part of it, since a *discount is not allowed in any circumstances!* Only *if more than 20* units are ordered, will there be any deduction. This part of the process may be expressed in more detail like this:

> COMPUTE *the total price*
> IF *more than 20 units are ordered THEN*
> > *deduct the discount to get new total*

By saying that the value of the variable *number* is the number of units ordered and introducing some simple rules of calculation known from arithmetic, we arrive at this description:

> *total:=number*price*
> IF *number>20 THEN*
> > *total:=total*95/100*

We also have to explain to the system that executes the program that the *condition*

> *number>20*

controls the deduction of the discount only, but should not apply to the rest of the program. The grand total must be printed out whatever happens. We now need to introduce a statement to indicate that the IF statement has nothing more to say, and we make it as simple as possible, using the one-word statement

> ENDIF

Having done this, we have finished the central part of the program.

You can have as many lines as you wish between the IF and the ENDIF statements. If the condition associated with the IF statement is met, the block of statements in the range from the IF to the ENDIF statement is executed, but if the condition is not met, the block is skipped.

Exercise 4.5 ☐
LOAD the program EXE45. RUN it with your own input. What condition must be met if

lines 90–150 are to be executed?. . . . .

Is the total price decreased or increased if the lines in question are executed?

. . . . What total price will the program output, if NUMBER equals

30 and PRICE equals 10? . . . ., and if NUMBER is 10 and PRICE is 100?. . . . .

Change the program such that a delivery charge is added only if the original amount (the suggested price) is less than £30. And do not forget that some of the texts have to be modified as well, so that the customer may have correct information about the rules. RUN and test your program.

★

The IF and ENDIF statements are also said to **control** the block of statements between them, since they delimit the block and the condition in the IF statement determines whether it is going to be executed or not. The statements in the block are sometimes referred to as the **range** of the IF–ENDIF combination. When the COMAL system prints out a program listing, statements in an IF–ENDIF range are always given an extra indentation compared to the IF and ENDIF control statements. Thus it is easy to identify the range at a glance.

The IF statement can also control *two blocks of statements.*

Exercise 4.6 □

LOAD the program EXE46. Check it by comparing it with the listing in the program booklet. The total amount is computed either in line 60 or in line 90. In what way are the

calculations done by line 60 different from those done by line 90? . . . .

. . . .

RUN the program four or five times using inputs of your own. You are told that PRICE has been assigned a value of 10 and that NUMBER is 5. Give the number of the line that

produces the output of the program: . . . . And what if PRICE is still set to 10,

but NUMBER has assumed a value of 20? . . . ., 15? . . . ., 30? . . . .,

or 19? . . . . As the program starts, line 10–40 are always executed. Which two lines

of the program are executed *only if* NUMBER is less than 20? . . . . and . . . .

And which lines are executed *only if* Number is greater than or equal to 20? . . . .

and . . . . Take a look at this diagram:

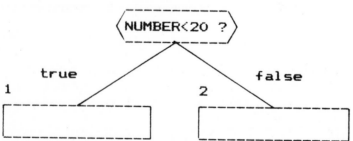

In the box to the left you should write the numbers of the lines executed, if the condition in the upper box (the **choice box**) *is met.* In the box to the right you should write the numbers of the lines that are executed, if the condition *is not met.*

★

By incorporating the ELSE statement with the IF–ENDIF range, this range is separated into two blocks, namely the statements between the IF statement and the ELSE statement, and the ones between the ELSE statement and the ENDIF statement. The former block (between IF and ELSE) is executed if the condition associated with the IF statement is met, and the latter (between ELSE and ENDIF) is executed if the condition is *not* met.

Conditions such as

NUMBER>20 or PRICE<100

are also called by the mathematicians **open statements** or **relational expressions**. If the condition specified by a relational expression is met, the expression is said to have the value "true", and if the condition is not met the expression is said to have the value "false". In computer science, relational expressions are normally called **Boolean expressions** (after the English mathematician George Boole), and in the rest of this book we shall adopt this convention. So just as numerical expressions may be computed to give numerical values, Boolean expressions may be evaluated to yield one of the two **truth values: true** or **false**.

THE **IF** STATEMENT CONSISTS OF THE KEYWORD IF FOLLOWED BY A **BOOLEAN EXPRESSION** [AND TERMINATED BY THE KEYWORD THEN].

Note: The last six words have been bracketed to indicate that you do not have to type the keyword THEN when writing an IF statement. You only have to press the RETURN key after the Boolean expression has been entered. The COMAL system automatically inserts the word if it is not there already.

THE **ENDIF** STATEMENT CONSISTS OF THE KEYWORD **ENDIF**.

THE **ELSE** STATEMENT CONSISTS OF THE KEYWORD **ELSE**.

A summary of the IF – ELSE – ENDIF statements, the structures they govern, and the effect they have is shown below:

IF ⟨a Boolean expression⟩ **THEN**
    THIS BLOCK OF STATEMENTS IS EXECUTED ONLY IF THE BOOLEAN
    EXPRESSION IN THE IF STATEMENT EVALUATES TO TRUE
ENDIF

IF ⟨a Boolean expression⟩ **THEN**
    THIS BLOCK OF STATEMENTS IS EXECUTED ONLY IF THE BOOLEAN
    EXPRESSION IN THE **IF** STATEMENT EVALUATES TO TRUE
ELSE
    THIS BLOCK OF STATEMENTS IS EXECUTED ONLY IF THE BOOLEAN
    EXPRESSION IN THE **IF** STATEMENT EVALUATES TO FALSE
ENDIF

Exercise 4.7
State the truth value of the following Boolean expressions, knowing that NUMBER=5, A=8, B=6 and C=2:

NUMBER>A: . . . ., NUMBER=A−3: . . . ., A=B+C: . . . .,

B/C=3: . . . .,   A<=B: . . . .,   NUMBER+B/C=8: . . . .,   B<=A: . . . .
★

A process as given in a program may also be depicted by means of a **structure diagram**. An example of such a diagram is shown in Exercise 4.6. In connection with IF statements two types of structure diagrams are considered:

The first one describes IF statements controlling only one block of statements (IF — ENDIF):

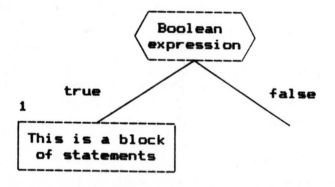

The second corresponds to IF statements controlling two blocks of statements (IF - ELSE — ENDIF):

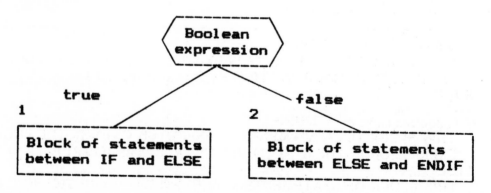

The box with the Boolean expression is called a **choice box**, and a rectangular box representing a block of statements is called an **action box**.

Exercise 4.8
Max Murphy is sent into town by his aunt. He is going to give a message to Paul Murphy. If Paul is at home, he must come round to Max's aunt at once. If, however, Paul is not at home, Max will put a note saying, "Come down to my aunt as fast as possible" into Paul's mail box. Fill in the action boxes of the diagram below such that the diagram describes what Max should do:

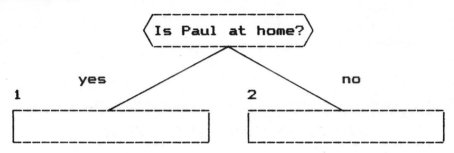

★

Exercise 4.9 □
In Atherton & Bramers General Store they have decided that customers who send for goods to be delivered, must pay a delivery charge of 75 pence, if the total value of the order is less than 10 pounds. You have been hired by Atherton & Bramer to write a program to do the following: As input it must accept the grand total of a customers order (in pounds), and it must output the amount of money the customer should pay. If for example the grand total of the order is £8.34, the output ought to be

```
GRAND TOTAL:                    8.34
INCLUDING DELIVERY FEE:         9.09

SINCE THE GRAND TOTAL OF YOUR ORDER
IS LESS THAN 10 POUNDS, A DELIVERY
CHARGE OF 0.75 IS ADDED.
```

If on the other hand the value of the order amounts to for example £15.50, the program should display

```
GRAND TOTAL:                    15.55

DELIVERY FREE BY COURTESY OF ATHERTON & BRAMER.
```

Your program might start like this:

```
0010 PRINT "ENTER TOTAL AMOUNT",
0020 INPUT TOTAL
0030 PRINT
0040 IF TOTAL<10 THEN
```

Design the program, type it in and test it.

★

In some of the exercises done so far we have used "<=" and ">" to denote *relational operators*. In COMAL there are six relational operators as follows:

    =   "is equal to"
    <   "is less than"
    >   "is greater than"
    <=   "is less than or equal to"
    >=   "is greater than or equal to"
    <>   "is not equal to"

Exercise 4.10 □
LOAD the program "DISCOUNT". Change the statement in line 60 into this:

    60 IF NUMBER>20 THEN TOTAL:=TOTAL*95/100

and remove lines 70–80 (DEL 70–80). RUN the program once or twice with some inputs of your own. A statement like the one now inserted is called a *compound statement,* since it is in fact made up of two statements.

★

If an IF statement controls only one block and that block has only one statement, this statement may be placed on the same line, as an extension to the IF statement. In this case *no* ENDIF should follow — the one-statement-block is terminated by the carriage return. It should be noticed that this statement:

    IF NUMBER=0 THEN PRINT "END OF SEQUENCE"; I:=8

is illegal, because two statements follow the keyword THEN on the same line, whereas this one:

    IF NUMBER=0 THEN FINISHED:=TRUE; TOTAL:=SUM

is legal, since one statement can hold several assignments.

        IF ⟨a Boolean expression⟩ **THEN** ⟨one single statement⟩

The keyword THEN must be typed in when this so called **compound IF statement** is applied.

5

Count to 1, count to 2, . . .

Most of the programs used with the exercises in this book have been stored on an external device such as a disk. A part of the disk where a program is stored, is called a **program file**. To get a **copy** of a program from a program file into the workspace, we use the LOAD command. The string that always follows the keyword LOAD is in fact the **name of the program file**. A command, such as

LOAD "EXE51"

means "take a copy of the program stored in the file EXE51".

AN AREA OF A DISK OR ANOTHER EXTERNAL DEVICE TO HOLD A PROGRAM IS CALLED A **PROGRAM FILE**.

Exercise 5.1 □
LOAD the program EXE51. Check it against the listing in the program booklet. RUN the

program. How many times are the lines 20–30 executed? . . . . Rewrite line 10 to become:

10 FOR NO:=1 TO 10 DO

RUN the program. How many times are line 20–30 executed now? . . . .
★

In the program in Exercise 5.1, two new statements are introduced:

FOR NO:=1 TO 5 DO   and   NEXT NO

The two statements go together just like the IF and ENDIF statements. Between them you may insert a block of statements with as many lines as you wish. In the program in Exercise 5.1, the FOR − NEXT combination works like this: First the **index-variable** NO is assigned the value 1 and then the statements in the block are executed. The NEXT statement is then encountered and the value of the index-variable NO is *increased by* 1, thus assuming a value of 2. Now the block of statements is executed again, and as the NEXT statement is encountered for the second time, NO assumes a value of 3. This goes on, until the block of statements has been executed five times. Then the index-variable assumes a value of 6, and the execution of the program continues with the statement following the NEXT statement. A part of a program designed to be executed repetetively is called a **loop**, and the one we are looking into now is called a **FOR − NEXT loop**.

Exercise 5.2 □
LOAD the program in the file EXE52. Check it against the list in the program booklet.

RUN the program. How many times is the poem displayed? . . . . How many lines

are contained between the FOR and the NEXT statements? . . . .

Rewrite line 10 to have the poem displayed 5 times. RUN the program.
★

As mentioned above, the variable found in both the FOR and the NEXT statement is called the index-variable. The NEXT statement always consists of the keyword NEXT followed by the name of the index-variable. The FOR statement is a little more complicated. Following the keyword FOR there is always an **assignment** setting the index-variable to its **initial value**. The keyword TO separates the initial assignment from the **terminal value**, and the whole thing ends up with the keyword DO.

FOR ⟨index-variable⟩:=⟨initial value⟩ **TO** ⟨terminal value⟩ [**DO**]
   This block of statements is executed for each of the following values of the ⟨index-variable⟩:
   ⟨initial value⟩, ⟨initial-value⟩+1, ⟨initial value⟩+2, etc., until the ⟨index-variable⟩ assumes a value greater than the ⟨terminal value⟩
   If ⟨initial value⟩ is greater then ⟨terminal value⟩ from the beginning the block is not executed at all.
NEXT [⟨index-variable⟩]

Note: The index-variable following the keyword NEXT has been bracketed to indicate that the COMAL system inserts it automatically if it has not been typed in. The keyword DO may also be supplied automatically by the system.
   Both the initial value and the terminal value may be given as **numeric constants**, **numeric variables**, or **numeric expressions**. You should notice that the value of the index-variable is always greater than the terminal value when the loop is finished. The block of statements between the FOR and the NEXT statements is also called the **range** of the loop.

Exercise 5.3 ☐

LOAD the program in the file EXE53. RUN it. Rewrite the statement in line 10 to become:

FOR TRIP:=1 TO LASTTRIP DO

and insert these lines in the program:

5 PRINT "HOW MANY TRIPS TO TAKE",
6 INPUT LASTTRIP

RUN the program using as input the values suggested below. For each input write down how many times the loop is executed.

If 3 is input, the loop is executed .... times.

If 8 is input, the loop is executed .... times.

If 0 is input, the loop is executed .... times.

If −5 is input, the loop is executed .... times.

Rewrite line 10 once more, now to become:

FOR TRIP:=FIRSTTRIP TO LASTTRIP DO

and insert the following lines:

3 PRINT "FIRST TRIP HAS NO.",
4 INPUT FIRSTTRIP
5 PRINT "LAST TRIP HAS NO.",
6 INPUT LASTTRIP

RUN the program again using the values in the form below as input. Fill in the blank spaces of the form.

FIRSTTRIP	LASTTRIP	The loop is executed
1	3	times
3	4	times
4	3	times
−3	0	times
−3	3	times

How many times is the loop executed if FIRSTTRIP is less than LASTTRIP? (give a general expression, using your head; the computer is not good at giving general expressions.)

. . . .

★

Exercise 5.4 □
Design, enter and RUN a program to display the following:

```
COUNT TO 1
COUNT TO 2
COUNT TO 3
COUNT TO 4
COUNT TO 5
DO NOT COUNT ON ME ANY MORE
```

In the program it might be a good idea to use a statement like this:

```
PRINT "COUNT TO ",NO
```

Now modify the program such that you may input the number it is going to count up to. You may start with these two lines:

```
5 PRINT "LAST NUMBER, PLEASE",
6 INPUT LAST
```

★

Exercise 5.5 □
Enter and run this program:

```
0010 FOR I:=1 TO 5 DO PRINT "COUNT TO ",I
0020 PRINT "DO NOT COUNT ON ME ANY MORE"
```

Rewrite it to display the following:

```
THIS WAS RUN NO. 1
THIS WAS RUN NO. 2
THIS WAS RUN NO. 3
THIS WAS RUN NO. 4
THIS WAS RUN NO. 5
WHICH WAS THE FINAL RUN!
```

Do not use more than two lines. RUN your program.

★

If the range of a FOR loop contains only one statement, this statement may be written as an extension to the FOR statement immediately following the keyword DO. When a one line FOR loop is used, there must be no NEXT statement, but the keyword DO must be entered to separate the control statement from its one-statement-block.

FOR ⟨index-assignment⟩ **TO** ⟨ terminal value⟩ **DO** ⟨one statement⟩

6
Odd or even

When you throw dice you cannot know in advance what the outcome of the game is going to be (unless there has been cheating). Numbers that come out in such a way that you never know what will come next, are called **random numbers**. The COMAL system can generate sequences of random numbers, and we can use that to simulate activities which involve unpredictable sequences of events, such as a game of chance with dice, cards etc.

Exercise 6.1 □
LOAD the program "ODDEVEN". LIST it and check the displayed list against the one in the program booklet. RUN the program.
★

In the program "ODDEVEN" from Exercise 6.1, the symbol "//" is found in several lines. Anything written on a line following that symbol is a **comment**, i.e. text used to identify and describe the program, but not executed by the system. Note that a comment may be any string, including for example a dotted line which could be used to separate two sections, and so illustrate the program structure.

THE SIGN "//" IS USED TO INITIATE **COMMENTS**.

Exercise 6.2
Find all the lines of the program "ODDEVEN" that contain a comment. Write these lines here:

10 //* ODD OR EVEN *// . . . .

20 // . . . .

. . . .

. . . .

. . . .

. . . .

. . . .

. . . .

. . . .

. . . .

One of the lines contains an *empty comment*. Give its number: . . . .
★

Exercise 6.3

Use the listing of "ODDEVEN" for this exercise. The main part of the game is done by a block of statements between a FOR and a NEXT statement (a FOR – NEXT loop).

Which line holds the FOR statement? . . . ., and which one holds the NEXT statement? . . . . What is the name of the index-variable in the FOR – NEXT loop?

. . . . What is the name of the variable whose value determines how

many games the program is going to play? . . . . In what line may

this variable be assigned a value? . . . . What prompt message does the program

display, when it expects a value of that variable to be entered?

. . . .
★

As we have seen, the block of statements between a FOR and a NEXT statement is executed repetitively, and the *values* of the expressions in the FOR statement determine how many times the range of a FOR–NEXT loop will be executed in succession. A part of a program to be executed repetitively is called a **loop**. To represent repetition in structure diagrams, we shall use an oval-shaped box:

```
 --------------------------
(  FOR I:=1 TO NUMBER DO  )
 --------------------------
```

The part of the diagram representing the range of the loop is then connected to this *repetition box*.

Exercise 6.4

This exercise is also about "ODDEVEN". Each time the FOR — NEXT loop is executed, the following happens:

1. You are asked to guess
2. The outcome of the game is determined
3. The result is displayed
4. The winner is announced

We may represent this in a structure diagram:

The actions referred to in the four boxes are executed as many times as the value of NUMBER indicates. If we compare the diagram with the program listing, we observe that the contents of the first action box correspond to lines 170–180 of the program, and the contents of the second action box to line 190. What lines of the program are

represented in the third action box? . . . ., and in the fourth action

box? . . . . What variable assumes a value as line 180 is executed?

. . . . What value do you have to enter, if your guess is 'even'?

. . . . In which line is the variable OUTCOME assigned a value?

. . . . Copy the statement on that line here:

. . . . Most of the output from the

program is text. In the last section of the program, however, two *variables* appear on the

output-list. Which ones? . . . . and . . . .

★

In the program "ODDEVEN" this assignment is found:

OUTCOME:=RND(0,1)

When the statement is executed, OUTCOME is assigned the value 0 or 1 *at random.*

Exercise 6.5 □
Type in this program:

```
0010 FOR I:=1 TO 10 DO
0020    RANNUM:=RND(1,5)
0030     PRINT RANNUM;
0040 NEXT
```

RUN the program several times. What numbers are displayed? . . . .

How many are output on each run? . . . . Rewrite line 20 to become

20 RANNUM:=RND(1,12)

RUN the modified program a few times. How many numbers does the program produce

on each run? . . . . Which numbers could be displayed? . . . .
★

Exercise 6.6
In the structure diagram from Exercise 6.4 an action box represents the process "DISPLAY RESULT", and another one the process "POINT OUT WINNER". The former represents lines 220–260, and the latter one lines 280–330 of the program "ODDEVEN". The structure diagram below illustrates the details of "DISPLAY RESULT":

What is "text 1"? . . . .

What is "text 2"? . . . .

The diagram below illustrates the program section "ANNOUNCE WINNER":

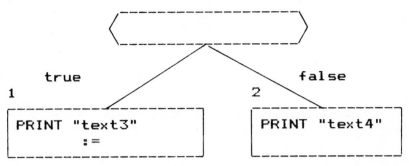

Fill in the choice box with the correct Boolean expression (condition). In one of the action boxes an assignment should appear. Complete it.

What is "text 3"? ....

What is "text 4"? ....

★

Exercise 6.7 ☐
RUN the program "ODDEVEN" once more. Each time a game is finished, the program outputs this message, "HERE IS ANOTHER ROUND". The message is, however, displayed

once too often. When does that happen?................................

....

Modify the program to prevent this. *Hint:* Use a compound IF statement. Then RUN the program to check that the modification works as required.

★

Exercise 6.8
Look at the listing of "ODDEVEN" again. In lines 130, 300, and 410–420, a variable

COUNTWIN appears. What is its initial value? .... What happens to its value, if

line 300 is executed? .... Under what condition does that happen?

.... What would you say is the role of COUNTWIN?.............

....

Suppose COUNTWIN has a value of 4 and NUMBER a value of 6. What then would be

the output of line 420?

. . . .

★

In the previous exercises we used random numbers in many places, and we saw that the RND function may take two arguments in COMAL; they must be integers such that the first one is less than or equal to the second one. The function returns an integer random number in the range between and including the two arguments.

THE EXPRESSION **RND(X,Y)**, WHERE **X** AND **Y** ARE INTEGERS, RETURNS AN **INTEGER RANDOM NUMBER** IN THE RANGE BETWEEN **X** AND **Y**.

Line 420 of "ODDEVEN" holds this statement:

PRINT "AND I HAVE WON ",NUMBER-COUNTWIN," ROUND(S)."

So far we have seen that the items or elements of an output-list may be *string constants* or *variables*. The above statement demonstrates that the list may also include *numeric expressions*.

Normally the elements of an output-listing are separated by *commas,* but in Exercise 6.5 you will have seen that the *semicolon* (;) may also be used. If a semicolon is used, the COMAL system always outputs *an extra space* between the displayed list items. Later we shall learn that the effect of the comma may be adjusted to cause the printout to be displayed in so called **windows** or **zones** (see the keyword ZONE).

THE **ELEMENTS** OF AN **OUTPUT-LIST** FOLLOWING THE KEYWORD **PRINT** MAY BE **STRING CONSTANTS, NUMERIC VARIABLES,** OR **NUMERIC EXPRESSIONS.**

NORMALLY THE ELEMENTS OF AN OUTPUT-LIST ARE SEPARATED BY **COMMAS, BUT SEMICOLONS** MAY BE USED, IN WHICH CASE A BLANK CHARACTER IS OUTPUT BETWEEN THE ELEMENTS.

The computer plays for peanuts

We have seen how our COMAL system can imitate a game by means of a function that generates **random numbers**. When the assignment

OUTCOME:=RND(0,1)

is encountered, OUTCOME assumes a value of 0 or 1 at random. In the program used in the preceding chapter a value 0 means that the outcome of the game is 'even', whereas a value of 1 stands for 'odd'. The system can only give us numbers. It is up to us to *define what the numbers imply.*

Exercise 7.1

For this exercise use the program listing in the program booklet. What does the program display if OUTCOME is equal to 1? . . . . What does it output if OUTCOME is equal to 2? . . . . What game is simulated by the program? . . . . How many games does the program perform? . . . . The structure diagram below illustrates the program. Fill in the empty boxes:

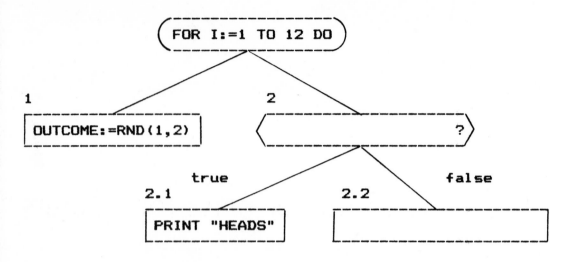

★

So far we have restricted ourselves to a study of games with only two possible **outcomes**: 'odd' or 'even', 'heads' or 'tails'. Many games have more than two outcomes. As an example, in a game of dice you can get six possible outcomes, and with a roulette wheel there are just as many results as there are colours or figures on the wheel. All games of this kind have, however, something in common. It is *a mere chance* what the result of the game is going to be. In a game of cards it is also a matter of chance what cards the individual players get, when the cards are dealt; but the way in which the game proceeds often depends on the talent and experience of the players.

In board games like "noughts and crosses", checkers (draughts), or chess, it is almost entirely the players' talents for and knowledge of the game that determines its final result; almost nothing is left to chance. Games, the outcome of which is mere matter of chance, are easy to simulate on a computer, whereas games in which human intelligence and experience are determining factors, are usually very difficult to simulate.

With a game, whose outcome is mere chance, it may be that some outcomes are more important to the final result of the game than others. If you throw dice, it may be that you are only interested in getting a six, while the rest of the possible outcomes are only looked upon as 'not sixes'. It is also conceivable that your only interest is whether the dice shows an odd number of pips or an even number of pips.

Exercise 7.2 □
LOAD and RUN the program for this exercise. LIST it and check the listing against the one in the program booklet. What are the possible outcomes of the game simulated by the

program?. . . . .

What kind of real game could be modelled by the program?. . . . .

How many such games does the program perform?. . . . .

Extend the program to count the number of sixes that come out. This compound IF statement might prove useful to you:

IF OUTCOME=6 THEN SIXES:=SIXES+1

You will of course need a proper statement to output the final value of SIXES accompanied by a suitable text, and also a statement to **initialize SIXES** before the counting starts. When you have made the extensions, RUN the program to test it.
★

In Exercise 7.2 we singled out a certain outcome by using a compound IF statement. Similar methods can always be used, since you may have as many IF statements as you like. Sometimes it is easier to obtain the result by *computation* using the value returned by the RND function. If we want to determine whether the outcome of the game in Exercise 7.2 is, say, 'odd' or 'even', we may of course ask if OUTCOME is equal to 2, 4, or 6, or if it is equal to 1, 3 or 5; but we might also make some *calculations* first to simplify the decision. To that end we may use the **arithmetic operator MOD**. In order to find out how it works, let us take a look at the expression

15 MOD 4

which returns the *remainder* of 15 divided by 4, that is to say 3. The word MOD is an abbreviation of *modulo* which means "what is left, when you measure"; as you know that is just the remainder.

Exercise 7.3 □
LOAD the program "EXE73". LIST it and check the displayed listing against the listing in the program booklet. RUN the program using input of your own choice, and set down the output of each round on the lines below:

. . . .

. . . .

. . . .

. . . .

. . . .
★
Exercise 7.4
Use mental arithmetic to calculate:
17 MOD 2 = ..., 26 MOD 2 = ..., 846 MOD 2 = ..., 9467 MOD 2 =

. . . . State a computational method to find out if a given number is odd or even:

. . . .

. . . .
★

Exercise 7.5
Use the program listing for Exercise 7.2 found in the program booklet. In this exercise we are going to design some extensions of it. Write down your suggestions on a programming sheet, but do not key anything in yet.

We want to count how many times an *even* number has occurred during a program run. To that end we introduce the statement:

IF (OUTCOME MOD 2)=0 THEN COUNTEVEN:=COUNTEVEN+1

with its own line number. What line number would you suggest? . . . . The counter COUNTEVEN must be initialized through the assignment:

COUNTEVEN:=0

Propose a line number for the assignment: . . . . After the games have been finished, we would like an output to appear as follows:

AN EVEN NUMBER CAME OUT 4 TIMES.

Write a suitable line to produce it:

. . . .

★

Exercise 7.6 □
Having done Exercise 7.5, your programming sheet should appear very much like the following, although your line numbers may be slightly different:

> 5 counteven:= 0
> 25 if (outcome mod 2)=0 then counteven:=counteven+1
> 55 print "an even number came out ", counteven," times."

LOAD the program "EXE72" and type in the lines to extend it. RUN it to check that it works as required.

★

X MOD Y MEANS: THE REMAINDER OF X DIVIDED BY Y.

Using the operator MOD it is easy to make out whether a number is odd or even. We shall make use of this facility to modify the program "ODDEVEN".

Exercise 7.7
In the following we shall try to teach the computer to play a game called "peanuts". In this game one player holds a number of peanuts in his hand. The other player tries to guess whether an odd or an even number of peanuts are hidden in his opponents hand. If he makes a right guess, the former player must give him the peanuts he has staked. On the other hand, if the guess is wrong, the player who holds the peanuts opens his hand to reveal how many peanuts he has staked and then receives an equal number from the loser. The computer is going to play the role of the player who holds the peanuts in his hand.

Find the listing of "PEANUTS" in the program booklet. The program is not complete, so do not try to RUN it yet. What is the name of the variable whose value determines the

number of games to be played? . . . . The variable STAKED is used by the program to hold the number of "peanuts" hidden in the program's "hand". Copy the line in which STAKED is assigned a value:

. . . .

How many "peanuts" at most may the program stake? . . . . In the program section –ODD OR EVEN– the variable OUTCOME is used to decide whether an even or an odd number of "peanuts" is staked. OUTCOME is, however, not assigned a value in the present state of the program. Think of a statement to assign a value of 0 to OUTCOME if STAKED is even, and a value of 1 is STAKED is odd. Write it down using a suitable line number:

. . . .

In the program section –WHO WINS?– the variable COUNTWIN is used to keep the score. If the user wins, the value of STAKED is added to COUNTWIN. If he loses, however, the value of STAKED should be subtracted from the value of COUNTWIN. Set down the appropriate assignment to do that:

. . . .

Suppose STAKED assumes a value of 5 and the user enters the number 0 to be assigned to GUESS. What then would be output by the two sections –ODD OR EVEN– and –WHO WINS?–?

. . . .

. . . .

. . . .

. . . .

Same question with STAKED equal to 3 and GUESS equal to 1:

. . . .

. . . .

. . . .

. . . .

★

Exercise 7.8 ☐

Having done Exercise 7.7, your programming sheet should look much like this:

235 outcome := staked mod 2
405 countwin := countwin − staked

LOAD the program "PEANUTS" and type in the statements suggested in Exercise 7.7. RUN the completed program. Compare the output from each individual run with those suggested in Exercise 7.7.

★

Exercise 7.9

This uses a listing of the exercise that was completed in Exercise 7.8. Suppose five games are played, and STAKED and GUESS assume, game by game, the values indicated below. State the value of COUNTWIN after each game in succession:

STAKED	GUESS	COUNTWIN
3	1	
1	1	
5	0	
2	1	
6	0	

In the last section of the program —FINAL RESULT— the conditional statement

        IF COUNTWIN>0 THEN

controls the printout of the final result of the game. What is the truth value of the Boolean expression in the statement if COUNTWIN has a value of −9? . . . . What printout results? . . . .

★

The operator MOD is often used along with another, namely DIV, which may be used to find the *integer quotient* of one number divided by another one. Thus the expression

        15 DIV 7

returns the value 2.

Exercise 7.10 ☐

These are the first six lines of a program to input an integer and a positive integer:

```
0010 PRINT "ENTER X (INTEGER ONLY)             ",
0020 INPUT X
0030 PRINT "ENTER Y (POSITIVE INTEGER ONLY) ",
0040 INPUT Y
0050 Q:=X DIV Y; R:=X MOD Y
```

If a value of 34 is input to X and a value of 5 is input to Y, the program should display the following:

$$34 = 5*6 + 4$$

Type in the six lines above and add one line with a PRINT statement to give the desired output. RUN and check the program.

If a value of −34 is input to X and a value of 8 to Y, we would like the program to output

$$-34 = 8*(-5) + 6$$

Extend the program to adjust the output in accordance with the sign of X.

★

X DIV Y MEANS: THE **INTEGER QUOTIENT** OF X DIVIDED BY Y.

8

Little boxes

When you try to solve a problem it is very often a good idea to cut it up into smaller sub-problems. In many cases it may be almost impossible to grasp the whole problem in one piece, but each of the smaller problems it is cut up into may prove easy to solve. Most real-life programs are quite large, and may contain hundreds or even thousands of statements. Such a program becomes very difficult to read and understand. In this chapter we shall introduce a method of packaging a program into smaller segments, each of which performs a specific well-defined part of the total process, which is to be carried out by the program as a whole.

Exercise 8.1
The structure diagram below illustrates the program "ODDEVEN":

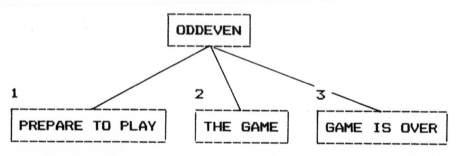

A listing of the program will be found in the program booklet. From the listing it is easy to see that the program consists three segments. This is illustrated by means of comments like this:

//--------------//

What are the numbers of the lines with that comment? . . . ., ..., and . . . .

★

It is very important to write a program in a way that makes it easy for others to read it and to understand what it does. Comments may serve as a means of making programs more understandable. This goes for comments that explain details of the program, as well as for null comments that separate one program section from another in the listing. But comments are passive statements; they do not in any way play a part in the processing itself. The system uses them only in the listing. Even if you use a lot of comments in a program such as "ODDEVEN", it still is a single long program. Genuine segmenting of a program must be done in a more radical way which we are going to look into now.

Exercise 8.2
The program to be used in this exercise is called "BIGNUTS". Find a listing of it in the program booklet. The program in question is a new edition of "PEANUTS", but this one has been segmented using **procedures** instead of the comments used before. The first procedure is INTRODUCTION. It begins in line 70 and ends in line 240. Copy the statement in line 70.

. . . .

Copy the statement in line 240:

. . . .

The second procedure is GAME. I what line does it start? . . . ., and in which line

does it end? . . . . The third procedure is FINITO; it begins in line . . . ., and

ends in line . . . .
★

In the program "BIGNUTS" that we met in Exercise 8.2, two new keywords are encountered, viz. PROC and ENDPROC. The two keywords are always followed by the *name* of the *procedure*.

A PROCEDURE IS INITIATED WITH A **PROC** STATEMENT AND TERMINA-
TED WITH AN **ENDPROC** STATEMENT.

PROC ⟨name of the procedure⟩

ENDPROC [⟨name of the procedure⟩]

THE **NAME** OF A **PROCEDURE** IS OF THE SAME FORM AS A VARIABLE
NAME.

Note. It is not allowed to have a variable and a procedure with the same name in the same program.

The first line of a procedure definition — i.e. the PROC statement — is called the *procedure head,* and the last statement of the definition — the ENDPROC statement — is called the *procedure tail.* The block of statements contained between a pair of PROC . —. ENDPROC statements is called the *body of the procedure.* The procedure body thus holds the statements to execute the process defined by the procedure.

When you want a program to perform a process, you start it with the command RUN. A procedure on the other hand must be called upon to do its task by means of a special statement. We speak of **calling a procedure.**

Exercise 8.3

We shall go on using the listing of "BIGNUTS". The procedure INTRODUCTION is called when the statement

    EXEC INTRODUCTION

is encountered. Copy the line with the statement that calls the procedure GAME:

. . . .

and the line holding the call for FINITO:

. . . .

★

A statement to call a procedure always begins with the keyword EXEC which is followed by the *name of the procedure* to be called. The word EXEC is an abbreviation of "execute". The statement

    EXEC INTRODUCTION

may be interpreted as "now execute the statements in the body of the procedure INTRO-DUCTION".

Note. In some versions of COMAL–80 the keyword EXEC may be left out. Thus to call INTRODUCTION the statement of only one word

    INTRODUCTION

will do.

AN **EXEC** STATEMENT IS USED TO **CALL** A PROCEDURE.

EXEC ⟨name of procedure to be called⟩

When the ENDPROC statement of a procedure is encountered, execution continues with *the statement following the one that called the procedure.* The *mainline program* of "BIGNUTS" consists of the following three statements:

```
EXEC INTRODUCTION
EXEC GAME
EXEC FINITO
```

This is how they are executed: First the procedure INTRODUCTION is performed. When its ENDPROC statement is encountered, the mainline program resumes with the statement

```
EXEC GAME
```

since this is the one following the statement that called INTRODUCTION. Now GAME is executed and then the mainline program resumes with

```
EXEC FINITO
```

causing FINITO to be performed.

Normally the user should not care about all this jumping to and fro. Just leave it to the COMAL interpreter to find its way about the program; it has been designed to do that job. Instead, simply suppose the whole procedure to be present at the place of the calling statement. If you write, say, EXEC INTRODUCTION, you intend of course to have a certain process performed, *at that point,* no matter *where the actual statements* are typed in. Large programs written for commercial or industrial purposes are often written by teams of programmers, each of whom writes some procedures. It is highly probable that each programmer does not know in detail how others have programmed their parts. The point is that this will not matter provided that the program has been packaged into procedures and everybody knows exactly what jobs are performed by the procedures he needs to call from his part of the program.

```
    . . .
    EXEC ⟨name of procedure⟩
 ──▶ ⟨the statement following the EXEC statement⟩
    . . .
    . . .
    . . .
    PROC ⟨name of procedure⟩ ◀

        THIS BLOCK OF STATEMENTS IS CALLED THE BODY OF
        THE PROCEDURE. IT IS EXECUTED WHENEVER THE PROCEDURE
        IS CALLED.

    ENDPROC [⟨name of procedure⟩]
    . . .
```

In a structure diagram, procedures are represented by boxes like this one:

```
 ╔═══════════════════════╗
 ║ Name of procedure     ║
 ╚═══════════════════════╝
```

In some programming languages, procedures are also called **subroutines**.

Exercise 8.4
The program "BIGNUTS" may be illustrated as follows:

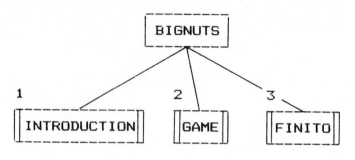

. . . .

Write down the line numbers of the *head* and *tail* of each procedure depicted on the lines below the boxes.

Inside the body of a procedure you may have calls to other procedures which in turn can call new procedures, and so on for as long as you like.

★

Exercise 8.5
In this exercise the work with "BIGNUTS" is continued. In the procedure GAME two other procedures are called. Locate them in the program listing. What are their names?

. . . . and . . . . Find the two lines from which

they are called and put down their line numbers: . . . . and . . . . The structure diagram below illustrates the procedure GAME. Fill in the empty procedure boxes:

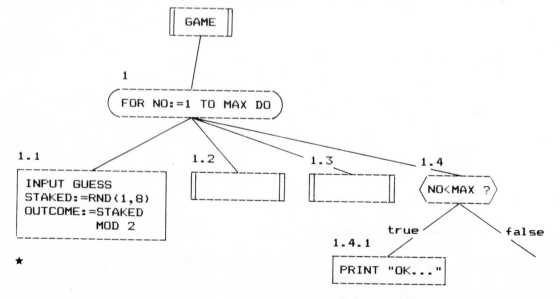

★

Note that very often PRINT statements are left out or only suggested in a structure diagram; you áre supposed to find them in the listing. There are no definite rules for this; it is done at the programmer's discretion. On the whole the boxes of a structure diagram are completed in an informal way. Eventually we shall reach a point where there are just enough details in the structure diagram to describe the algorithm for conceptual purposes, the exact details of the program being implied rather than spelled out.

★

It is a well established fact that large programs can not be written in a sensible way without making extensive use of procedures. A program that has been carefully segmented, using named procedures, is also easy to read because from the name of a procedure you normally get a strong hint as to what job it is doing. If the programmers have done their homework, the program will also be *easy to maintain*. Very often, if you have to modify it you only have to change one or two procedures, and it may not even be necessary to know the details of the other procedures.

Exercise 8.6 □
We are still working with "BIGNUTS". Draw a box around lines 290–300 and one around lines 310–320. Use the two blocks of statements thus delimited as the bodies of two new procedures GETGUESS and STAKENUTS, respectively. Type in the two procedures starting with:

```
750 PROC GETGUESS
760 PRINT "WELL, . . .
```

Then erase the original lines using the command

```
DEL 290–320
```

and insert calls for the two new procedures in place of them.

9
Guess my number

Of course a computer cannot "think". After all it is nothing but an automaton that will carry out our programs. You must tell it exactly what to do, and in return it will follow your orders without making any fuss. There is nothing extraordinary about its being able to generate random numbers. So can dice, and not many people believe that dice can think. It is our programs that make a computer look as if it thinks. All we do is exploit its ability to manipulate numbers with incredible speed.

However, numbers are of little significance until people *assign meanings to them,* and that is exactly what we are doing when we let the computer simulate a game. That the number 0 stands for "even" and the number 1 for "odd" is something *we* decide. It is sometimes said that we *interpret* the results our computer generates when it executes the processes we have programmed it to.

Exercise 9.1 ☐
LOAD and RUN the program "EXE91". How many games does the program perform?

. . . . What numbers can the program possibly "think of"? . . . .

★

Exercise 9.2
Use the listing of the program from Exercise 9.1 for this exercise. In which line is the

variable THINKOF assigned a value? . . . . Which line will allow the player to enter

his guess? . . . . What is the name of the variable that picks up the guess?

. . . . In what line is the head of GAME encountered? . . . .

Which line holds the tail of GAME? . . . . The head of TRYGUESS is in line . . . .

In one of the procedures a call to the other one is ecncountered. In what line? . . . .

Which procedure is called? . . . . What would the program display if

THINKOF is equal to 2 and GUESS is set to 1:

. . . .

. . . .

The structure diagrams on the next page represent the program and its procedures. Fill in the empty boxes with suitable texts.

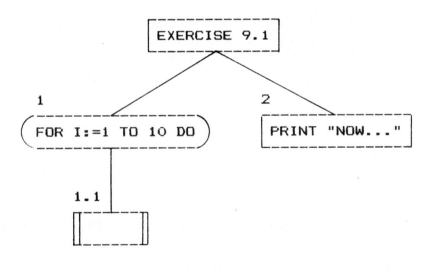

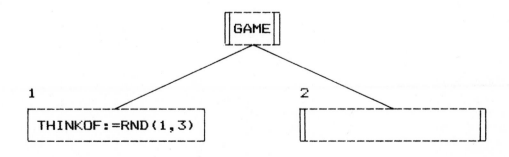

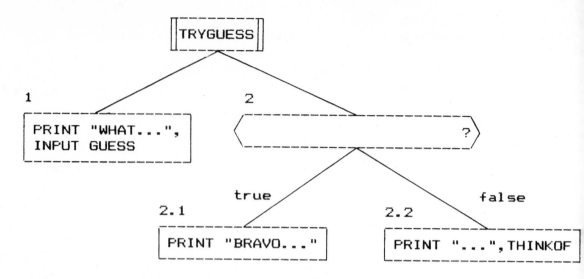

We want to plan some extensions of the program in order to improve it. We want it to count how many times the player guesses the number picked up by the RND function. A suitable name for the counting variable would be, say HITS, and each time the player succeeds in making a correct guess, the following statement must be executed:

HITS:=HITS+1

It must be inserted in the block of statements which is processed when the player hits the

computer's number. What line number would you suggest? . . . . Before the first round of the game starts, HITS must be initialized. Suggest a program line to do that,

and put it down here: . . . . The value of HITS should be output when the games are finished. The closing printout of the program should be replaced by a message, formatted like this:

YOU HAVE MADE 3 CORRECT GUESSES.

What line must be rewritten? . . . . Write down the program line to replace it.

. . . .

★

Exercise 9.3 ☐
LOAD the program "EXE91" and type in the changes and extensions suggested in Exercise 9.2. Then RUN the program to test it.

★

Exercise 9.4 ☐
LOAD the program "EXE94". RUN it once or twice. A listing of the program is found in the program booklet. Locate a statement that begins with the word REPEAT and another

one that starts with the word UNTIL. The first statement is encountered in line . . . .,

and the second one in line . . . .
★

What about p239?

In the program from Exercise 9.4 two new COMAL words are introduced, viz. REPEAT and UNTIL. REPEAT may stand alone, whereas UNTIL must be followed by a Boolean expression. The two statements cause the block of statements contained between them to be *executed repeatedly, until* the Boolean expression following UNTIL assumes a value of *true.*

Exercise 9.5
Use the listing of the program in Exercise 9.4 in this exercise. The block of statements between the REPEAT and the UNTIL statements has been enclosed in a box. This block is executed *repetitively, until* GUESS is equal to THINKOF, that is until the player has guessed the number, generated by the RND function. What line is executed when the

player types in his guess?. . . . .
The Boolean expression

GUESS=THINKOF

is used in two different statements. Copy them here:

. . . .

. . . .

What message is output by the program if GUESS is *not* equal to THINKOF?

. . . .

. . . .

. . . .

Pack the section of the program ranging from line 200 to line 280 into a procedure which you will call CONTROL.
Start writing the procedure with this line:

320 PROC CONTROL

and do not forget to terminate with the statement

ENDPROC CONTROL

Put down your suggestions on a programming sheet to be ready for typing in.

★

Exercise 9.6 □

LOAD the program "EXE94". Type in the procedure that was written in Exercise 9.5. Then delete the original lines (DEL 200–280) and insert the statement:

     EXEC CONTROL

in the program at an appropriate point.

★

Since a group of statements may be executed several times, what we have here is a **loop structure**. So far we have encountered two types of loops: FOR — Next loops and REPEAT — UNTIL loops. As usual the group of statements contained between the REPEAT and UNTIL statements is said to be the **range** of the loop. We may also talk about the block *within* the loop.

REPEAT
     THIS BLOCK OF STATEMENTS IS EXECUTED **REPEATEDLY**,
     UNTIL THE BOOLEAN EXPRESSION FOLLOWING THE KEYWORD
     UNTIL HAS ASSUMED A VALUE OF TRUE
UNTIL ⟨Boolean expression⟩

Note that since provision for the loop to be terminated is accomplished with the UNTIL statement, which is the last one of the loop, the range of it will always be executed at least once (unlike the FOR . . . NEXT loop).

In structure diagrams a REPEAT — UNTIL loop is represented, as before, by an oval shaped box:

```
 _____
(  REPEAT..UNTIL    )
(  GUESS=THINKOF    )
 ------------------
```

The part of the diagram representing the range of the loop is connected to the repetition box.

     In some cases you may choose between REPEAT — UNTIL loops and FOR — NEXT loops as you like, but as a rule it is more practical to use a FOR — NEXT loop when provision for the loop to be terminated may be done using an index variable. In the program in Exercise 9.4, it is the value of the index-variable I that determines if more games are performed or the program is going to be stopped. In the REPEAT — UNTIL loop of the procedure TRYGUESS, however, it is *not* possible to introduce an index-variable to control the loop and terminate it because you don't know as you enter the loop how often you are going to do it. Only if the value of GUESS is equal to the value of THINKOF should the loop be terminated. Here a FOR — NEXT loop could not be used.

Exercise 9.7
The structure diagram below describes the procedure TRYGUESS:

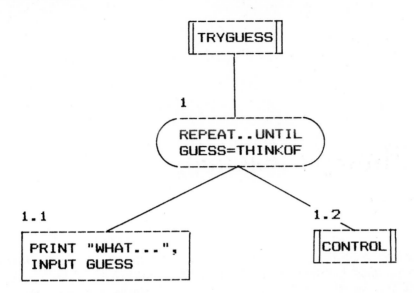

Draw one to represent CONTROL.

10

The arithmetic teacher

Computers may be used to teach. People talk about "computer assisted learning" or "computer programmed learning" and the like. You can write very small programs to put simple drill and practice exercises, or very large, complicated programs to manage the whole teaching of one or several subjects. In what follows we are going to look into a small program to set up tiny arithmetic exercises and check the pupils answers.

Exercise 10.1 □
LOAD the program "EXE101". RUN it. LIST the program. Locate the line in which two variables A and B are assigned values. Copy the line here:

. . . .

Also locate a line in which the variable RESULT is assigned a value. What line is it? . . . .

What value is assigned to RESULT if A is equal to 3 and B is equal to 5? . . . .
★

In the program from exercise 10.1 this line is encountered:

        70 A:=RND(1,5); B:=RND(1,5)

As you see there are *two* assignments on one line; the first one assigns a value of {1, . . ., 5} to A, and the second one assigns a value in ths same range to B. You may have as many assignments on a line as the line width permits; the individual assignments being separated by the *semicolon* (;).

> YOU MAY HAVE **SEVERAL ASSIGNMENTS** SEPARATED BY **SEMICOLONS** ON ONE LINE.

Exercise 10.2
Use the listing of the program from Exercise 10.1 for this exercise. In what lines are the

heads and tails of the following procedures encountered: EXERCISE? . . . . and

. . . ., GETANSWER? . . . . and . . . ., CONTROL? . . . . and . . . .

One of the procedures has an empty body. Write down its name: . . . .

We are going to complete it in accordance with the structure diagram below:

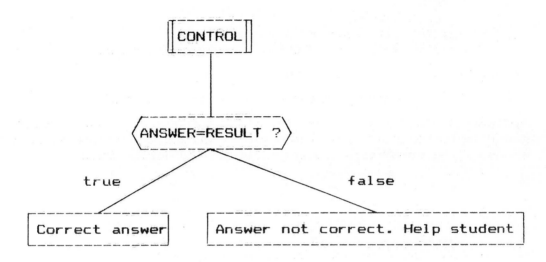

If the answer is correct, we want the program only to display the message

> **THAT'S CORRECT!**

If the answer is not correct, however, we want to tell the student the sad story but we would also like to give some help. If A is equal to, say 3, and B is equal to 4, and the student does not answer 7, the following message should appear:

> **YOUR ANSWER IS NOT CORRECT;**
>
> **4 + 3 = 7**

Suggest the program lines necessary for CONTROL to work in accordance with the structure diagram and the output specifications; write these lines down on a programming sheet.

★

Exercise 10.3 ☐
LOAD the program "EXE101". Type in the program lines that were suggested in Exercise 10.2. RUN the program to test it.

★

A procedure the body of which has not been filled in is called a **procedure stub** or simply a stub. Stubs are used when you want to test a program without having to finish all procedures. In Exercise 10.1 we were able to run and test parts of a program although one of the procedures had an empty body. The program would, however, not have worked had the head and tail of CONTROL not been present.

The program we have written during the previous exercises is not very patient with its pupils. If the answer to a problem is not correct at the first attempt, the pupil, without further notice, is given the right answer and the next exercise. We shall try to improve this harsh behaviour on the part of the program by modifying it to let the pupil have three tries, before the correct answer is eventually given. Let us start with this algorithm:

> *REPEAT*
> > *pose the problem*
> > *get the students answer*
> *UNTIL answer is correct OR three attempts have been made*

At the present level of description this statement occurs:

> *UNTIL answer is correct OR three attempts have been made*

Apparently we shall have to introduce a **counter** to keep track of the number of times the student has tried to answer. This counter must be *increased by one* each time an answer is entered. These considerations lead us to set up the following algorithm:

> *initialize counter to zero*
> *REPEAT*
> > *pose the problem*
> > *get the students answer*
> > *increase counter by one*
> *UNTIL answer is correct OR counter is equal to three*

Exercise 10.4

The structure diagram below represents a detailed description of an implementation of the algorithm suggested above. Write down the statements represented in the diagram to form a normal COMAL program segment. Do not forget that the UNTIL statement must terminate the loop initiated with the REPEAT statement.

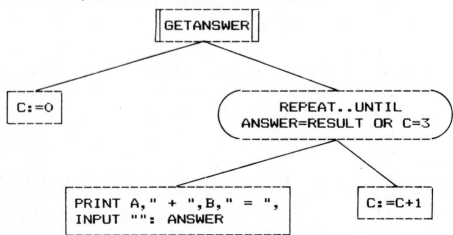

★

Exercise 10.5 □

LOAD the program "EXE105". In that version CONTROL has been completed. Enter with proper line numbers the statements necessary to complete GETANSWER according to the algorithm suggested in the program booklet and the structure diagram from Exercise 10.4. RUN it to see that it works correctly.

Type in the word RENUM and press the RETURN key. Now list the program and watch the numbers of the lines. Compare the listing now on the screen with the listing of the program "ADDITION" found in the program booklet.

★

In the previous exercise we have used the statement

UNTIL ANSWER=RESULT OR C=3

The Boolean expression

ANSWER=RESULT OR C=3

has been put together using two *simple* Boolean expressions "ANSWER=RESULT" and "C=3". The keyword OR that is used to combine the two expressions is called a **Boolean operator** and it has the same meaning and function as the so called *"logical or"* known from mathematics. Thus with the present expression we get a value of **true** if *either* the student has given a correct answer (ANSWER=RESULT) *or* three attempts have been made (C=3), and this is exactly what we intended to have.

Boolean expressions can be put together using the Boolean operators AND, OR, and NOT to produce other Boolean expressions. The three operators are defined as follows:

AND IS A BINARY OPERATOR WHOSE TWO OPERANDS ARE BOOLEAN EXPRESSIONS. THE RESULTING OPERATION IS TRUE IF **BOTH EXPRESSIONS ARE TRUE**, OTHERWISE IT IS **FALSE**.

OR IS A BINARY OPERATOR WHOSE TWO OPERANDS ARE BOOLEAN EXPRESSIONS. THE RESULT OF THE OPERATION IS TRUE, IF **EITHER OR BOTH OF THE TWO EXPRESSIONS IS TRUE**, OTHERWISE IT IS **FALSE**.

NOT IS A UNARY OPERATOR THE OPERAND OF WHICH IS A BOOLEAN EXPRESSION. IF THE VALUE OF THE EXPRESSION IS **TRUE** THE RESULTING OPERATION IS **FALSE**: IF THE VALUE OF THE OPERAND IS **FALSE**, THE RESULT OF THE OPERATION IS **TRUE**.

Exercise 10.6

Use the listing of the program "ADDITION" for this exercise. Suppose we want to redesign the program to give practice in multiplication instead of addition. Write down on a programming sheet the necessary replacements for program lines in the present program. To make the program more flexible we should also like to be able to change the maximum value of the factors which it outputs as it sets up a multiplication problem. Try to find out how this can be done. It might be a good idea to introduce a variable MAXFAC.

★

Exercise 10.7 ☐

LOAD the program "ADDITION" and type in the statements suggested in Exercise 10.6 to replace existing statements and extend the program. RUN the program to test that it works as required.

Type RENUM and press the RETURN key. LIST the program and watch the line numbers. Especially notice the lines added to the program to extend its usability. Then type in

RENUM 1000

press the RETURN key and LIST the program again. Watch the line numbers. How do they go?

. . . .

Finally key in

RENUM 15,2

and press the RETURN key. LIST the program and watch the line numbers. How do they go now?

. . . .

★

At the end of Exercises 10.6 and 10.7 we used the command RENUM. The word RENUM is an abbreviation of the word "renumber" and, as is seen from the exercises, the command causes the lines of the program to be numbered like this: 10, 20, 30, . . . The RENUM command is often used when you have finished typing in a program to make the listing "look pretty". In some cases however, use of the RENUM command is essential. Suppose we have to insert some extra lines in the midst of a program. We might end up having no room for the new lines, because the line numbers already there are too close together. Generally it is hard to push in an extra line between say, line 105 and line 106! The RENUM command may then be used to "open up" the program.

> THE **RENUM** COMMAND CAUSES THE PROGRAM LINES TO BE NUMBERED AS FOLLOWS: 10, 20, 30, ...

The RENUM command has some interesting modifications; thus the following command:

RENUM 50

causes the lines to be numbered like this: 50, 60, 70, . . . Using this command:

RENUM 15,2

generates the following sequence of line numbers: 15, 17, 19, 21, . . .

THE COMMAND **RENUM X**, WHERE **X** IS A POSITIVE INTEGER, CAUSES THE LINES OF THE PROGRAM TO BE NUMBERED: **X, X+10, X+20,** . . .
THE COMMAND **RENUM X, Y**, WHERE **X** AND **Y** ARE POSITIVE INTEGERS, CAUSES THE LINES NUMBERS OF THE PROGRAM TO BECOME: **X, X+Y, X+2Y, X+3Y,** . . .

11

Uncle Hannibal's X-mas cards

In this line:

      60 PRINT "ALFRED WATERMAN, DIVER."

the string to be printed out is inserted directly after the keyword PRINT. Each time the statement is executed *the same text* is displayed, and it can only be changed by rewriting the line. A text that has been set up in the program in that way is called a **string constant**. In many cases it would be very useful to be able to change a text or part of it without having to rewrite one or more program lines. This is where **string variables** come in.

Exercise 11.1
Take a look at this form:

    Name:. . . . .

    House No. . . . .   Street:. . . . .

    Town:. . . . .

Fill in the form. It has four fields. In one of them you are supposed to write a number, in the three others texts are expected. What are the titles of the three text fields?

. . . ., ..., and . . . .
★

    Most people who look at a form like the one shown in exercise 11.1 know that it has to be *completed* to mean something. Whoever has sent out the form would never know in advance what is going to be written on it — in which case it would be a little silly to send it out, by the way —. But you can see that a person's name is expected in the first field, a house number in the second field, a name of a street in the third, and the name and possibly postal code of a town in the fourth one. The title of a field tells you something about the *meaning* of the text or the number that may be filled in, but absolutely nothing about *what text* or *number* somebody might write in the field. Imagine that 3000 forms like the one shown in the exercise have been filled in. Each form will then hold *the same four fields,* but it is very unlikely that two of the forms come to carry the same texts and the same number.

We can have our computer system organize parts of the workspace in a way that is very similar to fields on a form.

Exercise 11.2 □

LOAD the program EXE112. Have a listing displayed and check it against the one in the program booklet. RUN the program to see how it works. In the program there are five

INPUT statements. Four of these take strings as input. What lines are they in? . . . .,

. . . ., ..., and . . . . One of them takes a number as input. In what line

is it found? . . . .
★

In the program from Exercise 11.2 these statements are found:

```
DIM NAME$ OF 25, STREET$ OF 20
DIM TOWN$ OF 20, CODE$ OF 10
```

When these statements are executed, the COMAL interpreter *sets aside* four **fields** in the workspace. The first one is labelled NAME$, the second one STREET$, the third one TOWN$, and the fourth one CODE$. The "$" sign that terminates each name indicates that texts rather than numbers are referred to. Each of them is followed by the keyword OF and a positive integer to tell the system *how many characters* each field must be able to hold. Thus the field that is called NAME$ may hold up to 25 characters, whereas the one referred to as STREET$ cannot hold more than 20 characters, which is also the case with the one called TOWN$. The first of the statements could be interpreted like this, "Set aside enough room in the workspace to hold up to 25 characters and label it NAME, then reserve another part to hold up to 20 characters and give it the name STREET". When the two statements have been executed, you may imagine that a small part of the workspace has been organized like this:

NAME $:

STREET $:

TOWN $:

CODE $:

Exercise 11.3
Some forms are designed in a way that only allows for a certain number of characters in the individual fields. This is one:

Name: |_|_|_|_|_|_|_|_|_|_|_|_|_|_|_|_|_|_|_|_|_|_|_|_|_|_|_|_|_|_|

Position: |_|_|_|_|_|_|_|_|_|_|_|_|_|_|_|_|_|_|_|_|_|

Address: |_|_|_|_|_|_|_|_|_|_|_|_|_|_|_|_|_|_|_|_|_|_|_|_|_|_|_|_|

Town: |_|_|_|_|_|_|_|_|_|_|_|_|_|_|_|_|_|_|_|_|

County: |_|_|_|_|_|_|_|_|_|_|_|_|_|_|_|_|_|_|_|

Code: |_|_|_|_|_|_|_|_|_|_|_|_|

How many characters may be used to give your name? . . . . How many characters may be used to enter your position? . . . .

★

A string constant is any sequence of characters that may be entered from the keyboard. Thus "FX678" and "APQ$%?()/+" are examples of string constants. However, most people would prefer to say that "THIS OLD MAN CAME ROLLING HOME" is a *text* rather than use such pompous words as "string constant". But in computer science it is practical to have a general and neutral name for any sequence of characters, even such nonsense ones as shown above. In this book we shall, however, also use the word "text" to refer to a string constant whenever it would be natural to do so. The double quotes sign (") has a special status since it is used to delimit string constants, i.e. to tell where a string constant starts and ends. The number of characters to appear between a set of delimiting double quotes is called the *length of the string*. Thus the length of this string (or text):

SALLY SINGS SAD SONGS

is 21 (do not forget that space is also a character).

A STRING CONSTANT IS ANY **SEQUENCE OF CHARACTERS** THAT MAY BE ENTERED THROUGH THE COMPUTERS KEYBOARD. VERY OFTEN A STRING CONSTANT IS CALLED A **TEXT**.
THE **LENGTH** OF A STRING CONSTANT (OR TEXT) IS THE **NUMBER OF CHARACTERS** IN IT.

Exercise 11.4 □
LOAD the program EXE112 again. RUN it and type in the following:

COLIN ST. GEORGE INGLEBY-MCKENZIE
45
SAINT JOHNS AVENUE NORTH
EARLY READING
RG6 1HY

Note the output from the program. What is the length of the name that is typed in?

. . . . How many of the characters in the name are printed out? . . . . Why is

that so? . . . .

. . . .
★

　　When a DIM statement is executed, space is reserved for a certain number of characters in each of the fields mentioned in the statement. If you try later on to store a string in a reserved field and that string is longer than the field, the excess characters are not stored but are lost without the user being warned by an error message. Space reserved for a string is referred to by means of a **string variable**. NAME$, STREET$, TOWN$, and CODE$ are examples of string variables. A string stored in a field named by a string variable is said to be the *value* of that variable. The variables we have been working with earlier, that are assigned *numbers* as values, can be called numeric variables. This means that from now on we may use two types of variables: **Numeric variables** that can assume **numeric values**, and **string variables** that may be assigned **strings** – or **texts** – as values. Names of string variables are known from names of numeric variables by the "$" sign that terminates them.

IN COMAL THERE ARE DIFFERENT **TYPES** OF VARIABLES. NUMERIC **VARIABLES** MAY ASSUME **NUMERIC VALUES**, AND **STRING VARIABLES** CAN BE ASSIGNED **STRINGS AS VALUES**.
THE NAME OF A STRING VARIABLE IS ALWAYS TERMINATED WITH THE "$" SIGN, BUT APART FROM THAT IT MUST CONFORM WITH THE SAME RULES AS THE NAME OF A NUMERIC VARIABLE.

Since fields for strings may differ in length, space must always be reserved for them in DIM statements. Another way of putting this is to say variables must be **declared**.

A **DIM** STATEMENT CONSISTS OF THE KEYWORD **DIM** FOLLOWED BY A LIST OF DECLARATIONS.

The word "DIM" is an abbreviation of "dimension" which also in every day language means the "size" of something. We may for example talk about "the dimensions of a room".

Exercise 11.5 □
LOAD the program EXE112. Change line 10 and 20 to become:

```
0010 DIM NAME$ OF 40, STREET$ OF 30
0020 DIM TOWN$ OF 30, CODE$ OF 10
```

RUN the program and enter the same name and address as in Exercise 11.4. Note the

printout. Why do we now get the full name and address displayed? . . . .

. . . .

How many declarations are written in line 10 and 20? . . . . In one of the PRINT

statements in the program, both a numeric and a string variable are used. Which line

holds that statement? . . . . What is the name of the numeric variable?

. . . . and that of the string variable? . . . .

★

Exercise 11.6
Hannibal Harris is very busy and incredibly forgetful. One of the things he always forgets about is sending his X-mas cards. So his nephew Havelock Harris has written a program to help him. A list of the program can be found in the program booklet under the name of "UNCLEXMAS". Use that listing with the following. The program uses four string

variables. What are their names? . . . ., ... ,

. . . ., and . . . . Three of these variables get

their values through user input. Mark them on your list above. The fourth one is assigned

the value of a constant in the program. Copy that constant here: . . . .

In the program there is a procedure PRINTOUT. In what line is its head? . . . ., and

its tail? . . . . From what line is it called? . . . .

Note: There is also a procedure CLEAR in the program. It is a service procedure to clear the screen and set the beginning of the printout. Its head looks like this:

        PROC CLEAR(X)

Here X is what is called a formal parameter which is simply a variable to be assigned a value during the call of the procedure. The procedure is called from different places in the program, e.g. by the statement

        EXEC CLEAR(3)

With the procedure called in this way, X is assigned a value of 3, and then the screen is cleared, and the cursor moved 3 lines down. Procedures with parameters will be explained later on. Service procedures like CLEAR are used in some of the following programs. You do not need to worry much about them at the moment — just use them as they are. Should you want to use them in programs of your own, simply copy them.

★

 When the following statement is executed:

        PRINT "A TOTAL OF ",NUMBER

the text between the quotes and the value of the variable NUMBER is displayed. If NUMBER has a value of say 8, this printout results:

        A TOTAL OF 8

The next statement is executed in a similar way

        PRINT "GENERAL MANAGER ",NAME$

If for example NAME$ has the value "MICHAEL HAWTHORNE", the statement generates this printout:

        GENERAL MANAGER MICHAEL HAWTHORNE

A variable always has its *value* printed out. This goes for both numeric variables and string variables. Evidently a numeric variable causes a number to be printed out, whereas a string variable causes a string to be output.

Exercise 11.7 ☐
All the X-mas cards Hannibal Harris writes end with the words:

        LOVE FROM
        HANNIBAL

LOAD the program "UNCLEXMAS". Rewrite one of the statements to have the cards signed with another name. RUN the program to test your modifications.

★

    A string variable can be used in a Boolean expression just like a numeric variable. Thus in Uncle Hannibals X-mas program this statement is found:

        UNTIL ANSW$="N"

The UNTIL statement holds the Boolean expression:

ANSW$="N"

which assumes a value of TRUE if ANSW$ is equal to "N", and a value of FALSE in all other cases. This is totally consistent with the way in which the following Boolean expression is interpreted:

NUMBER=5

It has a value of TRUE if NUMBER is equal to 5, and a value of FALSE in all other cases.

Note. When the COMAL system encounters Boolean expressions using the relational operators "<" and ">" the usual **lexicographical ordering** of strings is applied to interpret the expressions. Lexicographical ordering of texts is the one used in dictionaries, encyclopedia, and indices. The sign "<" then means "comes before", whereas ">" can be understood as "comes after".

12
The fourth form pupils

We give *names* to people, animals, things, and this helps us to think and talk about them, and to manage them. Very often we also use *numbers* as well as or even instead of names, particularly when we want to *order* things, people, or events in a special way. After a bicycle race we may have the following result:

No. 1: Spencer Sprocket
No. 2: Peter Pedal
No. 3: Simon Spoke

Numbers have been added to the names of the three winners to indicate in what *order* they have passed the finishing line. The three sportsmen also have an entrant number each. Thus Spencer Sprocket has the number 7 on his back — together with a sponsor's text saying, "Step on it — with Robertson's rush shoes" — and on Peter Pedal's back it says 15 in large red digits, while Simon Spoke carries the proud number 1 which does not prevent him from finishing third! As everyone knows, the number you are given when entering a game has nothing to do with the number you get as a result of the game.

Exercise 12.1
Below is shown a part of a register. The register contains the names of those fourth form pupils who are doing computer studies.

Subject: Computer Studies		Form Fourth

No.	Surname	First name(s)
1		
2	Jensen,	Lars Krohn
3	Kjaer,	Torben
4	Lorentsen,	Hans Joergen
5	Petersen,	Lars B.
6	Enoksen,	Hans Henrik
7	Gaml-Jensen,	Lars
8	Gerlach,	Tom
9	Hansen,	Pia
10		
11	Mortensen,	Holger
12	Nissen,	Frank
13	Schmidt,	Wenche
14	Sylvest,	Tina
15	Valeur,	Niels
16	Riemke,	Bjarne
17	Rubaek,	Steen
18		
19	Sylvest,	Claus
20		

How many pupils are doing computer studies? . . . . What is the name of pupil no. 4?

. . . . What is the name of pupil no. 9? . . . . What

is the number of the pupil named: Nissen, Frank? . . . ., and what is the number of

the pupil named: Schmidt, Wenche? . . . . Four of the fields are empty. Which ones?

. . . ., ..., ..., and . . . . In what follows we shall use "PUPIL(1)"

as short for "Pupil no. 1", "PUPIL(2)" for "Pupil no. 2" etc, and instead of "Pupil no. 3
has the name Kjaer, Torben", we shall write "PUPIL(3) = "KJAER, TORBEN". Complete
the following:

PUPIL(6) = " . . . . ",

PUPIL(16) = " . . . .",

PUPIL(. . .) = "SYLVEST, TINA", PUPIL(. . .) = "JENSEN, LARS KROHN".
★

The individual names in the register from exercise 12.1 are numbered. A set whose elements are numbered is called a *table* or an *array*. Many applications require the use of tables to store data in a convenient way. COMAL allows you to organize parts of the workspace as tables (arrays). As an example, if this statement is executed:

DIM PUPIL$(20) OF 30

20 fields of 30 characters each are reserved. Thus a part of the workspace is arranged in a manner quite similar to a page in a register, like the one shown in the exercise, but of course no names have been entered yet. You may picture to yourself that it looks like this:

The "$" sign following the name of the array indicates that a table of strings is referred to. Each individual entry or element of the table has a number which is called its subscript or index and is used to reference that element. If we want to refer to, say the 3rd element — i.e. the element with index 3 — we simply write PUPIL$(3). Thus the elements of the array may be individually referenced as PUPIL$(1), PUPIL$(2), PUPIL$(3), . . ., PUPIL$(20), and each of these elements may be used like a simple string variable. As an example if this statement is executed:

PUPIL$(16):="RIEMKE, BJARNE"

the string "RIEMKE, BJARNE" is stored in the element PUPIL$(16), or you could say that the *subscripted variable* PUPIL$(16) is assigned the value "RIEMKE, BJARNE". After the statement has been executed, we may imagine it looks like this in the workspace:

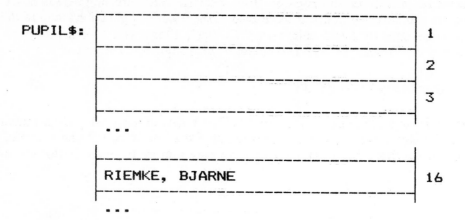

The other elements are still empty. If a statement like the following is executed:

INPUT PUPIL$(17)

the COMAL system as usual displays the input prompt and waits for us to type in something from the keyboard. If the text, say "RUBAEK, STEEN" is entered, we may fancy that it looks like this in the workspace afterwards:

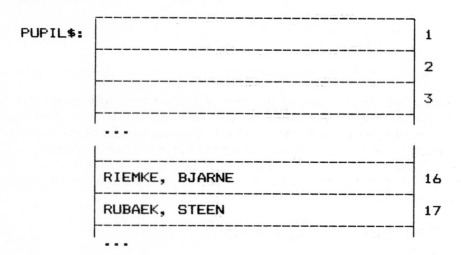

If subsequently we have this statement executed:

PRINT PUPIL$(16)

the following is displayed on the screen:

RIEMKE, BJARNE

since this is the text assigned to the element with index 16.

Exercise 12.2 ☐
Find the program listing for this exercise in the program booklet. Fill in this picture of
ART$ (articles) in accordance with the texts given in the program:

```
ART$:   ┌─────────────────────────────────┐  1
        ├─────────────────────────────────┤  2
        ├─────────────────────────────────┤  3
        ├─────────────────────────────────┤  4
        ├─────────────────────────────────┤  5
        ├─────────────────────────────────┤  6
        ├─────────────────────────────────┤  7
        ├─────────────────────────────────┤  8
        ├─────────────────────────────────┤  9
        └─────────────────────────────────┘  10
```

What is the maximal length of a string that may be assigned to ANSW$? . . . . Which

line allows you to enter a value of ANSW$ . . . . The value of ANSW$ determines

whether the REPEAT — UNTIL loop (200–330) is executed once more or stopped. What is

the value of ANSW$ when the execution of the loop is terminated?. . . . .

What is printed out if line 280 is executed and NO has a value of 3?

. . . .

What printout is produced by PROC REQUEST if NO is equal to 9?

. . . .

and what printout shall we see from the procedure if NO has a value of 6?

. . . .

The structure diagram below illustrates the procedure REQUEST. In some of the boxes only part of the contents have been filled in. You should complete them:

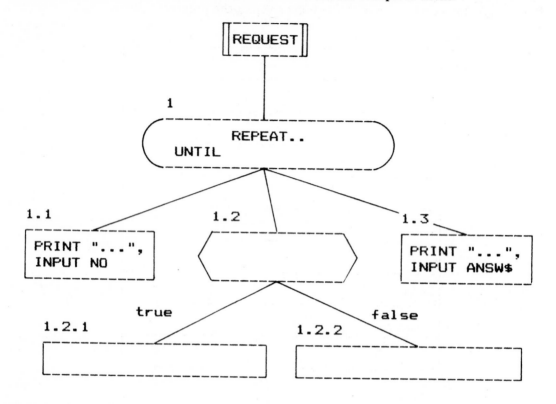

The program has been stored as the file "EXE122". LOAD it and test it. Check the answers you have written at the beginning of the exercise.

Note about structure diagrams: As usual statements like the one to clear the screen, and PRINT statements without output lists which are in the program only to improve the appearance of the output are left out in the diagram.

★

The index of an element of a table may be given as a constant, a variable or a numeric expression. If you use variables or expressions to indicate elements, you must of course make sure that they do not assume values beyond the range defined for the indices. If you try to reference elements not in the table, execution of the program is stopped and the system returns an error message. If, on the other hand, an expression returns a non-integer value, the COMAL system automatically converts it to an integer rounding it down.

In the program from Exercise 12.2 this statement is found:

```
ART$(3):="SOAP FLAKES"
```

In this case the index is given as a numerical constant. The following statement is also in the program:

PRINT "ARTICLE NO. ",NO,": ",ART$(NO)

Here an element of the table ART$ is referenced by means of the variable NO. By assigning different values to NO you may pick out any of the 10 elements of ART$.

A **TABLE** OR AN **ARRAY** IS A SET WHOSE INDIVIDUAL ELEMENTS ARE REFERENCED BY MEANS OF **NUMBERS**.

A TABLE MUST BE **DECLARED** IN A DIM STATEMENT.

THE NUMBER USED TO REFERENCE AN INDIVIDUAL ELEMENT OF A TABLE IS CALLED THE **INDEX** OF THAT ELEMENT AND MAY BE GIVEN AS A **CONSTANT**, A **VARIABLE**, OR AN **EXPRESSION**.

In the program from exercise 12.2, the following assignment is found:

ART$(6):=" "

To the right of the assignment the empty string – or the empty text – is specified. This is done, logically enough, by using two double quotes with nothing between them. The empty string always has the predefined length zero. As demonstrated in the exercise, the empty text may be used just like any other text. It is used in the Boolean expression held in the statement:

IF ART$(NO)=" " THEN

The expression returns a value of "true" if ART$(NO) has got the empty string as its value, i.e. if nothing has been stored in it. It is important never to confuse the empty string (" ") with the space (" ") which is of length 1 and has an effect on printout, which the empty string does not.

THE **EMPTY STRING** – OR **TEXT** – IS SPECIFIED BY THE SYMBOLS " "

THE **LENGTH** OF THE EMPTY STRING IS ALWAYS **ZERO**.

Exercise 12.3 □

Find the list of the program for this exercise in the program booklet. In the program

a string array and three string variables are declared. What is the string array called?

. . . . How many elements does it have? . . . . How many characters

can be held by each element? . . . . What are the names of the three string variables?

. . . ., ..., and . . . . Locate

the procedures TAKEIN, PRINTALL, and PRINTONE and put down the line numbers of

their heads and tails: TAKEIN: . . . . and . . . ., PRINTALL: . . . . and

. . . ., PRINTONE: . . . . and . . . . In what line is TAKEIN called? . . . .,

and PRINTALL? . . . ., and PRINTONE? . . . . The value of one specific variable

determines which of the three procedures is going to be called. What is the name of that

variable? . . . . Three possible values of the variable are given in a

prompt message displayed before the input of the value. What values does the program

suggest? . . . ., ..., and . . . .

The program is controlled by the main loop (40–150) which is a REPEAT – UNTIL
loop. What value must be assigned to ANSW$ to stop the execution of that loop?

. . . . What prompt message is displayed prior to the input of a

value to ANSW$ . . . . The input of names in PROC TAKEIN is also
controlled by a REPEAT – UNTIL loop terminated with the statement:

> UNTIL NAME$=" "

That is to say that the execution of the loop is stopped when NAME$ is equal to the
empty string. The empty string is of course not going to be provided with any number

and stored in the table as a name. What line holds the statement to prevent that? . . . .

Copy the Boolean expression in the statement: . . . .

The program is stored in the file EXE123. LOAD it and RUN it. When the program
prompts you with its

> WHAT JOB (ENTRY, LIST, REQUEST) ?

type ENTRY. Then think of some names and key them in. Also check the two other
commands LIST and REQUEST.

★

The different parts of the program in Exercise 12.3 are invoked by means of the words
"ENTRY", "LIST", and "REQUEST". Thus these words have a similar function in the
context of the program as words like "RUN", "LIST", and "NEW" has in the COMAL

system itself. By using a string variable (like JOB$) and having the value of this variable determine what procedures are executed, you may define as many commands as you like in any program.

The empty string can also be typed in, and this is done simply by pressing the RETURN key when the program prompts for data entry. Just as the double quote signals the end of a string constant, striking the RETURN key indicates that typing in a string has been completed. Now if no other keys have been touched before the RETURN key is hit, the system must of course interpret this as a text with no characters, i.e. the empty string.

Exercise 12.4 □

The program from Exercise 12.3 has one or two obvious weak points. In this exercise we shall try to improve the program in these respects. LOAD the program and RUN it. Type ENTRY when the program has displayed its prompt line of commands. Type in three names and number them 1, 2, and 3 respectively. Then use the command LIST to check that they have been properly stored in the array. When the the program displays its prompt line again, type ENTRY once more and key in another name with the number 3. Have another list of the students printed out and note that the name first entered as number 3 has now been overwritten by the name entered during the second round. This has happened without any warning, and if such a thing could happen in a real life program it might be most unfortunate, and give rise to serious mistakes, such as sending a bill to a wrong person. Maybe the name entered originally was not meant to be deleted at all, but by mistake a number already used has been typed in as the number of a new name. The program ought to give a warning when there is a risk that this might have happened. Let us try to consider what can be done to remedy this evident flaw.

A new name is stored in the table when the statement in line 250 is executed:

PUPIL$(NO):=NAME$

This, then, is the statement that may be "fatal", and we shall replace it with a call to a procedure that does not allow a new name to be stored just like that, but looks first to see if the element wanted is vacant and not occupied by another name. The structure diagram below pictures this procedure CONTROL:

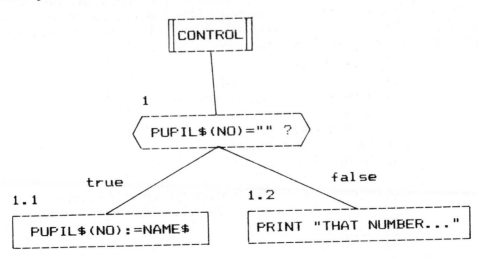

The procedure may also be represented in "pseudo COMAL":

>PROCEDURE CONTROL
>   IF the referenced element is empty THEN
>   store the name
>   ELSE //the element is in use//
>   give a warning
>   ENDIF
>ENDPROC CONTROL

How is the condition *"the referenced element is empty"* expressed in the structure

diagram? . . . . How is the statement *"store the name"* represented

in the structure diagram? . . . . The equivalent of *"give a warning"*
is only partially shown in the structure diagram. Think of a suitable text to complete
the message. Now type in the procedure CONTROL to extend and improve the program.
Start like this:

```
540 //
550 PROC CONTROL
    . . .
```

Also replace the statement that currently stores a name in the table STUDENT$ with a
call of the procedure.

RUN the program thus modified to test it. If it is in order, then store it on the disk or
cassette using the command:

```
SAVE "EXE124"
```

★

Exercise 12.5 □
In this exercise we shall further improve the program we worked on in exercise 12.4. We
no longer risk deleting the name of some pupil by mistake, but in return it has become
impossible to delete the name of a pupil no longer in the class, or correct a wrongly
entered name. This is of course unacceptable so we shall have to write a new procedure to
do that job. This procedure ERASE is outlined in "pseudo COMAL" below:

>PROCEDURE ERASE
>   type in the number of the pupil
>   IF the referenced element is empty THEN
>   tell the user that no pupil
>   with that number exists
>   ELSE //a name is stored in the element//
>   display the name of the student and
>   ask if it is correct (Y/N)
>   IF the answer is "Y" THEN assign the referenced element
>   the value of the empty string
>   ENDIF
>ENDPROC ERASE

Write the procedure in COMAL on a sheet of paper. Then LOAD the program "EXE124" and type it in after the procedure CONTROL. Rewrite the prompt line showing the various commands to include the new command "ERASE" and insert the following statement in a suitable place in the main loop:

IF JOB$="ERASE" THEN EXEC ERASE

After having finished the modifications, RUN the program and test it carefully. When it is working to specification, save it using the command:

SAVE "EXE125"

13

Apple, pear, plum

Each element of a string array has its own number or **index**. We have seen in the previous section that each individual element is used as a simple string variable. Thus statements like the following may be used:

```
PUPIL$(15):="VALEUR, NIELS"
PRINT PUPIL$(NO)
```

That is why an element such as PUPIL$(15) is also called a **subscripted variable**.

It was also mentioned earlier that the index of an element may be given as a numeric constant, a numeric variable, or a numeric expression. This last means that it is possible to identify a certain element by a calculation. The expression ruling this calculation simply appears in the brackets which follow the name of the array. If a variable, say NO, has a value of 3 then ARTICLE$(NO+6) indicates the 9th element of the array ARTICLE$.

Exercise 13.1 □
For this exercise use a small box containing at least 30 small objects such as counters, buttons or paper clips. Out of this box allow yourself 20 pieces of whatever you have collected and put them on the table by the computer. Then LOAD the program "EXE131" and RUN it. Each time the program asks you to

INSERT A COIN

take one of the "coins" on the table, put it in the box, and press the RETURN key. The program displays a certain combination of fruit names and how many coins you have won, if you are lucky enough. Each time you win you have a right to take as many counters out of the box as the program indicates. When you do not want to play any longer or you are out of counters, press the "N" key and the RETURN key to stop the program. You may of course "break the bank" if you can, and the larger the bank the harder it is to break. It is all up to you, since you create the condition yourself.

★

Exercise 13.2

Find the listing of the program for Exercise 13.1 in the program booklet. In line 10–20 an array of strings and some string variables are declared. What is the name of the array?

. . . . How many elements does it hold? . . . ., and how many

characters may each element have? . . . . What are the names of the string variables?

. . . ., ..., ..., and

. . . . Fill in this picture of FRUIT$ in accordance with the program list:

The two most important procedures of the program are THE' GAME and RESULT. The

procedure, THE'GAME begins in line . . . . and ends in line . . . ., and the

procedure RESULT has its head in line . . . . and its tail in line . . . . Copy the

statement in line 260 here: . . . . Is the line number part

of a statement? . . . . The function RND(1,6) returns at random one of the numbers:

1, 2, . . ., 6. This number is then used to indicate an element of FRUIT$. The string value

of this element is assigned to F1$. What string value does F1$ assume if RND(1, 6) returns

the number 3? . . . . And what value does F1$ assume if RND(1, 6)

returns the number 2? . . . . The function RND(1,6) is also used in

the next two lines of the program, and each time it is used one of the numbers mentioned above is returned. What string value is assigned to F2$ if RND(1,6) returns the number

5? . . . . What string value does F3$ assume if RND(1, 6) returns the

number 1? . . . . What printout is produced by line 300 if RND(1, 6)

has returned the numbers 2, 4, and 3 respectively on execution of line 260, 270, and

280?

. . . .

In THE' GAME three "fruits" are chosen. In RESULT, which fruits were selected is
examined, and the player is awarded his winnings, if any. The structure diagram below
illustrates the procedure. Some of the boxes have not been filled in. Finish the diagram
(As usual PRINT statements need not be written out in full, but can be indicated informally in some way):

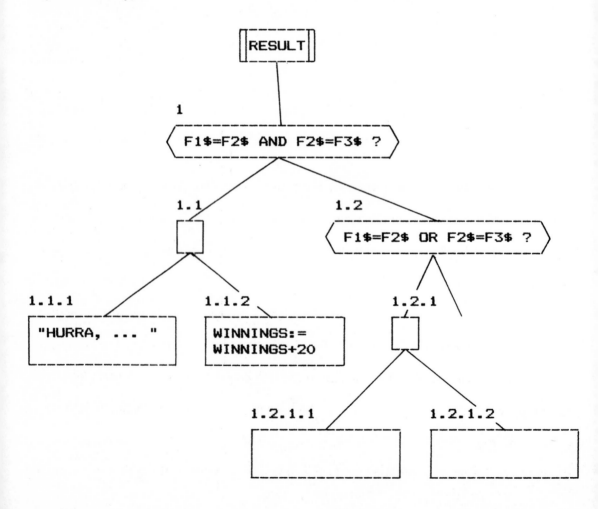

How many of the "fruits" are the same if the Boolean expression in the upper choice has

a value of "true"? . . . . How many of the "fruits" are alike if the upper Boolean

expression is "false" and the lower one is "true"? . . . . Put a cross by all the boxes
that picture statements executed if F1$ has assumed the value "LEMON", F2$ the value
"GRAPE", and F3$ the value "GRAPE". Put a circle by the boxes representing the
statements executed if F1$, F2$, and F3$ has the value "BANANA", "PLUM", and
"BANANA" respectively. Mark with a square the boxes picturing the part of the procedure executed if F1$, F2$, and F3$ are assigned the same value. If the procedure
ADIEU is going to be executed, a certain Boolean expression must assume the value of
"true". Copy that expression here:

. . . .
★

We have used random numbers to imitate (or simulate) some games. In the previous
exercises we had the system generate at random the numbers: 1, 2, . . ., 6, and this very
set of numbers has also been used to imitate a game of dice. By using a small array of
strings we have, however, managed to *mask the numbers* totally, thereby obtaining −
ostensibly − quite a different game. The whole difference is due to our using *words*
instead of naked *numbers*. We thus have made our way into the range of ordinary language
which is much more rich in means of expression than that of the numbers alone. The
above mentioned program imitates a gambling machine, and is also said to constitute a
model of such a machine. This model may serve various useful purposes. As an example
one might examine whether a real gambling machine built using the same principles
would be too greedy in law; there is a limit to how often it may win. In a few minutes, a
program like the one demonstrated in the exercise is able to play through so many games
that it would take several days to perform them on a real life automaton. The outcomes
of these "model experiments" (simulations) are easy to register and analyse, and thus you
can see if a "fair" gambling machine is likely to result.

Exercise 13.3 □
Use the program listing from Exercise 13.1 for this exercise. The program introduces two
variables which have not been used for anything yet, viz. STAKED and WINNINGS.
Locate the following statements and put down the numbers of the lines that hold them:

WINNINGS:=0; STAKED:=0   . . . .

STAKED:=STAKED+1   . . . .

WINNINGS:=WINNINGS+20   . . . .

WINNINGS:=WINNINGS+2   . . . .

What is the value of STAKED if thirty-two games have been played? . . . . What is the value of WINNINGS if five of these games have given the same first and second or second and third fruit, and one of the games has given the same fruit on all three places? . . . . What then is the value of the difference STAKED-WINNINGS? . . . . In the program this statement is encountered:

> STOP //STOP THE PROGRAM

In what line? . . . . Since the three last words form a comment, the statement itself consists only of the word "STOP". As is already explained in the comment, execution of the program is stopped whenever a STOP statement is encountered.

We are now going to plan a test of the program in order to examine whether it satisfies legal requirements with respect to "honesty". We want the machine to run automatically, i.e. without anyone pressing the RETURN key, until it happens that the three "fruits" are the same. This may be done by inserting an extra STOP statement in the section of the program that is executed when this happens. The statement must be inserted in such a way that the happy event is proclaimed and the counter variable WINNINGS is properly updated, What line number would you suggest to give such a STOP statement? . . . . The program should run without any outside intervention. This means that the statements in line 180 and 190 must not be executed. That might be done by simply deleting them, but you should avoid changing any statement in a program to be tested, because then you would be testing another program! Instead we simply short-circuit the two statements by inserting these two lines in the program:

> 175 GOTO INTERIM
> 195 INTERIM:

The GOTO statement in line 175 makes the system jump to the line with the label "INTERIM:". During execution the statements in line 180 and 190 are thus simply skipped.

LOAD the program in the file "EXE131" and insert the two test lines. RUN the program a few times and after each run have the values of STAKED and WINNINGS displayed. Take the values down and assess the program with respect to "honesty".

The test may be made even faster if you also short-circuit the printout from line 430–450. Try to do that (warning: the same label must not be used in two places), and RUN the program again.

Do not forget to delete the test lines after having finished your tests.

★

In the exercise use has been made of three new COMAL statements. The STOP statement consists of the word "STOP" only, and whenever it is encountered, the execution of the program stops immediately. A GOTO statement consists of the keyword GOTO followed by the name of a label. When a GOTO statement is encountered, control is transferred to the statement following the label statement referred to in that GOTO statement. A label is formatted like a variable name, and a label statement is no more than a label followed by the sign ":" (colon). Each label statement must be put on a line of its own, and no two lines may hold the same label statement. On the other hand the same label may be used in more than one GOTO statement.

A **STOP** STATEMENT CONSISTS OF THE KEYWORD **STOP**.

A **STOP** STATEMENT **TERMINATES THE EXECUTION** OF A PROGRAM.

A **GOTO** STATEMENT CONSISTS OF THE KEYWORD **GOTO** FOLLOWED BY THE **NAME OF A LABEL**.

WHEN A **GOTO** STATEMENT IS ENCOUNTERED **CONTROL IS TRANS-FERRED** TO THE STATEMENT **FOLLOWING THE LABEL STATEMENT** REFERRED TO IN THE GOTO STATEMENT.

A **LABEL** IS FORMATTED AS A **VARIABLE** NAME.

A **LABEL** STATEMENT CONSISTS OF A **LABEL** TERMINATED WITH THE **SIGN** ":" (COLON).

Exercise 13.4 □

Extend the program from Exercise 13.1 to use 8 "fruits" instead of 6. Also add some statements to have the program ask for the players name when it starts and then use this name in a short message when it stops. A message like this is suggested:

> DEAR JOHN,
>
> THANKS FOR THE GAME. YOU STAKED 42 COINS, BUT YOU WON 56. SO YOU HAVE MADE 14 COINS PROFIT ON THIS GAME. CONGRATULATIONS.

The message should of course be properly modified if the player loses. Test your program using the same method as in exercise 13.3. You may have to adjust the winnings if the program is too good at winning.

★

GOTO statements should be used for *special purposes only*, such as testing, tricky error cases and the like. You may jump *out of* any COMAL structure (except procedures) by means of a GOTO statement, but *never into* one!!!

14

Little Simon's English lesson

By means of arrays of strings we can connect numbers with texts. In COMAL it is also possible to work with texts given in the program without having to assign these texts to elements of a table. We can list the texts and then pick them up one by one as we want to use them. For this purpose DATA and READ statements are used.

A DATA statement begins with the keyword DATA followed by a list of constants. Each constant may be numeric or string. Here is an example of a DATA statement:

    DATA "SIMON HARRIS", 5,8,3

The list which follows the keyword DATA holds a string constant, and three numeric constants. The constants listed in a DATA statement are read by a READ statement. A READ statement begins with the keyword READ followed by a list of variables. Here is an example of one:

    READ NAME$,FIRST,SECOND,THIRD

The list which follows the word READ holds a string variable and three numeric variables.

Exercise 14.1 □
Little Simon Harris has problems at school. He keeps making mistakes in English with irregular verbs. His cousin Havelock Harris has written a program to help poor Simon improve his standards. The program is stored in the file "EXE141". LOAD it and RUN it. A listing of the program is given in the program booklet. Use it to answer the following:

How many DATA statements does the program contain? . . . . In what lines are they

found? . . . . There is also a READ statement in the program. In what

line? . . . . Copy the read statement here: . . . .
★

In the program from Exercise 14.1 there are seven DATA statements. Each holds two strings, the first one being a sentence, the second a single word. The only thing that matters for the COMAL system, however, is that a set of data is present with fourteen elements altogether. That some of these are long and others short is of no concern to the system. When the program is executed, the system sees all the data given in DATA statements as one list, beginning with the items in the DATA statement with the lowest line number and ending with the items in the DATA statement with the highest line number. In the program we have been looking at, COMAL simply sees this list of data:

"BACH *GOES* TO TOWN", "WENT", "LOTTIE *WINS* THE GAME", "WON", "THEY *SIT* BY THE FIRE", "SAT", . . ., "CHOSE"

When the program is executed and the READ statement is encountered, the first variable following the READ keyword is assigned the value of the first constant in the list of data. In this case TEXT$ thus assumes the value "BACH *GOES* TO TOWN". Then the next variable in the READ statement is assigned the value of the second element in the data list. In the present example WORD$ is put equal to "WENT". Then nothing happens with the list of data until a READ statement is encountered again. When and if this happens, the next constant is read, and this goes on until the last of the elements on the list is read or no more READ statements are encountered. In the program from Exercise 14.1 it happens to be the same READ statement that is executed several times, but that does not matter. Each time it is encountered, two new items of data are used. The list of data may be compared with a queue; the first customer is first served, then the second one, now the third one, and so forth until the whole queue has been served or the shop closes — this corresponding to the situation where there are no more READ statements with variables to which values have to be assigned. A list of data processed in this way is also called a **data queue**.

A DATA STATEMENT BEGINS WITH THE KEYWORD **DATA** FOLLOWED BY A LIST OF CONSTANTS.

THE **ITEMS** IN DATA STATEMENTS ARE ALWAYS ARRANGED AS **ONE QUEUE OF DATA**.

A **READ STATEMENT** BEGINS WITH THE KEYWORD **READ** FOLLOWED BY A LIST OF VARIABLES.

THE **VARIABLES** IN READ STATEMENTS PICK UP THEIR VALUES FROM A **DATA QUEUE**. THE DATA ITEMS ARE READ CONSECUTIVELY BEGINNING WITH THE FIRST ITEM.

If an attempt is made to read from a data queue after the last element has been read, execution of the program is stopped and an error message is output to inform the user that the READ statement is out of data. Later on we shall see that it is possible to start reading a data queue again after it has been totally or partly finished.

Exercise 14.2 □

Use the listing of the program for Exercise 14.1 for this exercise. The structure diagram below is supposed to represent the mainline program, i.e. line 40–60. Complete it.

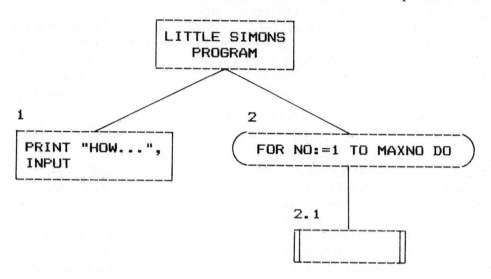

The procedure EXERCISE may be represented in "pseudo COMAL" thus:

> *PROCEDURE EXERCISE*
>   *initialize counter of attempts*
>   *get material for exercise*
>   *REPEAT*
>   *display the exercise*
>   *get the pupils answer*
>   *check the answer*
>   *UNTIL answer is correct OR*
>   *three attempts have been made*
> *ENDPROC EXERCISE*

The action *"initialize counter of attempts"* is actually programmed like this:

    "ATTEMPTS:=0".

How are the following actions programmed:

"get material for exercise":...

"display the exercise":...

"get the pupils answer":...

"check the answer":...

How is the following condition *"the answer is correct OR three attempts have been made* expressed in the program?

. . . .

Complete the structure diagram below:

```
                          ┌─────────┐
                          ║EXERCISE ║
                          └─────────┘
        1                          2
  ┌───────────────────┐     ╭──────────────────────────────╮
  │ ATTEMPTS:=0        │     │       REPEAT..UNTIL          │
  └───────────────────┘     ╰──────────────────────────────╯
                         2.1        2.2          2.3
                      ┌──────┐   ┌──────┐     ┌──────┐
                      │      │   │      │     │      │
                      └──────┘   └──────┘     └──────┘
```

In the program a variable HINT$ is declared and used. Locate the following statement:

> HINT$:=WORD$

In what line is it found? . . . . If WORD$ is assigned the value "WENT", what will

the value of HINT$? . . . . What prompt is displayed by procedure

HELP if ATTEMPTS is equal to 1 and WORD$ is equal to "SANG"?

. . . .

What prompt is displayed if WORD$ is still equal to "SANG", but ATTEMPTS is equal

to 3? . . . .

. . . .

. . . .

In the structure diagram below the blocks of statements to submit prompts are represented by PROMPT 1, PROMPT 2, and PROMPT 3. A person who wants to know more about the details will have to look in the program listing; a diagram is provided to give a general idea of the structure of a program. Complete the diagram:

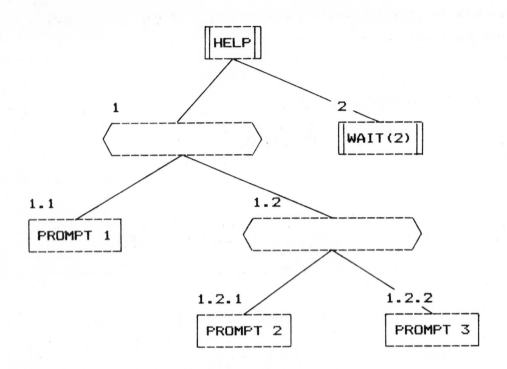

★

Strings may be held in arrays or DATA statements. They may also be joined together and assigned to one string variable. Joining texts together is an activity familiar to most of us. In fact it simply means that they are put together one after another. We can join together "LOTTIE'S CAT " and "IS CALLED SOPHIE." to get "LOTTIE'S CAT IS CALLED SOPHIE.". In COMAL you may join together or **concatenate** strings by using the "+" sign. When the following statement is executed

    TEXT$:="LOTTIE'S CAT "+" IS CALLED SOPHIE."

TEXT$ is assigned the value "LOTTIE'S CAT IS CALLED SOPHIE.". Note the space that has been introduced after the word "CAT" in the first of the two strings. If this were not done, TEXT$ would have the value "LOTTIE'S CATIS CALLED SOPHIE.". Each character counts when you come to strings! You may, however, obtain the same result by using this statement:

    TEXT$:="LOTTIE'S CAT"+" "+"IS CALLED SOPHIE."

In that case three strings have been concatenated, viz. "LOTTIE'S CAT", a space, and "IS CALLED SOPHIE.".
If we imagine that the string variable TXT1$ has been made equal to "BACON, BEEF", and the variable TXT2$ is assigned the value "HAM", the statement

    FOOD$:=TXT1$+" AND "+TXT2$

assigns the value "BACON, BEEF AND HAM" to the variable FOOD$.

In the program from Exercise 14.1 this statement is found:

ATTEMPTS:=ATTEMPTS+1

We know already that it increases the value of ATTEMPTS by one. In a similar way you may expand a given string by joining extra pieces of string to it. Let us imagine that the variable TEXT$ has the value "THE NOBLES FROM JUTLAND REFUSED TO COME" and T$ has the value "WHEN THE KING SENT FOR THEM.". The following statement

TEXT$:=TEXT$+", "+T$

then assigns the value "THE NOBLES FROM JUTLAND REFUSED TO COME, WHEN THE KING SENT FOR THEM." to TEXT$. Note that both a space and a comma has been inserted between the two main components of the text.

Exercise 14.3 □

Little Simon's teacher wants to know which verbs Simon has difficulty with, so that he can give him extra help. He therefore wants a "trap" inserted in the program to "catch" the words Simon has not got right even after a second attempt. To that end a string variable called TRAP$ is introduced. This variable should hold the words that have not been spelled correctly in an exercise. LOAD the program "EXE141" and insert this statement

TRAP$:=TRAP$+", "+WORD$

such that it is executed each time a word is misspelled on the second attempt. The variable TRAP$ should be declared to take a string of up to 40 characters. Each time Simon has used the program the teacher only needs to have the value of TRAP$ printed out to see what words have been "caught". RUN the program to test it.

★

STRINGS MAY BE **CONCATENATED** – JOINED TOGETHER – USING THE SIGN "+". **STRING CONSTANTS** AS WELL AS **STRING VARIABLES** MAY BE CONCATENATED.

15

In case of

Just round the corner in Wheel Street stands "Oldham's Grammer School". Local people simply call it "Oldham's". It has been owned by the Oldham's for 150 years, and its present headteacher, Eliza Oldham has a degree in Computer Science. Eliza's sister, Louise Oldham — usually referred to as "Aunt Louise" — is a mathematics teacher. Some of her students have difficulties in mental arithmetic, but now Eliza has written a program for the school's microcomputers in order that they may be used to support the students. The program is not quite finished, but most of it works and has already been put into service.

Exercise 15.1 □
A copy of the program written by Eliza Oldham is stored in the file "AUNTIE". A listing can be found in the program booklet. Try to RUN it. The program begins by asking for the name of the student. What does it actually write?

. . . . The student is then prompted to state which arithmetic

operation is going to be practised. How does the prompt go? . . . .

The student may also choose between different levels of difficulty. What is printed out by

the program to indicate that this choice may be entered? . . . .
★

Exercise 15.2
The prompts mentioned in Exercise 15.1 are submitted by statements in the procedure

ENTRY. This procedure has its head in line . . . . and its tail in line . . . . The

three PRINT statements that produce the requests are found in lines . . . ., ..., and .... Immediately after each of the three PRINT statements is an INPUT state-

ment which requires an answer from the person at the keyboard. The first one goes like this:

INPUT NAME$

In which line is it found? .... Thus the variable that is assigned the text entered is

called NAME$ and is a string variable. It is declared at the beginning of the program.

What is its greatest length? .... Which lines are holding the two INPUT statements

which require answers to the type of operation and the level of difficulty? .... and

.... What are the names of the variables used in the two INPUT statements?

.... and .... One of them is a string variable

which is declared at the beginning of the program. What is its greatest length ....
★

Exercise 15.3 □
The program for this exercise is stored in the file "FESTIVALS". A listing can be found
in the program booklet. Try to RUN it. Make it write a "Whitsun letter" first, then a
"Christmas letter", and finally an "Easter letter". In what way is it determined what kind
of letter the program should print out?

....

....
★

Exercise 15.4
Get a listing of the program for Exercise 15.3 ("FESTIVALS"). In which line is the head of

the procedure called WRITELETTER found? .... In WRITELETTER a statement

beginning with the keyword CASE is found. In what line? .... Three statements
beginning with the keyword WHEN are also present in the procedure. In what lines are

they found? ...., ..., and .... Further a statement consisting of the

keyword ENDCASE alone is found. In what line? ....
★

In the exercises, three new COMAL keywords have been encountered: CASE, WHEN, and ENDCASE. Statements beginning with these words go together like IF, ELSE, and ENDIF statements. IF, ELSE, and ENDIF statements are used when you want to control *two* blocks of statements where one or the other is going to be executed. The value of the Boolean expression in the IF statement determines which of the two blocks is processed. If you have to control more than two blocks of statements, the CASE, WHEN, and ENDCASE statements are used. The keyword CASE can be followed by a **numeric expression**, a **string expression**, or a **Boolean expression**, and it is the value of the actual expression that determines which one of the associated blocks is to be executed.

Note. From now on the word "**expression**" may also cover a **constant** or a **variable**. This is a somewhat broader sense than is usual in mathematics, but in computer science it is normally used that way. As examples of **numeric expressions** we thus have:

> 4, NUMBER, PRICE*NUMBER+15, (A+B)/2

and the following are examples of **string expressions**:

> "ELISABETH", NAME$, TEXT$+LINE$(I)+" "

while the items on the following line are examples of **Boolean expressions**:

> TRUE, NUMBER<100, ANSW$=WORD$ OR ATTEMPTS=3

Each block of statements in a CASE **structure** is initiated with a WHEN statement, i.e. the keyword WHEN followed by a **list of expressions**. When the CASE statement has been executed, and the expression in it is evaluated, the COMAL system starts scanning the WHEN statements looking for an expression with the same value as the one in the CASE statement. If an expression with a matching value is found in one of the WHEN statements, the block following that statement is executed. When that is finished, execution is continued with the statement following the ENDCASE statement. If more than one WHEN statement holds the same value — the last of the clumsy programmers has not yet died — it is always the WHEN statement closest to the CASE statement that has its block processed, and among the WHEN statements belonging with a certain CASE statement *one at most* is executed.

In the program from Exercises 15.3 and 15.4, the value of the variable FESTIVAL determines which one of the WHEN blocks is executed. If FESTIVAL has a value of 1, the block following

> WHEN 1

is executed, and if FESTIVAL is equal to 2, the block following

> WHEN 2

is processed. Finally if FESTIVAL has been assigned a value of 3, the system will start working on the block following

> WHEN 3

The ENDCASE statement is of course used to terminate the set of blocks that are controlled from the corresponding CASE statement. This is like an ENDIF statement terminating one or two blocks controlled by an IF statement. We have already introduced a way of illustrating an IF–ELSE–ENDIF branching in a structure diagram by means of a choice box, and now we simply extend that picture to represent a CASE structure as well. Thus the CASE–WHEN–ENDCASE in the program from Exercise 15.3 may be pictured like this:

Exercise 15.5
Fill in the boxes of the structure diagram below such that it represents the CASE structure in the procedure ENTRY from Aunt Louise's program (AUNTIE):

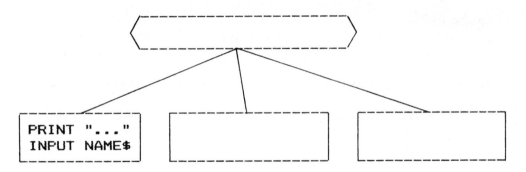

★

A statement like "CASE FESTIVAL OF" may sound a little strange at first. If, however, FESTIVAL is replaced by one of its values, say 2, the statements says "CASE 2 OF", and if that is further extended a little to become "CASE 2 OF THE FOLLOWING" the effect of it is expressed quite clearly.

Exercise 15.6
Locate PROC CONTROL in Aunt Louise's program. In this procedure a CASE structure

is found. Which line holds the CASE statement? . . . . In what lines are the three

WHEN statement found? . . . ., ..., and . . . . What line holds the END-

CASE statement? . . . . Also locate the CASE structure in procedure ERROR.

What printout is produced by the blocks controlled by the CASE statement if the variable

MATTER has a value of 3?

. . . .

What printout is produced if MATTER is equal to 1?

. . . .

. . . .

★

As mentioned before, a string expression may be placed after the word CASE in a CASE statement. If that has been done the expressions in the WHEN statements coming with such a CASE statement must of course also be of string type, i.e. string constants (texts between quotation marks), string variables, or string expressions.

Exercise 15.7 □
The program for this exercise is stored in the file "DOCTOR". A listing can be found in the program booklet. RUN the program. Then find the listing. In the program a CASE

statement is found in line . . . . The corresponding ENDCASE statement is found in

line . . . . What is the variable in the CASE statement called? . . . .

Is it a numeric variable or a string variable? . . . . In what lines are the

WHEN statements belonging to the CASE statement found? . . . ., ..., ...

and . . . . What is the value of COLOUR$ if the "doctor" arrives at this diagnosis?

```
        YOU ARE JUST FINE. PLEASE DO NOT WASTE MY TIME.
        DID YOU NOT KNOW THAT MONEY IS VERY TIGHT IN
        THE NATIONAL HEALTH SERVICE THESE DAYS.
```

Answer: . . . . Put down the string constants found in the other WHEN

statements: . . . ., ..., and . . . . In one of the four "cases" IF–ELSE–ENDIF branching is used. What is the value of

COLOUR$ if that block is processed? . . . .
★

Exercise 15.8

We shall return to Aunt Louise's program. In the procedure WORKSHOP, a CASE structure can be found. Its CASE statement is found in line . . . ., and its ENDCASE statement is found in line . . . . What is the string variable whose value controls the CASE structure? . . . . Put down the string constants used in the WHEN statements: . . . ., ..., ...,

and . . . . A CASE structure using the same variable can be found in procedure WRITEEXERCISE, only this time there are two string constants in each WHEN statement. Copy the two WHEN statements below:

. . . .

. . . .

The diagram below pictures the CASE structure. Fill in the line to the right.

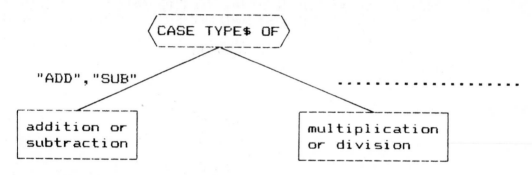

★

A CASE STATEMENT CONSISTS OF THE KEYWORD **CASE** FOLLOWED BY AN **EXPRESSION** [AND TERMINATED WITH THE KEYWORD **OF**].

A WHEN STATEMENT CONSISTS OF THE KEYWORD **WHEN** FOLLOWED BY A **LIST OF EXPRESSIONS**.

AN **ENDCASE** STATEMENT CONSISTS OF THE KEYWORD **ENDCASE**.

Note. The brackets enclosing the last six words in the definition of the CASE statement mean that you do not have to type in the keyword OF on entering a CASE statement. You only have to strike the RETURN key after having typed the expression. COMAL automatically supplies the keyword OF if it is not typed in (cf. the keyword THEN in an IF statement or the keyword DO in a FOR statement).

An IF statement or a CASE statement is cometimes called a **conditional statement**, because it holds the condition of the executing a specific block of statements. The expression following the keyword CASE, whose value determines what block is going to be processed, is also called the **case selector**. Each block of statements in a CASE structure may of course hold any kind of statements including new CASE, WHEN, and ENDCASE statements.

Here is a survey of the CASE multi-branching structure:

CASE ⟨expression (case selector)⟩ **OF**
WHEN ⟨list of expressions⟩
    THIS BLOCK OF STATEMENTS IS EXECUTED IF THE VALUE OF THE CASE SELECTOR IS EQUAL TO THE VALUE OF ONE OF THE EXPRESSIONS ON THE LIST
WHEN ⟨list of expressions⟩
    THIS BLOCK OF STATEMENTS IS EXECUTED IF THE VALUE OF THE CASE SELECTOR IS EQUAL TO THE VALUE OF ONE OF THE EXPRESSIONS ON THE LIST AND THE FIRST BLOCK HAS NOT BEEN EXECUTED

   . . .

WHEN ⟨list of expressions⟩
    THIS BLOCK OF STATEMENTS IS EXECUTED IF THE VALUE OF THE CASE SELECTOR IS EQUAL TO THE VALUE OF ONE OF THE EXPRESSIONS ON THE LIST AND NONE OF THE PREVIOUS BLOCKS HAVE BEEN EXECUTED

   . . .

ENDCASE

16

While not answering properly

The pupils at Oldham's very often type in something wrong when they use the micros for arithmetic exercises. They are not the only ones to do so. Any person who sits at a terminal and sends messages to a computer system makes mistakes. Those who have been working a lot with computers should hit the right keys most of the time, while others who are not so familiar with a keyboard make more mistakes. Louise Oldham has observed that two particular kinds of errors are often made. A wrong answer may be typed in because the pupil makes a miscalculation, and that type of error is easy to detect. You only have to compare the pupil's answer with the correct result, which is calculated by the computer in a split second. But maybe the pupil simply "stumbles over" some key and presses a wrong one. As a result "A58" might be typed in, even though the pupil knows very well that the correct answer is 58. As we have seen from many examples, COMAL makes a sharp distinction between strings (texts) and numbers, and there is no doubt that "A58" is a string, whereas 58 in this case is a number. The second kind of error, where the wrong kind of data is entered, is very hard to deal with, because it is not the program but the system itself which protests, and "the system" is not always as easy to converse with as your own program.

Exercise 16.1 □
LOAD and RUN the program "FESTIVAL". When the sender and the recipient have been entered, the program prints out

　　　　1=XMAS / 2=EASTER / 3=WHITSUN

and waits for the user to type in the number 1, 2 or 3. Try as an experiment to type in 4.

What happens . . . .

. . . .

Start the program again and enter a sender and a recipient. When the program asks for "Xmas, Easter, or Whitsun" try to type in a letter, e.g. "A", instead of the numbers 1, 2, or 3. What happens this time? . . . .

. . . .

. . . .

★

In Exercise 16.1 experiments with two types of error are made which both causes the system to react with an error message. But otherwise they are very different. In the first instance the program is stopped after the message has been submitted, but in the second instance you are allowed to re-enter your answer after the warning has been given. In some cases this may be inconvenient, because it may "mess up" the layout on the screen, but as a rule it can be overcome by simply explaining to the user of the program that the answer should be typed in again. However, the first type of error is fatal, because it makes the system stop executing the program. It may be that the person sitting at the terminal does not know how to restart it, and furthermore a lot of data already entered may get lost if the program is restarted using the RUN command. We shall therefore have to improve our program so that it will not be stopped by this type of error. In Exercise 16.1 the program is stopped if a number other than 1, 2, or 3 is entered. Let us try to examine how we can prevent this happening:

> *INPUT festival*
> *IF festival is not equal to 1, 2, or 3 THEN*
>   *PRINT that an error has been made, and*
>   *INPUT festival*

Thus, if the value of "festival" keyed in is illegal, a warning is printed out, and a second chance to enter a value for "festival" is offered. All right, but what happens if an illegal value is entered on a second attempt? Should we do it like this?

> *INPUT festival*
> *IF festival is not equal to 1, 2, or 3 THEN*
>   *PRINT that an error has been made, and*
>   *INPUT festival*
>   *IF festival is not equal to 1, 2, or 3 THEN*
>   *PRINT that an error has been made, and*
>   *INPUT festival*

It is quite obvious that in case a stubborn person or even a drunk has sat down at the terminal this may never end. But out analysis reveals that each time an illegal value of festival is entered the following action should be taken:

> *PRINT that an error has been made, and*
> *INPUT festival*

We therefore try this approach:

> *INPUT festival*
> *WHILE festival is not equal to 1, 2, or 3 DO this*
> > *PRINT that an error has been made, and*
> > *INPUT festival*

Exercise 16.2 □
LOAD the program stored as "FESTIVAL" and have a list displayed on the screen. The

statement that handles the input of a value of FESTIVAL is found in line . . . .
Type in the following program segment between the INPUT statement just located and
the procedure call following it:

```
WHILE NOT (FESTIVAL=1 OR FESTIVAL=2 OR FESTIVAL=3) DO
    PRINT "ONLY 1, 2, OR 3 MAY BE ENTERED!"
    PRINT "YOUR ANSWER, PLEASE",
    INPUT FESTIVAL
ENDWHILE
```

It is of course very important that these statements are correctly numbered, and it is
obvious that they should have numbers in the range from 141 to 149. To make it easier,
you can type in this command:

```
AUTO 141,1
```

The COMAL system answers by displaying

```
0141
```

and then allows you to enter the first statement. When this has been done and the
RETURN key is pressed, COMAL writes

```
0142
```

and gives you an opportunity to key in the second statement. You can go on like that
until the last of the statements (ENDWHILE) has been entered and the system displays

```
0146
```

Since you have no more statements to enter simply strike the RETURN key (or, on
some systems, press the ESC key). This stops the numbering and makes the system return
to the normal "command mode". By using the AUTO command you may minimize the
risk of "falling outside" the range of numbers. RUN the program to check your extensions.
Type in various illegal values of FESTIVAL to see whether the "trap" works properly.

★

With the WHILE and ENDWHILE statements, the third — and last — of the loop
structures in COMAL has been introduced. As you may remember, the two other ones
are the REPEAT — UNTIL loop and the FOR — NEXT loop. The effect of the WHILE
— ENDWHILE loop may be described informally, like this: When the WHILE statement
is executed the truth value of the Boolean expression following the WHILE keyword is

calculated. If it returns a value of TRUE the block of statements held between the WHILE and the ENDWHILE statements is executed, and the WHILE statement is then executed again. Thus the block controlled from the WHILE statement is processed repetitively as long as the expression in the WHILE statement evaluates to TRUE. If the expression has a value of FALSE, the block of statements in question are skipped, and sequential execution is continued with the statement following ENDWHILE (or stopped if there are no statements after ENDWHILE).

In some way the WHILE — ENDWHILE structure resembles the IF — ENDIF structure, but the block controlled by the IF statement is executed once at most, whereas execution of a WHILE block is repeated as long as the Boolean expression following the WHILE keyword evaluates to TRUE. Also note that the block in a WHILE loop is not executed at all if the Boolean expression has a value of FALSE when the WHILE statement is encountered for the first time. As an example, that is what happens if a legal value of FESTIVAL is entered in the program from Exercise 16.2. Of course this is how it should be. If a correct value of FESTIVAL is typed in no error message should be produced. You might say that it would be best never to have the WHILE–ENDWHILE loop executed, but many years of experience with computer systems has shown that anyone who does not take measures against any imaginable error is far too naive. Computer people tend to say that "any mistake that can possibly be made sooner or later will be!".

THE **WHILE** STATEMENT CONSISTS OF THE WORD **WHILE** FOLLOWED BY A BOOLEAN EXPRESSION [AND TERMINATED WITH THE WORD **DO**].

THE **ENDWHILE** STATEMENT CONSISTS OF THE WORD **ENDWHILE**.

A summary of the functioning of a WHILE — ENDWHILE loop is shown below:

```
WHILE (Boolean expression) DO
    THIS BLOCK OF STATEMENTS IS EXECUTED REPETITIVELY
    AS LONG AS THE BOOLEAN EXPRESSION IN THE WHILE
    STATEMENT IS EVALUATED TO TRUE
ENDWHILE
```

In a structure diagram a repetition box is used to represent the WHILE — ENDWHILE loop just like the one used to picture the REPEAT — UNTIL and the FOR — NEXT loops. The box is often drawn and filled in according to this model:

```
 ------------------------
(           WHILE          )
(    <Boolean expression>  )
 ------------------------
```

As an illustration a structure diagram representing the WHILE — ENDWHILE loop from Exercise 16.2 is shown below:

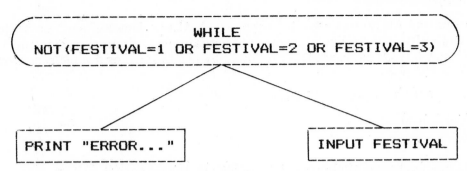

From the above, it may look as though WHILE loops are used mainly to prevent input of wrong or illegal data. However, there are many problems that are better solved using WHILE loops rather than REPEAT or FOR loops. This is because one often needs to have a loop which in some cases is not executed at all, as in the above example.

Exercise 16.3 □
The program for this exercise is stored as "EGGS". A list is found in the program booklet.

RUN it once or twice. Find the listing. In what line is a WHILE statement found?........

and its ENDWHILE statement? .... How many times is the WHILE loop executed

if the variable EGGS has a value of 10?........, 20?........, 6?........, 5?........,

3?........, 7?........
Try to replace the WHILE loop with a REPEAT loop if possible. Type in your suggestion, if any, and test your program using as input the values listed above.
★

A clear picture of the difference between a WHILE loop and a REPEAT loop can be obtained by representing them in simple flow charts:

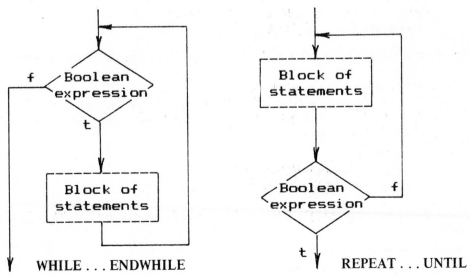

The command AUTO was used in Exercise 16.2. As was demonstrated this is a command to have COMAL supply line numbers automatically when entering a program. The word AUTO may be used either alone, or followed by one or two positive integers seperated by a comma. Its format thus is:

AUTO [⟨integer⟩] [,⟨integer⟩]

If the command

AUTO

is used the numbering will become 10, 20, 30, etc. If a command such as

AUTO 110

is used the line numbers generated will be 110, 120, 130, etc.

If the command

AUTO 110,5

is applied the sequence will be 110, 115, 120, etc. The command

AUTO ,5

generates the line numbers 10, 15, 20, etc.

In Exercise 16.2 we introduced a WHILE loop to catch faulty input. This is a method that may be applied generally. However, in programs where a multi branching CASE structure is used and the case selector takes its value from input, illegal values may often be met in a very simple way.

EXERCISE 16.4 ☐

LOAD the program "DOCTOR" and RUN it. WHEN the program has displayed its prompt:

WHAT IS THE COLOUR OF YOUR FACE
(PALE/PINK/BLUE/YELLOW)?

try to type in the word "RED". The system stops running the program and submits an

error message. How does the message go? . . . .
Now look at the program listing. The last statement in the body of the procedure DIAGNOSIS is the ENDCASE statement. Insert the following statements immediately before the ENDCASE statement:

OTHERWISE
   PRINT "I NEVER CURE PEOPLE
   PRINT "WHOSE FACES ARE ",COLOUR$

RUN the program again and type in one or two colours not on the list suggested by the program.

★

In the CASE structure a final block of statements may be included, initiated with the keyword OTHERWISE. This extra block is processed if the value of the case selector is not found in any of the WHEN lists. We sometimes call it a "default case".

THE **OTHERWISE** STATEMENT CONSISTS OF THE WORD **OTHERWISE**.

Thus the description of the CASE structure given in Chapter 15 may be extended to become:

CASE ⟨expression (case selector)⟩ **OF**

. . .
>   ⟨all the **WHEN** statements with
>   their blocks of statements⟩

. . .
OTHERWISE
>   THIS BLOCK OF STATEMENTS IS EXECUTED IF THE VALUE OF THE
>   CASE SELECTOR IS NOT FOUND ON ANY OF THE LISTS FOLLOWING
>   THE WHEN STATEMENTS
ENDCASE

It is worth mentioning that if the case selector does not match any of the expressions following the WHEN statements and no OTHERWISE block is present, the system stops the program and issues an error message. If there is any risk that such a situation may come up, an OTHERWISE block should be introduced. The block following the OTHER-WISE statement *may be empty,* but normally an error message is inserted to warn the user if he goes beyond the scope of the program.

Exercise 16.5
Look at the list of "FESTIVAL". In its structure it looks a lot like "DOCTOR". We have seen that "FESTIVAL" will be stopped if an "unauthorized" festival is entered, and we have taken precautions against that by introducing a WHILE loop to catch faulty input. Try to explain why we cannot use an OTHERWISE statement, as we did in "DOCTOR", to catch illegal input to "FESTIVAL". If you cannot find out, try to LOAD "DOCTOR", insert an OTHERWISE block in the proper place, and RUN the modified program.

. . . .

. . . .

★

The method of using an OTHERWISE block to catch faulty input should be used only where the CASE structure stands alone and is not an integrated part of a larger process. In complicated segments, other and more adequate methods should be used for error handling as is demonstrated in the following sections. Finally, it should be mentioned that OTHERWISE blocks may be used for other purposes than to trap errors. It may, of course, be used simply to indicate what should be done otherwise.

17

Of messengers and flags

A program as long as "AUNTIE" must be broken down into procedures if you are not going to get lost in the details. Eliza Oldham knows that and even maintains that if a procedure grows to a length of more than ten lines, you ought to consider seriously the possibility of breaking it down in more procedures. The building up of a program by means of short, easy to grasp procedures also has other good points.

Exercise 17.1
In the gateway to Oldham's there is a fire alarm. Beside it a sign with the following instructions have been nailed to the wall:

IF A FIRE IS DETECTED

DURING LECTURE HOURS:
    PRESS THE FIRE ALARM
    ACTIVATE THE SCHOOL BELL BY PRESSING
    THE YELLOW BUTTON BESIDES THE ALARM.

DURING THE DAY OUTSIDE LECTURE HOURS:
    PRESS THE FIRE ALARM
    WARN THE PORTER (ENTRANCE ROUND THE CORNER).

DURING THE NIGHT:
    PRESS THE FIRE ALARM
    WAKE UP THE PORTER (ENTRANCE ROUND THE CORNER)
    TURN ON THE LIGHTS OUTSIDE THE GATE
    BY PRESSING THE SWITCH BESIDES THE GATE

You should know that the lights outside the gate light up the school's name so that it is very easy to identify the building and the gateway.

In any case a certain action should be taken. Which one? . . . .

. . . .

What is it that determines which of the three alternative instructions to follow? . . . .

. . . .

★

When a procedure has been written, it is there once and for all, and may be called from anywhere else in the program as often as you like. Imagine we need to run a certain process on three different places in a program, and that this process can be programmed in ten lines. If that process is packed as a procedure, we may simply call it from the three different places in the program where it is needed. If we do not use a procedure we shall, however, have to write the ten lines three times altogether, and a modest use of mental arithmetic should return the result that you now need thirty lines.

Procedures may also be used when you want to have several closely related processes collected under one name. Which segment of the procedure is going to be executed may depend on the program line from which it is called. The procedure call can be made context dependent.

Exercise 17.2
Use the listing for Aunt Louise's program ("AUNTIE") with this exercise. In line 70 of the

program three string variables are declared, viz. NAME$, ... , and

. . . . The first one has been declared to hold up to . . . . characters,

the second one may hold up to . . . . characters, and the third one can hold . . . .

characters only. In line 140 and 150 five numeric variables have their values assigned. Put down the names of those numeric variables together with their values:

. . . . := . . . . := . . . .,

. . . . := . . . . := . . . .,

and . . . . := . . . .

Locate the procedure TAKEIN and copy its head:

. . . .

At the beginning of the program the MAINLINES are found. Among these are three calls of TAKEIN. Copy the three calling statements:

. . . .

. . . .

. . . .

The following structure diagram should represent TAKEIN. Complete it.

```
            ╔══════════════════╗
            ║ TAKEIN(MATTER)   ║
            ╚══════════════════╝
               ╱            ╲
         1    ╱         2    ╲
      ╔════════╗     ╭──────────────────────────────────╮
      ║ ENTRY  ║     │             WHILE                │
      ╚════════╝     ╰──────────────────────────────────╯
                         ╱                  ╲
                2.1     ╱            2.2      ╲
            ╔════════════╗       ╔════════════════╗
            ║            ║       ║                ║
            ╚════════════╝       ╚════════════════╝
```

In what line is the head of ENTRY found?. . . . . . . .What line holds the head of ERROR?

. . . . From the body of ENTRY the procedure CONTROL is called. From what line?

. . . . In what line is the head of CONTROL found?. . . . . In all three procedures, ENTRY, CONTROL, and ERROR, this statement:

        CASE MATTER OF

is found. Locate the three lines and put down their numbers here: . . . ., ...,

and . . . . Now go back to procedure ENTRY. Which lines are executed if

MATTER has a value of 1? . . . .,

MATTER has a value of 2? . . . .,

MATTER has a value of 3? . . . .

★

In Exercise 17.2 we have seen that the variable MATTER is used as a *case selector* in each of three procedures used directly or indirectly by TAKEIN. The process executed by each one of these procedures depends on the value of MATTER. The variable MATTER first appears in the statement

> PROC TAKEIN (MATTER)

i.e. in the head of the procedure TAKEIN. A variable that appears like that *has its value assigned at the same time as the procedure is called.* Thus the assignment comes with the call and depends on it. The first call of TAKEIN is made with the statement:

> EXEC TAKEIN (THISNAME)

When this call is evoked two things happen: The procedure TAKEIN starts as it used to do, but at the same time the variable MATTER is assigned the value of THISNAME. Since THISNAME has a value of 1, MATTER is also set to 1. The second time TAKEIN is called this statement is in charge:

> EXEC TAKEIN (THISTYPE)

and now MATTER is assigned the value of THISTYPE which is 2. Finally TAKEIN is called by the statement:

> EXEC TAKEIN (THISLEVEL)

whereby MATTER is assigned the value of THISLEVEL, namely 3.

Variables like THISNAME, THISTYPE, THISLEVEL, and MATTER, that appear in brackets following the procedure name in a procedure head or in a procedure call, are called **parameters**. Since parameters may occur in two different types of statements and in two rather different roles, those in EXEC statements are called **actual parameters**, whereas the ones in procedure heads are named **formal parameters**. An actual parameter *has a value* (the actual value), whereas a formal parameter *is assigned a value* during the procedure call. You may think of the actual parameter as a "sender" of the value and the formal parameter as the "receiver" of it. The word "formal" is of course used because a parameter of the type in question has no value until the procedure to which it has been attached is called.

Exercise 17.3
One of the last procedures in "AUNTIE" is called TABULATOR. Its head contains a

formal parameter. What is its name?........ It is called from three different places in

the program. What are the names of the three actual parameters used?

. . . ., ..., and . . . .

★

The value of a formal parameter is not known until the procedure that holds it is called, and after the procedure has been finished the value of the formal parameter is forgotten again. In fact, the COMAL system does not even know that it ever existed. A variable that is introduced as a parameter in a procedure head is therefore called a **local variable**.

Exercise 17.4 ☐
Type in this small program:

```
INPUT N
EXEC PRINTOUT (N)
//
PROC PRINTOUT (NUMBER)
   PRINT NUMBER
ENDPROC PRINTOUT
```

Now RUN the program. After it has stopped, try to ask for the value of N (use the command PRINT N) and then the value of NUMBER (PRINT NUMBER). What is the

name of the actual parameter? . . . ., and the formal parameter?

. . . . Explain the message from the system:. . . . .

. . . .

. . . .

★

An actual parameter represents a value and may therefore be a constant, or variable or a formula, in one word **an expression**. A formal parameter on the other hand must be **a variable**, since a value is assigned to it.

Exercise 17.5
Below is shown a procedure head:

```
PROC MOVEPOINTER (DISTANCE)
```

This procedure is called from three different places in a program using the following statements:

```
EXEC MOVEPOINTER (6)
EXEC MOVEPOINTER (J)
EXEC MOVEPOINTER (J + 2)
```

If J has a value of 7, what is the value of DISTANCE after each of the three calls?. . . . .

. . . ., and . . . . In "AUNTIE" a procedure called WINDOW can be found (one of the last in the program). What are the names of the two formal parameters in this procedure?.................... and .... can .... It is called from many different places in the program, because it is used to clear certain parts of the screen. Locate three lines from which it is called, and put down the line numbers and the values of the actual parameters in each case.

Line:.......... ; actual parameters: .... and ....

Line:.......... ; actual parameters: .... and ....

Line:.......... ; actual parameters: .... and ....

From WINDOW the procedure SCREEN is called. Give the names of the two actual and the two formal parameters involved in the call. The actual parameters are:

.... and ....: and the formal parameters are:

.... and ....

★

AN **ACTUAL PARAMETER** ALWAYS APPEARS IN THE STATEMENT FROM WHICH THE PROCEDURE IS CALLED AND MAY BE **ANY TYPE OF EXPRESSION**.

A **FORMAL PARAMETER** ALWAYS APPEARS IN A PROCEDURE HEAD AND MUST BE A **VARIABLE**.

AT THE TIME THE PROCEDURE IS CALLED, THE VALUE OF EACH ACTUAL PARAMETER IS ASSIGNED TO THE CORRESPONDING FORMAL PARAMETER.

You may look upon parameters as "messengers", from the mainline program to a procedure or from one procedure to another.

Note. The parameters we have looked at so far can only take messages one way, from the actual parameter to the formal parameter. COMAL also offers another type of parameter that can carry messages both ways, but we are not going to use them until later on.

In procedure TAKEIN in Aunt Louises's program, this statement is found:

    WHILE NOT OK DO

Normally you would expect a Boolean expression (a condition) to follow the keyword NOT, as in

    NOT NUMBER=5

The latter expression returns a value of TRUE if NUMBER is not equal to 5, and a value of FALSE if NUMBER is equal to 5. In COMAL you may, however, use a *numeric variable in place of a Boolean expression*. The COMAL system interprets a variable that takes the "role" of a Boolean expression in the following way: If the variable has a value *different from zero*, it is taken for the Boolean value TRUE, but if it is *set to zero*, it is looked upon as a Boolean expression with a value of FALSE. Using this convention the following makes sense:

> NOT OK

Exercise 17.6

Put down the truth value (TRUE or FALSE) of the following Boolean expressions, given that OK has a value of 1, FOUND a value of 0, and NUMBER a value of 5:

FOUND AND OK: . . . ., NUMBER<5 AND OK: . . . .,

FOUND AND NOT OK: . . . ., NUMBER<=5 OR FOUND: . . . .,

NOT (FOUND AND OK): . . . .

★

In procedure CONTROL in Aunt Louise's program this statement is found:

> OK:=(TYPE$="ADD" OR TYPE$="SUB")

In this example the expression to the right of the assignment is a Boolean expression, whereas the variable OK is a normal numeric variable. At a first glance this may look like a type conflict, like the one that occurs if you try to assign a numeric variable the value of a string expression. The reason why the statement above is nevertheless legal in COMAL is that internally the system uses numeric values to represent truth values. Thus the numeric value *0 is equivalent to* FALSE, and a value of *1 is equivalent to* TRUE. When the statement displayed above is executed, OK is assigned a value of 0 if the Boolean expression to the right is evaluated to FALSE, whereas OK is set to 1 if the expression returns a value of TRUE.

Exercise 17.7

Let us imagine that during the execution of the program AUNTIE we have encountered the statement:

> EXEC TAKEIN(THISTYPE)

During the call the variable MATTER is assigned the value of THISTYPE, i.e. 2. What printout is submitted by the procedure ENTRY?

. . . .

Now fancy that the word "ASD" is typed in. What variable gets this word assigned as its

value? . . . . From ENTRY the procedure CONTROL is called to check the input. Since MATTER still is equal to 2 the case under WHEN 2 is executed, whereby OK and LACKS are assigned values. What value is assigned to OK? .... What truth value does that imply? .... What value is assigned to LACKS? ...., and what truth value does that represent? .... ENTRY and CONTROL are now both finished, and execution goes on with the WHILE statement in line .... The Boolean expression NOT OK is part of that WHILE statement. Since OK has a value equivalent to the truth value ...., NOT OK must be taken to have the value .... Therefore the WHILE loop is executed, giving as a result the error message:

. . . .

and a repeated call of the procedure . . . .

★

When a numeric variable replaces a Boolean expression it is also called a **Boolean variable**. However, it should not be forgotten that it is still also a numeric variable, even though it is being used in a somewhat different manner.

A NUMERIC VARIABLE MAY BE USED IN PLACE OF A BOOLEAN EXPRESSION. A VALUE OF **ZERO** IS THEN TAKEN FOR **FALSE**, AND A **NON-ZERO** VALUE IS TAKEN FOR **TRUE**.

A **BOOLEAN VARIABLE** IS A NUMERIC VARIABLE THAT IS BEING USED IN PLACE OF OR TO STORE THE VALUE OF A BOOLEAN EXPRESSION.

WHEN A BOOLEAN EXPRESSION IS EVALUATED COMAL RETURNS A VALUE OF 1 IF THE EXPRESSION IS TRUE, AND A VALUE OF 0 IF THE EXPRESSION IS FALSE.

A Boolean variable is sometimes called a *"flag"*, and we say that the flag is *"set"* if the variable has a value equivalent to TRUE, and the flag is *"reset"* if the variable has a value that may be taken as FALSE. You may like to imagine how the procedure CONTROL can set a flag to be seen all over the program by the rest of the procedures.

Exercise 17.8
Below is shown a dialog between a user and Aunt Louise's program. For each line, put down the number(s) of the line(s) that has/have generated the program's part of the line. Also underline the answers typed in by the user.

```
WHAT IS YOUR NAME? JOHN                    _____

MOST PEOPLE HAVE BOTH A FIRST NAME         _____
AND A SURNAME. PLEASE GIVE BOTH!           _____

WHAT IS YOUR NAME? JOHN ATHERTON           _____

ENTER TYPE (ADD, SUB, MUL, DIV)? MUM       _____

NO SUCH TYPE OF EXERCISE!                  _____

ENTER TYPE (ADD, SUB, MUL, DIV)? MUL       _____

NO SUCH TYPE OF EXERCISE!                  _____
MUL AND DIV ARE NOT YET INSERTED           _____
PLEASE PICK OUT ADD OR SUB                 _____

ENTER TYPE (ADD, SUB, MUL, DIV)? ADD       _____

ENTER LEVEL (1, 2, 3)? 33                  _____

NO SUCH LEVEL OF EXERCISES!                _____

ENTER LEVEL (1, 2, 3)? 3                   _____
```

Write a list of all the procedures that have been involved in the conversation:

. . . .

. . . .

. . . .

★

   The number 0 may be used meaning FALSE, and the number 1 may mean TRUE. If you want a variable, say OK, to act in the role of a Boolean expression with a value of TRUE, you may use the assignment:

```
OK:=1
```

To make it plain that a truth value is meant, COMAL offers two built in constants: TRUE and FALSE. TRUE has a constant value of 1, and FALSE a constant value of 0. If this is utilized, the assignment above may be written:

```
OK:=TRUE
```

Now anyone can see what is meant.

> **TRUE** AND **FALSE** ARE TWO BUILT IN CONSTANTS THE VALUES OF WHICH ARE **1** AND **0** RESPECTIVELY.

TRUE and FALSE are called **Boolean constants**.

18

Mark my work

At a meeting at Oldham's, the parents have asked that the pupils should bring a report home each term instead of once a year, which is how it used to be done. However, only the subjects: English, Mathematics, and French should be marked. A marking scale of 0 to 5 is to be used. An absolutely unacceptable standard is marked with 0, whereas a highly laudable standard is rewarded with a 5. Miss Oldham does, however, not want to burden the school's secretary and right-hand woman, Miss Goldberg, with additional work, and the parents' committee is therefore asked to buy the school a microcomputer to do the routine work necessary, the record and print out marks. The parents' committee accepts this, and on the next staff meeting it is agreed to handle the recording of marks and printout of reports as follows:

After end of term when examinations have been finished and the students papers marked, the teachers must type in the results. The class lists will be permanently stored on the microcomputer's disk ready to be used each time a teacher comes in to record marks. When all the marks have been recorded the system is supposed to print out reports.

Exercise 18.1 ☐
LOAD the program stored as "ENROL" and RUN it. Give the system a few seconds to read some data from the disk. Its menu is then displayed:

```
1=ENROLL
2=LIST
3=STOP
```

Type 1 and press the RETURN key. A procedure to set up a new class list is called. Follow the program's instructions and enter five names (you may think this is a very small class, but Oldham's is highly exclusive). Key in the names using the following format:

```
JOHN ATHERTON
```

Strike the RETURN key twice to stop entry. The program resubmits the menu, and you should type 2 to check the list you have entered. What numeric value has the program

inserted in place of marks?........ When you have finished your inspection, stop the program by typing 3 after the menu has reappeared. (WARNING: if you use a tape recorder, you should rewind the data tape before asking the program to stop). Give the system a few seconds to write your mark book on the disk (tape).

Now LOAD the program stored as "ENTERMARKS" and RUN it. It should start displaying the following menu:

        1=ENTER MARKS
        2=LIST MARKS
        3=STOP PROGRAM

Type 1 and press RETURN and then mark the pupils in one of the subjects: English, Mathematics, or French at your own option. Use LIST MARKS to check your entry. Then stop the program using the same procedure as before (don't forget about the data tape if you use one!).

★

When starting up a system like the one we are now looking at we must get the names of the pupils stored to be ready for use, when the teachers bring their lists of marks in. Data that is entered and stored to be at the user's disposal on a longer term, is called **recorded data**. A program, such as "ENROLL", is used primarily to *create* a new class list, which is then stored on a disk or a tape. "ENROLL" may be used occasionally to enroll a new pupil in a class, but otherwise it is not used until the beginning of the next term, and the data entered by means of it is supposed to remain fixed for a long period. After a teacher has entered the results of an end of term examination, the marks are stored, too, and are now acting as registered data. The states and processes may be pictured like this:

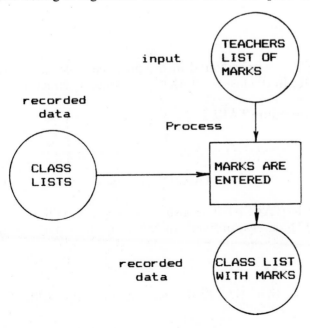

While working with the program "ENTERMARKS" a copy of the registered data is held in the workspace in two tables. These tables are filled in when the program starts, using the data stored on disk or tape, and when the program is stopped, updated copies of the tables are recorded on disk or tape to be ready for the next run.

During execution of one of the programs used to administer the mark books, the pupils' names are stored in a strings array. The school has three classes: 1st, 2nd, and 3rd year, and in each class there may be only eight pupils. As long as the program is used for educational purposes there is, however, no reason to have more, since our main purpose is to study the processes inherent in managing a set of registered data, and the main principles involved in solving such problems can be demonstrated and learned using small amounts of data, without the examples being unrealistic.

The table that holds the names of the pupils in one form, is declared in the program using the statement

DIM NAME$ (MAX) OF 20, ANSW$ OF 11

To make the whole affair as simple as possible, the pupil's number is at the same time the index of his name in the array of strings NAME$. Thus the pupil whose name is the first one in the array, has the serial number 1, the one whose name comes next, has the serial number 2, etc. This of course has its drawbacks, since there may be a pupil with the serial number 1 in each of the 1st, 2nd and 3rd forms, but so far the staff at Oldham's think they can overcome this without the aid of the computer system. If a pupil leaves in the middle of a school year, the student's name is deleted from the array of names simply by replacing it with the empty string. New pupils are admitted to the school only if a place is vacant. In the computer system this is represented by an empty string in a table of names.

Initially the system is run as a pilot project and used to handle the 1st year only. The programs are prepared for use with the 2nd and 3rd years also, but have been adjusted temporarily to display an error message if an attempt is made to enter names or marks of pupils in the 2nd or 3rd years.

Exercise 18.2
A listing of the program "ENROL" can be found in the program booklet. Find the procedures TAKEIN and CONTROL. In the head of TAKEIN a formal parameter MATTER$ is found. How is it used in the procedure TAKEIN? . . . .

. . . .

The procedure CONTROL is called from TAKEIN in line . . . . Even though

MATTER$ is a local variable to TAKEIN it is also known to CONTROL, since it is called before the tail of TAKEIN is encountered. In this program it may assume three

string values. Which ones? . . . . , ...   and

. . . . Imagine that MATTER$ has assumed the value "CLASS", and suppose the user enters the number 9 as a value of CLASS, CONTROL then takes

over, and values are assigned to two numeric variables. Which ones? . . . .

and . . . . The two numeric variables are both used as Booleans. On

the given assumptions what truth value is assigned to the first one? . . . .; to the

second one? . . . .

Find the procedure NEWCLASS. The procedure starts by calling TAKEIN to allow the
user to enter the number of the class in question. Then INITCLASS is called, and after
that you are allowed to enter the pupil's names. First PUPILNO is set to one in

line . . . ., and you are allowed to enter the name of the first pupil.   Control is then

taken over by a WHILE loop. Copy the Boolean expression in the WHILE statement:

. . . .

What part of the expression represents the fact that you may stop the entry of names by

pressing the RETURN key twice in succession? . . . ., and what

part of the expression shows you that no more than eight pupils are allowed in a class?

. . . . Try to write a REPEAT loop to replace the WHILE loop:

. . . .

. . . .

. . . .

. . . .

. . . .

. . . .

. . . .

. . . .

. . . .

. . . .

19

Uncle Hannibal's shop

As we already know, Uncle Hannibal has a bakery with a shop, and now he has found out that he might also be able to sell a few delicatessen items, since installing a deep freeze. Because Hannibal is a jovial person with a fairly good nose for business, he quickly has good sales of delicatessen foods, but has a hard time keeping the accounts of the sales. Hannibal's customers are used to having bills sent out, but as we know he is a little forgetful and unfortunately he does not always remember to have a bill written. Since he still has his micro computer, we might try to help him by writing a program to print the bills.

Exercise 19.1 □
LOAD the program stored as "HANNIBAL". A program listing can be found in the program booklet. In what line is the following statement found

　　　READ ARTICLE$ (I), PRICE (I)

. . . . . . Below is a copy of "This Week's Special Offers", which Uncle Hannibal advertised in "Oddington Weekly":

　　　HONEY ROAST HAM . . . . 2.29 per lb
　　　ROAST BEEF. . . . . 2.19 per lb
　　　DANISH BACON . . . . 1.99 per lb
　　　GARLIC SAUSAGE . . . . 1.29 per lb
　　　CAMEMBERT. . . . . 1.79 per lb
　　　CREAM CHEESE . . . . 1.38 per lb

Add some DATA statements to the program to hold this week's special offers. Start like this:

　　　DATA "HONEY ROAST HAM", 2.29, "ROAST BEEF", 2.19
　　　DATA . . .

Note that both numeric and string constants are queued in the DATA statements. Now test the program by RUNning it.

What line holds this statement?

> DIM ARTICLE$(10) OF 20, PRICE (10)

. . . .

In which line is this statement found?

> AMOUNT (LINE):=PRICE (ARTNO)*QUANTITY (LINE)

. . . .

★

At the beginning of the program about "Hannibal's Shop" ("HANNIBAL") this statement is encountered:

DIM ARTICLE$ (10) OF 20, PRICE (10)

When this statement is executed, storage is first set aside for an array of strings ARTICLE$ that may hold 10 strings of up to 20 characters each. Then a place for an array of numbers is reserved, able to hold 10 numbers. We may picture that a part of the workspace is arranged like this:

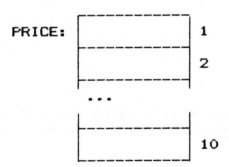

Each of the ten entries may hold *a number*. When an array of numerics is declared no length is given of the individual entries (no "OF-part"), because numbers of the type (reals) we are using have a fixed size in our system. A number always takes up 4 or 5 bytes — depending on the COMAL version you are using — and the system automatically sets aside the requisite space for the individual numeric values.

After the program has been executed using the data given in the exercise, we may picture that this is how it looks in a part of the workspace:

PRICE:		
	2.29	1
	2.19	2
	1.99	3
	1.29	4
	1.79	5
	1.38	6
		7
		8
		9
		10

The individual entries of an array of numbers are selected by means of **indices** in the same way as the entries in an array of strings. In the statement

READ ARTICLE$ (I), PRICE (I)

the I'th entry in the array of strings ARTICLE$ is assigned a string value, and the I'th entry in the array of numerics is assigned a numeric value. The index of an entry in an array of numerics may be given as a numeric expression in just the same way as an entry in an array of strings.

Exercise 19.2
In the program "HANNIBAL" a series of numeric and string arrays are declared. Copy their names on the lines below, and for each individual array state its type — string or numeric — and the number of entries set up:

. . . .

. . . .

. . . .

. . . .

. . . .

Locate the procedure GETORDER and finish the structure diagram below:

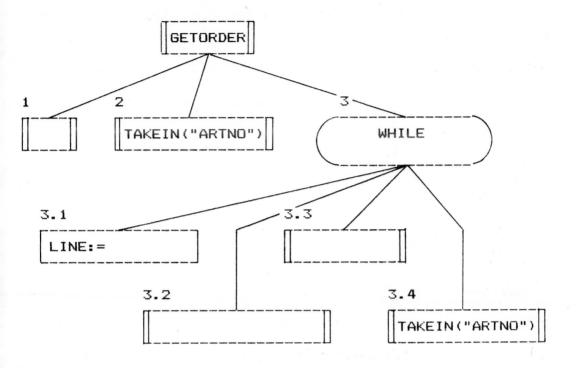

★

Exercise 19.3

In this exercise we shall presuppose that the data suggested in Exercise 19.1 have been added to the program "HANNIBAL". After a customer has been served, the program displays the following:

```
QUANT.    ARTICLE                  AMOUNT
-------------------------------------------
  2 LB    HONEY ROAST HAM           4.58
  1 LB    DANISH BACON              1.99
  2 LB    CREAM CHEESE              2.76
                                  --------
                        TOTAL:      9.33
```

The calculations and assignments needed to fill in an invoice such as the one above are undertaken by the procedure INVOICELINE. How many times has that procedure been

called in this case? . . . . What values has the variable LINE assumed during the

process? . . . . What values has the variable ARTNO assumed?

.................For each of the three calls of INVOICELINE put down the values of the following variables:

TEXT$(LINE): ....

....

....

PRICE (LINE): ...., ..., and ....

QUANTITY (LINE):........., ..., and ....

AMOUNT (LINE): ...., ..., and ....

TOTAL: ...., ..., and ....

How many times has the procedure TAKEIN been called? .... What values has the formal parameter KINDOF$ assumed during these calls?................... and

.... The section of TAKEIN executed when KINDOF$ assumed the value of "ARTNO" contains a REPEAT — UNTIL loop. Copy the statements in its interior (range) below:

....

....

....

After the REPEAT loop, a Boolean variable FINISHED is encountered. It is obviously set to TRUE only if ARTNO is equal to zero. FINISHED is used by one of the statements in

GETORDER. In what line is that statement found?........ And now a hard one: What goes wrong if someone replaces the WHILE loop in GETORDER by the following REPEAT loop:

```
0390 LINE:=0
0400 REPEAT
0410    EXEC TAKEIN("ARTNO")
0420    LINE:=LINE+1
0430    EXEC TAKEIN("QUANTITY")
0440    EXEC INVOICELINE
0450 UNTIL FINISHED
```

★

Exercise 19.4 ☐
Type NEW and enter the following program:

```
0010 INPUT X
0020 PRINT TAB(X),"START AT ",X
0030 PRINT "----!----!----!----!----!"
0040 PRINT "     5    10   15   20   25"
```

RUN it a few times. Use the following data as input: 1, 5, 10, 8, 20, 15, and 17. Also invent some data of your own. Watch the output carefully after each run.
Type NEW and enter the following program:

```
0010 INPUT X
0020 PRINT "INTEGER PART OF ",X," IS ",INT(X)
```

RUN the program using the following data as input: 6, −3, 4.8, 3.9, 3.1, −4.4, −6.7.

Invent some of your own. What is returned by the following: INT (3.456)?. . . . .,

INT (−3.456)?. . . . ., INT (0.52)?. . . . ., and INT (−0.52)?. . . . .
★

In the previous exercise we have looked at the function TAB. It is used to set the start position of the next output. Thus the statement

PRINT TAB (10), "NAME OF ARTICLE"

displays the text "NAME OF ARTICLE" starting in column 10.

THE FUNCTION TAB IS USED TO **POSITION THE START OF A PRINTOUT.** TAB (X) SETS THE START OF A FOLLOWING PRINT ELEMENT TO BE IN COLUMN X.

The argument of the TAB function is a numeric expression. If the expression does not return an integer value it is truncated before the position is set. If a variable PLACE has a value of, say 10, the statement

PRINT TAB((PLACE+1)/2), "WRITINGS"

displays the text following the TAB function from position 5 and on.

Note: that the positions on a line are supposed to start from one.

We have also been looking at the function INT in exercise 19.4. This function return the nearest integer that is less than or equal to the argument. If the argument is positive, its fractional part is truncated (not rounded), but if the argument is negative, it is rounded down.

INT (X) RETURNS THE NEAREST INTEGER THAT IS LESS THAN OR EQUAL TO X.

In mathematics INT is known as "the integer part of".

Exercise 19.5
In this exercise we shall take a closer look at the procedure WRITEBILL in the program "HANNIBAL". Locate this line:

　　　"QUANT.", TAB (10), "ARTICLE", TAB (30), "AMOUNT"

Give the exact printout from that line using the positions indicated under the line below:

. . . .

　　5　　　10　　　15　　　20　　　25　　　30　　　35　　　40　　　45　　　50

Now find the function LGTH. What is returned by LGTH if X assumes a value of 45.35?

. . . ., 4.95? . . . ., 234.55? . . . ., and 0.95? . . . . Look at the last line of the body of procedure WRITEBILL. At what position does the printout of the value of TOTAL start, if TOTAL has a value of 5.43? . . . ., 10.89? . . . ., and 0.456? . . . .

★

Exercise 19.6 □
In the procedure INITIALIZE of "HANNIBAL" this statement is found:

　　　UNTIL EOD //END OF DATA//

In what line? . . . ., Type NEW and enter this program:

```
0010 REPEAT
0020   READ X
0030   PRINT X;
0040 UNTIL EOD
0050 DATA 2,3,4,5,6
```

RUN the program to see how it works. Rewrite the statement in line 40 to become:

UNTIL X=0

What error message is displayed by the system when this program is run?

. . . .

Rewrite the statement in line 50 to become

DATA 2,3,4,5,6,0

RUN the program. The number 0 does not belong to the original queue, but only serves as a "stop" indicator. It is, however, printed out with the others. By using the function EOD the use of such "tricky values" can be avoided.

★

The function EOD (END OF DATA) is a Boolean function. It returns a value of FALSE when the reading of a data queue starts, and a value of TRUE when the last item of the queue has been read. The statement

UNTIL EOD

found in "HANNIBAL" may read, "UNTIL no more data in the queue".

THE FUNCTION **EOD** (END-OF-DATA) IS A BOOLEAN FUNCTION. IT RETURNS A VALUE OF FALSE WHENEVER THE READING OF A DATA QUEUE STARTS, AND A VALUE OF TRUE WHEN THE LAST ELEMENT OF THE QUEUE HAS BEEN READ.

In "HANNIBAL" the following statements are found:

INPUT "TYPE RETURN ": CODE$

and

INPUT "> ": ARTNO

When an INPUT statement is set up like that, the text given before the colon (:) is used as a prompt instead of the question mark normally displayed by the system. This user defined prompt may also be the empty string, as in

INPUT " ": RESULT

This may prove useful in cases where the question mark would be irrelevant for some reasons or other. The user prompt may be any string expression. We thus have

---

INPUT ⟨string expression⟩: ⟨input list⟩

20
Aunt Louise keeps a register

As mentioned before the parents' committee asked that the following three subjects should be marked each term: English, Mathematics, and French. Thus for each pupil three numbers – the marks – must be typed in and stored. At Oldham's they used to keep lists of marks, but it was only done once a year and then of course manually since they had no computer. The lists used to look like this:

No.	Name	En	Ma	Fr
1	Atherton, John	9	10	7
2	Bramer, Max Victor	11	11	9
3	Hamilton, Hugo Wilhelm	8	3	10
. . .				

As may be seen from the sample list, a different scale of marks was used. The lists used to be kept at Miss Oldham's office and the reports were written by Miss Goldberg in person. In some ways the new arrangement is similar to the old one, but it implies that the marks are typed in by the teachers, to be stored first in the computer's workspace and later on an external device (disk or cassette). However, the idea of holding the marks in a table is maintained, i.e. the old lists are used as a **model** in the new system. In the programs designed for Oldham's Grammar School three arrays are set up using a statement like this:

DIM MARK (MAX,3), SUBJ$ (3) OF 11, KEY (MAX)

Let us take a look at the first one, viz. MARK. The variable MAX has a value of 8, and as soon as the statement is executed storage for a **two dimensional array** is first set aside. It may be pictured like this:

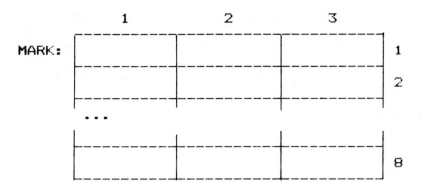

The array MARK holds 8 rows of 3 entries each (arranged like the seats in a theatre). Each entry can hold *one number.* When you want to insert a number into a two dimensional array or to retrieve one, you must give *two indices,* i.e. two numeric values. The first one indicates the row you must look into, and the second one points out the exact entry in that row where you can insert your number or retrieve one that has already been inserted. This is the same procedure that is often used to find a seat in the theatre. On your ticket two numbers are given. The first one tells you which row you are going to sit in, and the second one is used when you make your way through to the place you have paid for (Imagine a person who tries to do it the other way round!!).

Exercise 20.1

After the 1st year teachers have typed in their marks, part of MARK may be pictured like this:

	1	2	3	
MARK:	2	4	0	1
	0	3	2	2
	5	4	3	3
	3	4	2	4

What value is held in MARK(3,2)?........ MARK(4,3)?........ and MARK(2,1)?

....

What mark has been given to pupil number 2 in English?........, pupil number 1 in

Mathematics? ...., pupil number 4 in French?........

Give the numbers of all the pupils that have been given 4 in Mathematics:

. . . ., 2 in French: . . . ., and 5 in English:

. . . . What pupils have been given the mark 3 and in what subjects

(give pupil number and subject)?. . . . .

. . . .

★

The two indices to point out a certain entry in a two dimensional array may be given as numeric expressions (constants, variables, or formula). Each individual entry, or "element" may be used just like any simple variable. Thus if PUPILNO is equal to, say 5, and SUBJNO is equal to, say 3, the following statement

        PRINT MARK(PUPILNO,SUBJNO)

prints out the number held in *row number 5, element number 3*. When the following statement is encountered:

        INPUT MARK(4,2)

the prompt "?" appears and a number to be stored in *row number 4, element number 2* may be entered.

Exercise 20.2

Use a listing of the program "ENROLL" with this exercise. In what line is the array

MARK declared? . . . . In the same line an array of strings is declared. What is its

name? . . . . How many elements does it hold? . . . ., and how

many characters can be held in each element? . . . . Immediately following the declarations the elements of the said array of strings are assigned values. The first element

is assigned the value . . . ., the second element is assigned the value

. . . ., and the third element is assigned the value . . . .

What is the index of the element that is assigned the value "MATHEMATICS"? . . . . Each time a new class is enrolled the procedure INITCLASS is executed. The procedure

has its head in line . . . ., and its tail in line . . . . Its body consists of four lines. Copy the lines here:

. . . .

. . . .

. . . .

. . . .

What are the names of the two variables used to indicate the elements of MARK?

. . . . and . . . . What is the name of the variable

used to indicate the elements of NAME$?. After the procedure has

been executed what is the value of MARK(2,3)?. . . . . and of NAME$(2). . . . .

In the procedure PRINTOUT this line is encountered:

> PRINT SUBJ$(SUBJNO), ": ",TAB(25) ,MARK(PUPILNO,SUBJNO)

The line is in the range of a FOR loop. What printout is displayed from that loop if PUPILNO is equal to 4 and the marks given in exercise 20.1 are used?

. . . .

. . . .

. . . .

★

Exercise 20.3

The structure diagram below represents the procedure INITCLASS. Complete it.

★

Exercise 20.4 □

LOAD the program "WORDGAME". LIST it and compare with the listing in the program booklet. RUN it.

Use the list with the following. What is the value of each of the following entries of MYWORD$ after the program has been started?

MYWORD$(1):. . . . .

MYWORD$(2):. . . . .

MYWORD$(3):. . . . .

When the program has written, say

TYPE IN YOUR 1. WORD:

the user is expected to enter a word he thinks is on the program's list. Then the program must find out if one of its words has been hit. This is done by comparing the user's word with those of the program. It takes four lines, holding an assignment and a WHILE loop, to do this job. Copy the lines below:

. . . .

. . . .

. . . .

. . . .

Put down the Boolean expression in the WHILE statement:

. . . .

What is the truth value of this expression if YOURWORD$ is equal to "CAT" and I is

equal 1? . . . ., 2? . . . ., 3? . . . ., 4? . . . . What is the truth value of the

expression if YOURWORD$ is equal to "DOVE" and I is equal to 1? . . . ., 2? . . . .,

What is its truth value if YOURWORD$ is equal to "DOG" and I is equal to 3? . . . .,

4? . . . ., 5? . . . . Insert five words of your own in the DATA statement (the last in the program), and have some of your friends RUN the program. Delete (DEL) the three lines that hold the WHILE loop and insert this statement to replace them:

WHILE YOURWORD$<>MYWORD$ (I) AND I<5 DO I:=I+1

RUN the program. Consider the possibility of replacing the WHILE loop with a REPEAT loop. If you think it can be done, then modify the program according to your suggestion and test it.

Note. The method applied to look for the user's word among those of the program is called *linear search*. As you have seen, it is very simple, and we have all tried to use it, when going over a list looking for a certain item. We simply take the items on the list one by one as long as the one we are looking for is not found and the last item has not been encountered.

★

Exercise 20.5

Use the listing of the program "ENTERMARKS" with this exercise. Find the procedure CONTROL in the program. Most of CONTROL consists of a CASE structure that uses MATTER$ as case selector. Copy the lines that are executed if MATTER$ has a value of "SUBJECT":

. . . .

. . . .

. . . .

. . . .

. . . .

What is the value of the counter I when the loop is started?. . . . . What then is the

value of SUBJ$(I)?. . . . . How many times is the loop executed if

ANSW$ has the value "MATHEMATICS"?. . . . ., "ENGLISH"?. . . . ., "DANISH"?

. . . ., "SCIENCE"?. . . . ., "FRENCH"?. . . . . What is the value of the

counter I after the loop has been terminated if ANSW$ is equal to "FRENCH"?. . . . .,

"ENGLISH"? . . . ., "GERMAN"? . . . ., "ARITHMETIC"?. . . . . What

numeric value is assigned to OK if ANSW$ is equal to "ENGLISH"?. . . . ., "FRENCH"?

. . . ., "GERMAN"?. . . . . Just as in Exercise 20.4 the WHILE loop can be

rewritten to take up one line only. Put down how you propose it be done:

. . . .

★

Exercise 20.6 ☐

LOAD the program "ENTERMARKS" and RUN it (users of music cassettes: make sure you have inserted the data cassette into the unit). The program reads some data from the external device (disk or cassette), and after a few seconds this menu is displayed:

>   1=ENTER MARKS
>   2=LIST MARKS
>   3=STOP PROGRAM

Pick out 2 and have a list of the pupils displayed. It ought to be the ones you have entered in exercise 18.1. When the menu is resubmitted, choose 1 and mark "your" pupils in the subject English. After you have finished that job, have another list displayed to check your entries. Then stop the program.

★

Since the programs in the system have been written to administer all the marking business at Oldham's, entering the marks is of course a very important part of the system. The marks are typed in by the individual teachers and you cannot expect them to be computer experts. Therefore the whole process of having the marks captured must be very carefully planned so that any operation is clearly prompted and mistakes are prevented as far as possible. After the marks have been entered they may be used in any way — whether it has been foreseen or not — so we must do as much as we possibly can to avoid faulty information being held in the system. Let us see what happens when Lousie Olsen, who is mathematics teacher for the 1st year, wants to enter the marks resulted from this term's examination. In the procedure ENTERMARKS this statement

>   EXEC TAKEIN ("CLASS")

is first executed (You should use the listing of "ENTERMARKS" with the following). The procedure TAKEIN is called and the formal parameter in the head of this procedure is assigned the value "CLASS". This evokes the first case with the statement

>   INPUT "CLASS (1,2,3): ":CLASS

Thus the program produces this prompt:

>   CLASS (1,2,3):

and waits for Louise to enter a number. The number she enters is assigned as a value to the variable CLASS. Then procedure CONTROL is called, and since MATTER$ still has got the value "CLASS" the following statements are executed:

>   OK:=(CLASS=1)
>   LACKING:=(CLASS=2 OR CLASS=3)

If CLASS is equal to 1 — the correct value in this case — OK is assigned the value 1 (=TRUE), and LACKING is assigned the value 0 (=FALSE). If, however, Louise by some mistake types in the number 2 — she also teaches mathematics to the 2nd year — OK is assigned a value of FALSE, because CLASS is NOT equal to 1, but LACKING is assigned a value of TRUE. You should recall that the program has not yet been designed to handle the markings of 2nd and 3rd years, so even if Louise does not really make a mistake — 2nd year does exist — it still is necessary to set a special flag to tell her that she is asking too much. If numbers other than 1, 2, or 3 are entered, both OK and LACKING assume a value of FALSE. Thus the Boolean variable OK is only assigned a value of TRUE if CLASS is equal to 1. In any other case it assumes a value of FALSE. The bulk of procedure TAKEIN is in the range of a REPEAT loop, and you cannot get out of it until OK has assumed a value of TRUE, since the closing statement of the loop is

> UNTIL OK

If it is discovered in procedure CONTROL that an error has been made on input, OK is set to FALSE and the procedure ERROR is called in

> IF NOT OK THEN EXEC ERROR (4)

This procedure has not been finished, but here the Boolean variable LACKING may be used to have a more detailed message output, telling the user that the value entered is not really faulty but the program has not yet been tuned to handle it.

When the number 1 has been entered and is accepted by CONTROL, TAKEIN is called again this time using

> EXEC TAKEIN ("SUBJECT")

The formal parameter in the head of TAKEIN now assumes the value "SUBJECT" and the following statements are executed:

> PRINT "ENTER NAME OF SUBJECT:"
> PRINT "(ENGLISH, MATHEMATICS, FRENCH)",
> INPUT ">": ANSW$

The program therefore displays this message:

> ENTER NAME OF SUBJECT:
> (ENGLISH, MATHEMATICS, FRENCH)>

and waits for one of the subject names to be entered. The name entered is assigned to ANSW$. Now the segment of CONTROL following the statement

> WHEN "SUBJECT"

is executed. We have analysed this segment in Exercise 20.5, and we have seen that OK assumes a value of TRUE only if ANSW$ is equal to one of the three names of subjects and that the variable SUBJNO gets the value 1 if the subject name ENGLISH is entered, the value 2 if MATHEMATICS is typed in, and the value 3 if the answer is FRENCH. Any other text sets OK to FALSE and the program displays an error message and a renewed request for a subject name is submitted.

When Aunt Louise has typed in the correct class level and the correct name of the subject, SUBJNO has a value of 2 and the statements

> PRINT "YOU MAY NOW ENTER PUPILS' MARKS IN ",
> PRINT SUBJ$ (SUBJNO)

are executed to display the message

> YOU MAY NOW ENTER PUPILS' MARKS IN MATHEMATICS

and she may begin to type in the marks she has given.

Exercise 20.7
Find the procedure ENTERMARKS in the program "ENTERMARKS". In this procedure a FOR loop is found that handles the entry of marks for each individual pupil in one subject. It is possible that a pupil number is vacant, corresponding to an empty line in the register. What is the value of NAME$ (PUPILNO) if PUPILNO indicates a number that is

unused?.................... Locate the statement that is used to prevent marks from being entered to non-existing pupils. Copy it here:

. . . .

It is much easier for most people to identify a person if a name is used than if a number

is used. This fact has been considered in TAKEIN. In what line can that be seen?........
★

In some of the exercises in this section we have seen that a WHILE loop may some-times be written in one line. Normally a WHILE loop is initiated with a WHILE statement followed by a block of statement and terminated with an ENDWHILE statement. If, however, only one statement is found in the range of the WHILE loop, that statement may be written on the same line as the WHILE statement immediately after the keyword DO. Thus we get this structure:

WHILE ⟨Boolean expression⟩ DO ⟨statement⟩

Note that the ENDWHILE is omitted when this notation is used. This one-line WHILE loop may be compared with the one-line FOR loop we have met earlier. It may be used in cases like the one given by

WHILE ANSW$<>NAME$ (I) AND I<4 DO I:=I+1

where the very short assignment statement would be textually dominated by the two control statements if the three line version were used. It is, however, often a mere matter of taste which one to use, the one-line or the multi-line version.

21

Little John takes a notice home

When all the quarterly marks have been typed in, enough data have been collected to print out the reports. These data are held in two arrays: The string array NAME$ and the two dimensional array of numerics MARK. The name of a pupil is associated with the marks of that pupil by means of a pupil number. If we know the number of a pupil, we can get access to the name of the pupil and the marks given to him in the three subjects. Thus the *key* to the information about a pupil is that *pupil's number.* If we want to know the name and marks of, say pupil number 4, we only need to ask the system to print out NAME$(4) together with MARK(4,1), MARK(4,2), and MARK (4,3). No system that processes assemblies of registered data fails to have one or more "look up" procedures, or "windows" through which the present status of information can be seen.

Exercise 21.1 □
LOAD the program stored as "CORRECT". When the program has finished reading data from the external device (disk or cassette) this menu is displayed:

```
1=CORRECTIONS
2=LOOKUP
3=STOP
```

Pick out 2 and follow the program's instructions to have the mark book of some pupil displayed. Against the name of each subject the program prints the mark given to the pupil in that subject. The first letter of the name is found at column 1. At what column is

the first character of the mark found?. . . . .

★

Exercise 21.2

Below is shown an informal representation of the procedure DISPLAY:

```
PROC DISPLAY
    IF a pupil with that number is found THEN
        get the pupil's name from the array;
        and display number and name;
        PRINT headline for mark book;
        FOR each of the three subjects DO
            PRINT subject name and mark given;
    ENDIF
ENDPROC DISPLAY
```

How are the following actually programmed:

"a pupil with that number is found":

. . . .

"FOR each of the three subjects DO
  PRINT the subject name and mark given":

. . . .

. . . .

. . . .

. . . .

★

Normally the **separator** comma (,) is totally neutral in PRINT statements. Thus the statement

        PRINT 8,2,3

displays the following

        823

when executed. The statement

        PRINT "DEAR",NAME$

prints out this text

        DEARUNCLE RICHARD

if NAME$ has the value "UNCLE RICHARD". Therefore you must remember always to insert the requisite spaces in your texts. The statement above should of course go like this:

> PRINT "DEAR ",NAME$

However, the functioning of the comma may be changed by means of a system variable called ZONE. If ZONE is set to, say 10, the items on the output list are displayed in 10-character windows, the first window beginning at column 1, the second one at column 11, the third one at column 21, etc. All quantities are left-justified in each window. If the length of an item is 10 or greater, as many windows as necessary are used. With ZONE set to 10 the following statement

> FOR I:=1 TO 5 DO PRINT I,

produces the printout

1   2   3   4   5

With ZONE still set to 10 and the variable QUANTITY set to 35 the following statement

> PRINT "NUMBER OF UNITS: ",QUANTITY

displays the following message:

> NUMBER OF UNITS: 35

ZONE IS A SYSTEM-VARIABLE THAT DEFINES THE **LENGTH OF THE WINDOWS** USED WITH PRINTOUT.
IF **ZONE** HAS THE VALUE X, THE FIRST WINDOW STARTS AT COLUMN 1, THE SECOND ONE AT COLUMN X+1, THE THIRD ONE AT COLUMN 2*X+1, ETC.

The default value of ZONE is 0. That is the reason why a comma normally has no effect at all on the printout, but only serves as a **separator** between the individual output-list items.

Exercise 21.3 □
Type in the following program:

```
0010 ZONE 5
0020 FOR I:=1 TO 5 DO
0030    PRINT I,
0040 NEXT I
0050 PRINT
0060 PRINT "----!----!----!----!----!----!----!----!"
0070 PRINT "    5   10   15   20   25   30   35   40"
```

RUN it. Then rewrite the first line to assign a value of 10 to ZONE and RUN the program again. Also try the program with other values of ZONE.
Rewrite the PRINT statement to become

> PRINT "LENGTH FIFTEEN.",

and RUN the program with ZONE set to 5, 10, 15 and 16 respectively. When finished reset ZONE to 0 by using the command

> ZONE 0

★

Exercise 21.4 ▯
LOAD the program "REPORTS" and RUN it. The program starts prompting

> 1=SCREEN
> 2=PRINTER

Of course you are only allowed to select the printer if one has been connected to your system.
On the list of the program locate the following statements:

> SELECT OUTPUT "LP" and
> SELECT OUTPUT "DS"

They are found in line . . . . and line . . . ., respectively.

★

If a printer is included in the system the statement

> SELECT OUTPUT "LP"

causes printout to be directed to that **printer** instead of the screen. "LP" is an abbreviation of "Line Printer". The system will continue to send the printout of a program to the printer until it encounters the statement

> SELECT OUTPUT "DS"

which resets the system to "screen mode". "DS" stands for "Data Screen". Both statements may be used as commands. If for example the command

> SELECT OUTPUT "LP"

is given, a following LIST command will direct the listing to the printer.
The syntax of the SELECT statement is given by

> SELECT [OUTPUT] "⟨name of an output device⟩"

THE **SELECT OUTPUT** STATEMENT IS USED TO DIRECT OUTPUT TO A SPECIFIED DEVICE.

22

Agathe Goldberg intervenes

At the beginning, Agathe Goldberg was not meant to work with the new system at Oldham's. But it soon becomes apparent that a lot of tasks can only be properly attended to by her. First of all the pupils' names must be typed in at the re-opening of school. Occasionally a pupil may leave in the midst of a school year, and a new pupil may be admitted to the institution. Inevitably, teachers make mistakes when entering a list of marks, and of course one must be able to correct that. It is not very practical to have the teachers do all these jobs because they are only expected to have very short sessions with the terminal. Miss Goldberg on the other hand is at the office most of the time, so she agrees to look after these details. In other words, she is going to **maintain** the data base which is the necessary prerequisite for the whole marking affair and printout of reports.

We have been looking into the procedure ENROL which is used to create a new class list. In that procedure this statement is found:

FOR SUBJNO:=1 TO 3 DO MARK (PUPILNO, SUBJNO):=−1

At the same time that a pupil is being registered the three entries in the marking list belonging to that pupil are each assigned a value of −1. In this way it is indicated that, so far, no marks have been entered for the pupil in question. It is an often used trick to choose a numeric value outside the proper range of the variable to indicate that no final assignment has taken place. Anyone who spies the value −1 knows for sure that this is no real mark, but instead some "dummy number". If on the other hand one fails to assign such an improper but nevertheless well defined value, there is the risk that entries will hold numbers that can be misunderstood, such as remnants of now obsolete marks.

Exercise 22.1 □
LOAD the program "CORRECT" and RUN it. Allow the system a few seconds to read the data it needs and display its menu:

        1=CORRECTIONS
        2=DELETE
        3=LOOKUP
        4=STOP

Pick up 2 and delete record number 1. Then use 3 to check that the pupil's record has gone. Stop the program by answering 4 when the menu has come up and have the system reveal what it has really done by using the commands:

        PRINT NAME$(1)

and

        FOR I:=1 TO 3 DO PRINT MARK(1,I)

What has happened to the name of the pupil?

. . . .

What about the marks? . . . .

LOAD the program "ENROL" and register a new pupil as number 1. Use the list facility of "ENROL" to check that the pupil has been accepted by the system, and take note of the dummy marks the pupil has been given.

★

When a pupil is leaving, his record is cancelled simply by setting the name entry equal to the **empty text** (""). No other action is taken by the program, and therefore the entries of MARK are left unaltered for the time being. If pupil number 1 had been given the mark, say 3, in English, the entry MARK(1,1) still holds that value even after the pupil's name has been erased. The entry does not get its value changed until a new pupil is admitted and registered as number 1. When that happens, the three relevant elements of MARK are set to −1, as we have seen before.

The program "CORRECT" also allows to correct faulty marks. Let us see how that can be done.

Exercise 22.2 □
LOAD the program "CORRECT" and RUN it. When the program is running and has displayed its menu, choose 1 (CORRECTIONS) and correct some mark at your own option.

★

Exercise 22.3
Find the list of "CORRECT" in the program booklet and locate the procedure CORREC-TIONS. Below is an informal pseudo language description of it:

```
PROCEDURE corrections
    get pupil's number
    display pupil's record
    any corrections?
    IF the answer is "yes" THEN
        enter the subject
        enter the correct mark
    ENDIF
END corrections
```

How are the following processes or conditions actually programmed:

"get the pupil's number"? . . . .

"display pupil's record"? . . . .

"any corrections?"? . . . .

"the answer is "yes" "? . . . .

We would like to improve the program such that more corrections can be performed without having to go via the menu each time. This can be done by simply introducing the following statements into procedure CORRECTIONS. Suggest a line number for each:

. . . . .REPEAT

. . . . .INPUT "MORE (Y/N)? ":ANSW$

. . . . .UNTIL ANSW$="N"

★

Exercise 22.4 ☐
LOAD the program "CORRECT". Insert the lines suggested in Exercise 22.3. To improve readability, you may also insert a statement to clear the screen and one to define the field in which the prompt "MORE (Y/N)?" should appear.

★

One morning as Agathe Goldberg starts to work on some records, she discovers that one of the teachers has been rummaging about in her files. She finds this beyond endurance, and asks Miss Oldham "to take immediate precautions against recurrence of such intolerable intrusion into her working conditions!"

Exercise 22.5 ☐

A few weeks before the episode just mentioned occurs, Miss oldham has had the opportunity to help Uncle Hannibal to solve a similar problem. Uncle Hannibal has started taking orders by telephone. He types in the orders as he gets them, and has them printed out. Each afternoon the ordered commodities are packed and delivered to the customers. One night someone had sneaked into his shop, started his computer, and used its program to order delicatessen goods and have them sent out the next day without Hannibal's knowing anything about it. This dirty deed is repeated several times, and as Hannibal finally finds out by the end of the month, it is too late. The bird has flown. LOAD the program "HANNIBAL" and insert the following lines immediately before the call to procedure INITIALIZE:

```
INPUT "KEY, PLEASE ": KEY
IF KEY<>723511 THEN
   PRINT "UNKNOWN KEY!"
   STOP
ENDIF
```

RUN the program.

★

A number that must be entered before you are allowed to use a program is called a **protection key**, and you could say that the program has been supplied with a program controlled lock. In this example the key is very primitive, because anyone who can list the program can find out what key should be used. However, many people who use programs do not know anything about the system as such or how to list and read the programs, and real life programs that are sold to be used professionally can only be listed by those who have written them and have access to the so called "source text". Later we shall see that there are other and much more subtle methods to implement keys or **passwords**.

Exercise 22.6 ☐

Miss Oldham does not want to protect all of the program "CORRECT" but only the procedure CORRECTIONS. LOAD the program "CORRECT" and replace the statement

```
IF JOBCODE=1 THEN EXEC CORRECTIONS
```

with the statements

```
IF JOBCODE=1 THEN
   TAKEIN ("KEY")
   IF KEYOK THEN EXEC CORRECTIONS
ENDIF
```

Then insert the following statements in a suitable place in the procedure TAKEIN:

```
WHEN "KEY"
   INPUT "KEY, PLEASE ": KEY
```

and the following in CONTROL:

```
WHEN "KEY"
    KEYOK:=(KEY=723511)
    OK:=TRUE
```

Test the program. When it works as required, introduce a similar lock on ERASE.
Why must the variable OK assume the value TRUE whether the key fits the lock or not?

. . . .

We want the key to be changed to 725070. Put down the new version of the statement
that must be rewritten:

. . . .

23

Uncle Hannibal also makes progress

Uncle Hannibal is still having difficulties with his Xmas cards. As time has passed, more people expect to get an Xmas greeting from him. The program ("UNCLEXMAS") he has been using so far has grown too troublesome for him. For each card sent out, he has to enter the name of the recipient from a list which, incidentally, does regularly get lost. Eliza has therefore suggested that he puts down the names in DATA statements in the program, so that the list of names becomes a part of the program itself.

Exercise 23.1
Find the listing of the program "XMASCARDS" in the program booklet. Put down names and lengths of the four variables that are declared at the beginning of the program:

. . . . has length. . . . .

. . . . has length. . . . .

. . . . has length. . . . .

. . . . has length. . . . .

In the program a REPEAT – UNTIL loop is used. The REPEAT statement is found in

line . . . ., and the UNTIL statement is found in line . . . . The body of the loop

among other things holds a READ statement, found in line . . . . The variable in the

READ statement is called . . . . In what lines are the corresponding

DATA statements found? . . . . and . . . . What value is assigned to RECIPIENT$

when the loop is executed the first time? . . . . What is the value of

the function EOD after the first assignment has taken place?. . . . . What is the value

of RECIPIENT$ when the loop has been executed the last time?. . . . .

What then is the value of EOD? . . . . In what line is the value of RECIPIENT$

used?. . . . . During a certain run through the loop, the printout of the program
begins like this:

ODDINGTON, 14 DECEMBER 1980

DEAR LITTLE JOHN,

. . .

How many Xmas cards will the program have printed out when the one above is finished?

. . . .

★

Exercise 23.2 □

LOAD the program "XMASCARDS" and RUN it. In real life a program like that can only
be used if the system includes a printer. If one is available the program should be modified
like this:
Delete the statement

INPUT "PRESS THE RETURN-KEY: ":ANSW$

and insert the following statements

SELECT OUTPUT "LP"
SELECT OUTPUT "DS"

at the beginning, and at the end, respectively, of the body of the procedure WRITECARD.
Now test the program again. If the individual printouts are not properly separated on the
paper, adjust the parameter in the statement

EXEC WRITEFROM (5)

at the beginning of procedure WRITECARD.

★

However, Hannibal also manages to mess up things with this new program. When he
has to modify the DATA statements, he regularly deletes one or two statements from the
rest of the program, though he never knows how that happens. After having listened to
Hannibal's complaints for a year or two, Eliza finally decides to rewrite the program to
allow data to be stored separately on the external device.

Exercise 23.3
Find the listing of the program "XMASFILE" in the program booklet. The program has a strong resemblance to "XMASCARDS", but the section with the REPEAT − UNTIL loop has been the subject of a substantial modification. Copy the UNTIL statement on the line below:

. . . .

Also copy the statement coming just before the REPEAT statement:

. . . .

In the range of the REPEAT loop a statement beginning with the word READ is found. Copy that statement below:

. . . .

Following the UNTIL statement, a line holding just one word is found. Which word?

. . . .

★

The program and its data is now held separately on the disk (or cassette). An area of a disk holding a program is called a **program file**. Similarly, an area of an external device holding a set of data is called a **data file**. The data file that holds uncle Hannibal's list of names is called "XMAS". We may picture that the names are stored in a queue in almost the same way as in a DATA statement:

XMAS: | ELIZA | LOUISE | MAX | ROY | LITTLE JOHN | WINNIE | CURT HUGO | . . .

The elements, i.e. the names, can be retrieved only in the same **order** in which they have been written, and always *from the beginning*. Before you start to read the elements in a data file, a channel to the file must be opened using a statement like

        OPEN FILE 2, "XMAS",READ

When this statement is executed, a channel of communication to the file "XMAS" is *opened*, and the channel is given the number 2. The keyword READ terminating the statement signals that the channel may be used for *reading only*. The process of reading an element of the file is performed by a READ FILE statement that may look like the following:

        READ FILE 2: RECIPIENT$

The keyword FILE following READ reveals that data to be retrieved is held in a file as opposed to a queue contained in DATA statements. The constant 2 of course refers to the channel that was opened with the OPEN statement above. When the statement is executed the first time, RECIPIENT$ is assigned the value "ELIZA" which is the first element in the file. The second time the statement is executed, RECIPIENT$ assumes the value "LOUISE", etc. It can be seen that this is exactly analogous to what happens when the statement

READ RECIPIENT$

is used to read data from a data queue.

When the last element in a data queue has been read, the Boolean function EOD (End–Of–Data) assumes the value TRUE. Another Boolean function in COMAL 80 assumes the value TRUE when all the elements of a data file have been retrieved. The function is called EOF (End–Of–File). Since a program can hold only one data queue, EOD needs no argument. But several data files may be opened at the same time, each of them with its own individual channel number, and therefore it is necessary for EOF to have the channel number as an argument. As an example, the statement

UNTIL EOF (2)

may be interpreted as: "UNTIL the end of the data file with the channel number 2 is reached".

When the program has finished picking up data from a data file, the channel that has been used must be *closed*. This has to be done whether or not all of the elements in the data file have been read. For this a CLOSE statement is used, which may consist either of the word CLOSE alone:

CLOSE

or of the words CLOSE FILE followed by a channel number:

CLOSE FILE 2

In the former instance all files are closed, whereas the latter statement only closes a file that has been opened with the channel number 2.

It may be useful to compare the following program fragment:

```
REPEAT
    READ RECIPIENT$
    EXEC WRITECARD
UNTIL EOD
```

with this one:

```
OPEN FILE 2, "XMAS", READ
REPEAT
    READ FILE 2: RECIPIENT$
    EXEC WRITECARD
UNTIL EOF (2)
CLOSE
```

The two REPEAT — UNTIL loops have been designed in an almost identical way: First a value for RECIPIENT$ is retrieved and a Christmas card is written, then another value is picked up and assigned to RECIPIENT$ and a new Christmas card is displayed, etc. until all names on the list have been used. The only difference is that in the former instance the names have been queued in DATA statements, and the loop is finished when EOD has the value TRUE, but in the latter case the names are stored in a data file, and the loop terminates when EOF(2) has the value TRUE.

Exercise 23.4 ☐
Load the program "XMASFILE". If your system includes a printer, carry out the modifications suggested for "XMASCARDS" in Exercise 23.2.
★

Data held in DATA statements is typed in with the program. Data held in a data file, on the other hand, must be stored by means of some specific program statements. These statements are similar in structure to those used when data items are retrieved from a file, but other keywords may be used.

Exercise 23.5
Use the list of the program "ENTERNAMES" with this exercise. One of the statements of the program begins with the word OPEN. Copy the statement below:

. . . .

Another statement begins with the word WRITE. Copy it below:

. . . .

The program holds a WHILE loop. What is the value of RECIPIENT$ when the loop is

terminated?. . . . . What number has been used for the

communication channel to the file "XMAS"?. . . . . The structure diagram below represents the program "ENTERNAMES". Fill in the empty boxes:

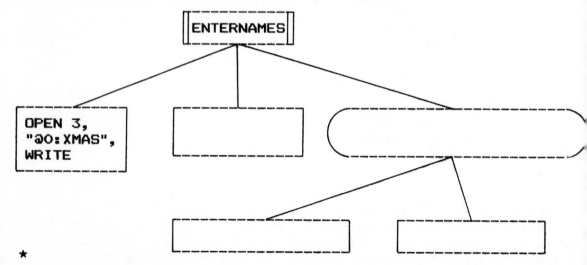

★

Exercise 23.6 □
LOAD the program "ENTERNAMES". RUN it and type in some names. Have a catalogue of the files displayed by using the command

      CAT 0

Note that a file with the name "XMAS" has been created. Now LOAD the program "XMASFILE" and RUN it.
★

    Data retrieved from a data file is also said to be **"read from"** the file. For you to read some data from a file, it must of course be stored first. The process of storing data in a data file is also called **"writing to"** the file. To open a channel for writing, a statement like the following is used:

    OPEN FILE 3, "@0:XMAS",WRITE

A channel, with the number 3, is opened to the file "XMAS" so that it may be used for writing to the file. This can be seen from the keyword WRITE that terminates the statement. There is one minor problem involved in opening a file for writing: The file may exist already. The three characters "@0:" that precede the file name in the OPEN statement indicate that the file is going to be created on disk drive number 0, and if a file with the same name exists already, then the old version is to be deleted and a new one created. If the character "@" is left out and the file exists already, the program is stopped with an error message. By the way, instead of continuing to talk about "opening a channel to a file", we shall from now on simply say that we are "opening a file".
    The process of writing to a file is performed by a statement like

    WRITE FILE 3: RECIPIENT$

The statement is found in the small program "ENTERNAMES":

```
0010 DIM RECIPIENT$ OF 30
0020 OPEN FILE 3,"@0:XMAS",WRITE
0030 INPUT RECIPIENT$
0040 WHILE RECIPIENT$<>"" DO
0050   WRITE FILE 3: RECIPIENT$
0060   INPUT RECIPIENT$
0070 ENDWHILE
0080 CLOSE
```

First the file "XMAS" is opened for writing using channel number 3. Then an INPUT statement to take in a value of RECIPIENT$ is found. Imagine that the name "LOTTIE" is entered. Since that is a string different from the empty string, the WHILE loop is executed and the statement:

    WRITE FILE 3: RECIPIENT$

writes the value of RECIPIENT$ in the file opened as number 3, i.e. "XMAS". We may picture the result like this:

XMAS: ‖LOTTIE|

Then the next string may be entered and assigned to RECIPIENT$. Let us imagine that the user types in "MICHAEL". Since this is not the empty string, the WHILE loop is executed again and the WRITE statement stores the recent value of RECIPIENT$ in the file. After that the situation may be pictured like this:

XMAS: ‖LOTTIE | MICHAEL|

This goes on until the user simply presses the RETURN key and thus enters the empty string. This terminates the WHILE loop and the file is closed. The "walls" shown in the picture indicate "markers" inserted automatically by the system so that it will later be able to distinguish one string from another. When the last string has been stored and the file is closed, the system inserts a special **end-of-file marker**. (Later on this marker can be used by the system to assign the value TRUE to the EOF function when the last element in the file has been read.) Let us imagine that the last name entered is "TIM". Part of the file may then be pictured like this:

XMAS: ‖LOTTIE | MICHAEL   ...   TIM | end-of-file‖

Of course data files may hold both strings and numerics, there may be any number of them, and they may come in any order, just as in DATA statements.

Exercise 23.7
Find the listing of "HANNIBAL" in the program booklet. In procedure INITIALIZE a READ statement is found. Copy it below:

. . . .

Each week, after the list of "This Week's Special Offers" has been worked out, the names of the articles and prices are typed in to be held in the DATA statements terminating the program. These DATA statements must be updated once a week. That is not particularly practical, and after Hannibal has heard about data files he decides to try to use them in his program. Two things must be done: Some statements in the program must be replaced by others in order that data can be retrieved from a data file instead of being picked up from a data queue, and an auxiliary program must be written to store data in the data file. In the main program the following statements must be inserted or used to replace existing statements. Add suitable line numbers:

. . . .   OPEN FILE 2, "OFFER", READ

. . . .   READ FILE 2: ARTICLE$ (I), PRICE (I)

. . . .   UNTIL EOF (2)

. . . .   CLOSE

As a model for the program that is going to write the names of the articles and the prices in the file "OFFER", the small program "ENTERNAMES" from Exercises 23.5 and 23.6 may be used. You only have to change the name of the file and introduce two variables ARTICLE$ and PRICE instead of RECIPIENT$. Below a part of the program is set up. Finish it and add line numbers:

. . . .   DIM ARTICLE$ OF 20

. . . .

. . . .   INPUT "NAME OF ARTICLE: ":ARTICLE$

. . . .   WHILE . . . .

. . . .   INPUT "PRICE: ":PRICE

. . . .   WRITE FILE 3: . . . .

. . . .   INPUT "NAME OF ARTICLE: ":ARTICLE$

. . . .   ENDWHILE

. . . .
★

Exercise 23.8 □
Load the program "HANNIBAL" and type in the statements from the first part of Exercise 23.7. When that has been done, save the program by using the command

        SAVE "NEWSHOP"

Type NEW and key in the small auxiliary program finished in Exercise 23.7. When that has been done save that one, too, by using the command:

        SAVE "ENTEROFFERS"

RUN it and type in the articles and prices used in Exercise 19.1. When that has been done LOAD the program "NEWSHOP" and RUN it. Type in some orders and check that the entered article names and prices are used correctly.
Have the system display a catalogue of disk 0 (CAT 0) and locate the data file "OFFER".
★

Data files whose elements may be stored or retrieved one by one in order are called **sequential files**. It is important to notice that you may read from or write to a sequential file using a **specified channel**, but you cannot open a channel to do both, i.e. channels to a sequential file may be used for **one-way communication only**.

A SEQUENTIAL FILE IS A DATA FILE, IN WHICH YOU MAY READ OR WRITE THE ELEMENTS **IN ORDER ONLY**.

AN **OPEN STATEMENT** IS USED WHEN YOU WANT TO **OPEN A CHANNEL TO A DATA FILE**.

An OPEN statement has the following syntax:

       OPEN FILE ⟨channel number⟩, "⟨file name⟩",WRITE

when the file is opened for writing, and this syntax:

       OPEN FILE ⟨channel number⟩, "⟨file name⟩", READ

when the file is opened for reading.

A **WRITE STATEMENT** IS USED TO **STORE DATA** IN A DATA FILE.

A WRITE statement has the following syntax:

       WRITE FILE ⟨channel number⟩ : ⟨list of data⟩

A **READ STATEMENT** IS USED TO **RETRIEVE DATA** FROM A DATA FILE.

A READ statement has the following syntax:

       READ FILE ⟨channel number⟩ : ⟨list of variables⟩

Note that the list in a READ FILE statement may hold variables only, not constants or expressions. It is obvious that this is how it must be, when you consider the effect of the statement. In some versions of COMAL 80, the list in the WRITE statement may only hold variables, too. This does not matter much, since constants are almost never used in WRITE statements anyway.

A **CLOSE** STATEMENT IS USED TO **CLOSE A FILE** AFTER HAVING FINISHED READING OR WRITING IN IT.

If you want to close all files that have been opened, use

       CLOSE

If, however, you want only to close one specific file, use

CLOSE FILE (channel number)

When the latter is used, only the file opened with the channel number referred to in the statement is closed.

When a file is closed after writing is terminated, the system inserts an end-of-file mark in it. This mark may be used later on to set the value of the Boolean function EOF to TRUE when the last item of the file has been read.

THE **FUNCTION EOF** (END-OF-FILE) IS A **BOOLEAN FUNCTION**. EOF(X) RETURNS A VALUE OF **TRUE** WHEN THE **LAST ELEMENT IN THE FILE** OPENED WITH CHANNEL NUMBER X **IS READ**.

THE **SAVE** COMMAND IS USED TO **STORE** A COPY OF THE PROGRAM PRESENTLY IN WORKSPACE ON THE DISKETTE (CASSETTE).

24

Louise and Agathe
put their heads together

During her Christmas holidays in Oddington Aunt Louise has seen how Hannibal has his data stored in data files.

Exercise 24.1
Use the listing of the program "NEWSHOP" with this exercise. The procedure INITIALIZE retrieves data from the data file "OFFER". In what line is the statement that opens the

file held?. . . . ., and in what line is the statement that closes the file found?. . . . .
Copy below the program lines that make up the REPEAT — UNTIL loop of the procedure:

. . . .

. . . .

. . . .

. . . .

In a specific week Hannibal has only four articles to offer. After they have been typed in and stored, we may picture the file "OFFER" to look like this:

| METTWURST | 1.89 | MEATBALLS | 1.56 | MINCHED PORK | 1.22 | EGG-ROLLS | 1.95 |

What is the value of ARTICLE$(3) when the reading is finished?. . . . .,

PRICE(3)?. . . . . . . .ARTICLE$(1)?. .:. . . . ., PRICE(2)?. . . . . Is
the file "OFFER" opened again after INITIALIZE has been finished (if "yes" then in

what line)?. . . . .
★

Exercise 24.2

Use the listing of "XMASFILE" with this exercise. In what line is the file "XMAS"

opened?........, and in what line is it closed?........ The printout of the Xmas cards

is controlled by a REPEAT – UNTIL loop which starts in line .... and ends in line

.... What is the name of the procedure that performs the printout of the cards?

.... Is it executed after all the names have been retrieved, or is it

executed each time a name has been picked up from the file?

. . . .

Try to explain why all the names of the articles and the prices must be retrieved before
the rest of the program "NEWSHOP" is executed, whereas in "XMASFILE" you are
allowed to retrieve the names one by one as they are used:

. . . .

. . . .

. . . .

. . . .

. . . .

★

By putting their heads together Louise and Agatha find out that the file "OFFER"
must be structured like this:

OFFER:	ROAST OF VEAL	1.59	ROLLED BEEF	1.79	. . .

When the program starts, the data elements are retrieved by the program and assigned to
two arrays ARTICLE$ and PRICE. After that the file is not used again until the program
is restarted or new offers are typed in. During the rest of the run only the two arrays are
used. In the program "XMASFILE" it is different. One name at a time is retrieved and
assigned as a value to the variable RECIPIENT$. Then a card is written to the person
whose name has just been picked up. Now another name is read from the file and a card is
written to the person in question. This line of action is followed until all the cards have
been written. Thus the program "XMASFILE" keeps its data file open and uses it during
the whole run. Louise and Agathe realize that sequential files may be used in two different
ways. You may choose to have the file open during the total process and read or write in
it whenever needed. You may also choose to read – or write – all of the elements once
and for all, and then use arrays that hold a copy of the file during the main part of the

run. The last method has its obvious advantages: By having data held in arrays when performing major parts of the program they may be *accessed directly* in *any order,* and that is impossible while they are contained in a sequential file. Also, in an array as opposed to a sequential file you may *read* or *write as you like.*

Variables or arrays used to hold copies of data files are called **file buffers**. As is seen from the remarks above, file buffers may be bery different in size. You may have buffers that can hold only one data element at a time, but you can also set up arrays as buffers to hold a copy of the whole file. You may of course also have buffers that will hold copies of more or less extensive subsets of the data file. Since one individual data element also represents a subset, we can say in general that

---

A **FILE BUFFER** IS A SET OF VARIABLES OR ARRAYS USED IN CONNECTION WITH READING OR WRITING A FILE. THE BUFFER HOLDS A **SUBSET OF THE DATA** THAT HAS BEEN READ FROM OR IS GOING TO BE WRITTEN TO THE FILE.

Exercise 24.3 □
Use the listing of the program "ADDRPGR" with this exercise. In the procedures PRINTADDR and TAKEIN, find a READ FILE and a WRITE FILE statement, respectively. What are the names of the variable and the array used as buffer for the file "ADDRESSES"?

.... and .... Modify the procedure PRINTADDR so that the user may have one specific address displayed without having to look at the preceding ones. You are not supposed to make any alterations whatsoever to the file buffer. Have the program produce a prompt like this:

ADDRESS NO.?

and wait for the user to enter a number, say 3, to indicate that he wants the third address displayed.
LOAD the program "ADDRPGR" and type in the modifications and extensions you have suggested. Test the program.
★

Some of the advantages of using large file buffers have been mentioned already: Fast and direct access to data, since it is held in the workspace, and the possibility to read or write in the buffers as you please without having to open or close various communication channels. The only drawback to large buffers, perhaps to hold a copy of a whole file, is of course that they occupy valuable workspace.

Exercise 24.4
Use the listing of the program "ENROLL" with this exercise. Find the procedure START-SYSTEM and copy the statements of its body on the lines below:

. . . .

. . . .

. . . .

. . . .

. . . .

. . . .

Two arrays are used as file buffers. What are they called? . . . . and

. . . . What channel number is used? . . . . Let us imagine that PUPILNO has
assumed a value of 3 and that we have reached this part of the file:

| . . . | MAX BRAMER | 5 | 5 | 2 | . . . |

Put down the elements of NAME$ and MARK that have values assigned to them during
the execution of the two lines in the range of the FOR loop. Also write down the values
that are used:

. . . . is assigned the value. . . . .

. . . . is assigned the value. . . . .

. . . . is assigned the value. . . . .

. . . . is assigned the value. . . . .

Now find the procedure STOPSYSTEM in the listing of "ENROLL". Copy the statements
of its body on the lines below:

. . . .

. . . .

. . . .

. . . .

. . . .

. . . .

. . . .

★

The structure of the file "MARKBOOKS" may be pictured like this:

MARKBOOKS: | ROY ATHERTON | 5 | 4 | 1 | MAX BRAMER | 5 | 5 | 2 | ...

Each name is followed by three marks, and even though the individual elements are separated by the same token, introduced by the system, it is obvious that the elements belong together in groups of one name and three numbers. This cannot be seen from the file itself, but it is easily seen in the program from the way in which data are stored and retrieved. In procedure STOPSYSTEM the storing of data is undertaken by the program segment:

```
1170    FOR STUDENTNO:=1 TO MAX DO
1180      WRITE FILE 2: NAME$(STUDENTNO)
1190      FOR SUBJNO:=1 TO 3 DO WRITE FILE 2: MARK(STUDENTNO,SUBJNO)
1200    NEXT STUDENTNO
```

For each individual student number, the student's name followed by the three marks that have been allotted to him by the end of the previous quarter are written in the file "MARKBOOKS", opened with channel number 2. In a similar way retrieving is undertaken by the segment:

```
1080    FOR STUDENTNO:=1 TO MAX DO
1090      READ FILE 2: NAME$(STUDENTNO)
1100      FOR SUBJNO:=1 TO 3 DO READ FILE 2: MARK(STUDENTNO,SUBJNO)
1110    NEXT STUDENTNO
```

As is seen, it is the **buffer** that defines the structure of the file. It is obvious that reading in the file must take place according to exactly the same pattern that was used during writing, if you are not going to have the buffer loaded with pure nonsense afterwards, or have the program stopped with an error message even before the buffer has been filled in. If, furthermore, you write in the file immediately after, it is more than likely that you may just as well start to set up a brand new data base.

Data elements that belong together due to the way in which they are used make up a subset of the file which is usually called a **record**. The individual elements of a record are called **fields**. In "MARKBOOKS", the name of a pupil, with his three marks constitute a record of four fields: One text field and three number fields. An element of the array NAME$, say NAME$(3), together with the three corresponding elements of MARK, MARK (3,1), MARK (3,2), and MARK (3,3), form a **record buffer** for the file.

A RECORD IS A SUBSET OF A DATA FILE IN WHICH THE INDIVIDUAL ELEMENTS GO TOGETHER BECAUSE OF THE WAY IN WHICH THEY ARE USED.

Notice that the structure of a file is defined by the way it is *written*.

Data items which belong together as one record do not necessarily have to be stored alongside one another in a file. One could organize "MARKBOOKS" in a way substantially different from the one used in "ENROLL".

Exercise 24.5

Instead of having data in "MARKBOOKS" stored according to the system: A name, three marks, then another name followed by three marks, etc., you might just as well have them come like this: First all the names and then all the marks such that the first three marks belong with the first of the names, the following three marks with the second name, etc. It may be pictured like this:

ROY ATHERTON	MAX BRAMER	...	COLLEEN KITCHEN	5	4	1	5	5	2	...

The illustration shows the two first and the last pupil name, and the two first set of marks, and we can see that ROY ATHERTON has been given the following marks: 5 in English, 4 in Mathematics, and 1 in French, whereas MAX BRAMER has been given 5 in English, 5 in Mathematics, and 2 in French. COLLEEN KITCHEN's marks are the last three numbers in the file, coming just before the end-of-file mark, but that cannot be seen in the picture. To have the names and the marks organized in the file according to that system, it is necessary to rewrite the main FOR loop of the procedure STOPSYSTEM to become:

```
FOR I:=1 TO MAX DO WRITE FILE 2: NAME$(I)
FOR I:=1 TO MAX DO
   FOR J:=1 TO 3 DO WRITE FILE 2: MARK(I,J)
NEXT I
```

Similar corrections will have to be made in STARTSYSTEM, since it is now necessary first to retrieve all the names and then all the marks, and not alternately a name and three marks. As in STOPSYSTEM four lines must be rewritten. Write your suggestion for the new segment below:

. . . .

. . . .

. . . .

. . . .

★

Exercise 24.6 ☐

In this exercise we shall try to have the procedures STARTSYSTEM and STOPSYSTEM modified according to the suggestions from Exercise 24.5. But we shall have to do it in all of the programs "ENROLL", "ENTERMARKS", "CORRECTION", and "REPORT". To avoid typing in the same eight lines several times, we shall use a special facility in COMAL 80. Use the following method: Type NEW to clear the workspace. Then type in the four lines to replace the FOR loop in procedure STARTSYSTEM. Take a look at the list of "ENROLL". The four lines to be replaced are numbered 1320–1350. Type in the command

```
RENUM 1320,10
```

in order to have the four lines just entered numbered 1320–1350. This done, store the segment using the command:

> LIST "INTERIM"

Then LOAD the program "ENROLL". As soon as it has come into workspace, type in the command:

> ENTER "INTERIM"

The old lines 1320–1350 are now replaced by the ones stored in "INTERIM". You can check that this is the case by having a listing of the program displayed. Save the new version by using the command

> SAVE "ENROL01"

Type NEW to clear the workspace and enter the four line segment into workspace by using the ENTER "INTERIM" command once more. Get the list of "ENTERMARKS" and locate the four lines to be replaced. They ought to be in line 1080–1110. Renumber the four lines in workspace to match the lines they are going to replace in "ENTER-MARKS" by using the command

> RENUM 1080,10

and store the segment by using

> LIST "@0:INTERIM"

Now LOAD the program "ENTERMARKS" and then ENTER the segment "INTERIM". LIST the program to see that the four lines from "INTERIM" have replaced the original lines in "ENTERMARKS". Finally save the new version by using

> SAVE "ENTERMARKS01"

Use the same procedure to update "CORRECTION" and "REPORT". Update the procedure STOPSYSTEM in each of the four new programs according to the suggestion made in Exercise 24.5 by using the same method as has just been demonstrated.

It is of course no good trying to run the updated programs, as long as the data file "MARKBOOKS" is not reorganized too. Its present structure no longer matches the arrangement of the buffer. To reestablish compatibility use the following program to convert the file:

```
0010 DIM NAME$(8) OF 30, MARK(8,3)
0020 OPEN FILE 2,"MARKBOOKS",READ
0030 I:=0
0040 REPEAT
0050    I:=I+1
0060    READ FILE 2: NAME$(I)
0070    FOR J:=1 TO 3 DO READ FILE 2: MARK(I,J)
0080 UNTIL EOF(2)
0090 CLOSE
0100 MAX:=I
0110 OPEN FILE 2,"@0:MARKBOOKS",WRITE
```

```
0120 FOR I:=1 TO MAX DO WRITE FILE 2: NAME$(I)
0130 FOR I:=1 TO MAX DO
0140   FOR J:=1 TO 3 DO WRITE FILE 2: MARK(I,J)
0150 NEXT I
0160 CLOSE
```

The first part of the program retrieves the data from the file according to its present format and fills in the arrays NAME$ and MARK. The second part of the program stores the data in a new version of "MARKBOOKS" and at the same time deletes the present version. After having RUN the conversion program (maybe you should save it first; it might prove useful some other day), the programs "ENROL01", "ENTER-MARKS01", "CORRECTION01", and "REPORT01" may be run.

★

A program can be stored using the command

LIST "⟨file name⟩"

If a program has been stored using the LIST command it can be retrieved using the command

ENTER "⟨file name⟩"

The difference between the SAVE/LOAD commands and the LIST/ENTER commands is a little technical, but for most purposes the following should do. When a program is retrieved through the ENTER command, a program line already in workspace is only affected if it happens to have the same line number as one of the lines that come in. In that case the old line is overwritten by the newcomer, just as if the new line were typed in from the keyboard. Thus the ENTER command may be used to **merge** a program in workspace with programs or program segments stored on an external device (disk or cassette).

You may also choose to have the names in one file and the marks in another one. That is to say you may have different fields of the same record stored in different data files.

Exercise 24.7
In this exercise we shall go on changing the program that administer the marking at Oldham's. We shall modify the procedures STARTSYSTEM and STOPSYSTEM in order to have the names of the pupils and the marks in two different files. One file is "PUPILS", and the other one is "MARKS". After the quarterly list of marks have been entered, you may imagine part of the new files to look like this:

PUPILS: | BARRY SMITH | JOHN COXBY | . . .

MARKS: | 4 | 5 | 0 | 3 | 2 | 1 | . . .

The first three marks have of course been given to the first pupil, Barry Smith, and the following three marks have been given to the second pupil, John Coxby, etc. What mark has been given to Barry Smith in Mathematics?........, and what has been given to

John Coxby in English?........ The body of both STARTSYSTEM and STOPSYSTEM must now be totally rewritten. Below are shown some of the statements that may be used to set up the new interior of STOPSYSTEM. Suggest statements to fit in the empty lines:

```
0010 OPEN FILE 2,"@0:PUPILS",WRITE
0020 FOR I:=1 TO MAX DO WRITE FILE 2: NAME$(I)
0030 CLOSE FILE 2
0040 OPEN FILE 2,"@0:MARKS",WRITE
```

. . . .

. . . .

. . . .

. . . .

On the lines below suggest statements to make up the body of STARTSYSTEM, after the new configuration of data files has been introduced:

. . . .

. . . .

. . . .

. . . .

. . . .

. . . .

. . . .

. . . .

★

Exercise 24.8 □
Use the same line of action as used in Exercise 24.6 to change the procedures STOPSYSTEM and STARTSYSTEM in the programs "ENROLL", "ENTERMARKS", "CORRECTION", and "REPORT", and save the new versions as "ENROL02", "ENTER-NAMES02", "CORRECTION02", and "REPORT02", respectively. Also write and run a program to move data from "MARKBOOKS" to "PUPILS" and "MARKS". RUN the new set of programs to test your modifications.
★

Very often it can be a great advantage to have the different fields of a record stored in separate files. In some situations one might be interested in putting the fields together in a different way and thereby setting up new record structures. Perhaps Eliza Oldham some day would like to do some statistical analysis of the marks in one subject for a whole class. In that case she will not need the names of the pupils but only their marks, and they are of course easier to retrieve if they are held in a file of their own.

In any event it is the **buffers** and the way in which they are used *that determine the structure of the records.* In large data bases, information is very often parcelled out in many different data files, and the individual records are set up by means of different *relations between the buffers.*

Self-tests

CHAPTER 1

Test 1.1
Look at this program line

    30 PRINT "HE CAME ROLLING HOME."

The line consists of two parts, a . . . . and a . . . .

There is a COMAL keyword on the line. What is it? . . . . There is also

a string constant on the line. Write it here: . . . .

Does the string constant include the double quotes (yes/no)? . . . .

Test 1.2

What command would you use it you want the system to *execute* a program? . . . .

Which command causes the system to display a program listing on the screen?. . . . .

What command is used to erase the program at present in the workspace? . . . .

A program called JACOB is on the disk. What command must be used to have this program

copied into the workspace?. . . . .

Test 1.3

Paul McMurphy has written this program

```
0010 PRINT "DEAR UNCLE BILL,"
0020 PRINT "MUMMY SENDS HER LOVE"
0030 PRINT "        LOVE FROM PAUL."
```

Paul's mother does not think it is good enough for Paul to write such a short letter. He therefore extends the program to write a letter of four lines. The third line goes like this:

SHE SAYS SHE IS FINE.

Finally he adds two more statements to have an empty line printed out immediately below the first line and another one before the line with the words, 'LOVE FROM PAUL.' What program lines would you suggest Paul should add?

. . . .

. . . .

. . . .

Test 1.4

Arthur McMurphy has written the following program:

```
0010 PRINT "ROW, ROW, ROW YOUR BOAT"
0020 PRINT "GENTLY DOWN THE STREAM."
0030 PRINT "MERRILY, MERRILY, MERRILY, MERRILY,"
0040 PRINT "LIFE IS BUT A DREAM."
```

Arthur want to erase the two last lines. What command should he use to do that?

. . . .

CHAPTER 2

Test 2.1

Look at this line:

50 INPUT SIZE

Its statement begins with the keyword . . . ., followed by the variable

name . . . . When the statement comes to be executed the system

displays the symbol . . . . , and waits. What is the operator (the one sitting at the keyboard) expected to do? . . . .

. . . .

Test 2.2
Max has written this program to Roy:

```
0010 INPUT DATE
0020 INPUT AMOUNT
0030 PRINT
0040 PRINT "          MILTON KEYNES, ",DATE
0050 PRINT
0060 PRINT "DEAR ROY,"
0070 PRINT
0080 PRINT "WITH THIS LETTER I ENCLOSE"
0090 PRINT AMOUNT," POUNDS, TO PAY FOR THE BOOK,"
0100 PRINT "BORGE TOOK WITH HIM TO DENMARK."
0110 PRINT
0120 PRINT "          BEST WISHES"
0130 PRINT "          MAX"
```

The program uses two variables. What are their names? . . . . and

. . . . Give the numbers of the lines that allow you to enter values

of the two variables: . . . . and . . . . The following values are entered: 791501
and 65.75. When that has happened we may imagine that it looks like this in the workspace:

DATE: [   ]

AMOUNT: [   ]

In which line is the value of the variable DATE printed out? . . . . and, in which line

is the value of AMOUNT printed out? . . . . How many characters does the string

constant in line 40 contain? . . . . How many elements does the output listing

following PRINT in line 90 contain? . . . . In the program four PRINT statements

with *empty output lists* are found. In which lines? . . . . , ... , ... ,

and . . . .

Test 2.3

With what keyword does a statement that allows data to be entered begin?

. . . . Which keyword initiates a statement that is used to print out

data? . . . . When a variable gets a new value the previous one is

deleted. We may also say that it is . . . .

Test 2.4
The following PRINT statements are given:

```
10 PRINT "QUANTITY"
20 PRINT QUANTITY
```

Which one prints out a string constant? . . . .

CHAPTER 3

Test 3.1
Look at this line:

```
0050 QUANTITY:=30; TYPE:=3; PRICE:=34.85
```

The line number is . . . . It holds a statement with three . . . .

What are the name of the three variables in the statement? . . . . , ,

. . . . and . . . . What is the value of PRICE after

the statement has been executed? . . . .

Test 3.2
Look at this program line:

```
0030 TOTAL:=QUANTITY*PRICE+VAT
```

What is the sign ":=" called? . . . . What is the part of the statement

to the right of the ":=" called? . . . . Write down the following signs:

addition: . . . . , subtraction: . . . ., multiplication: . . . ., division: . . . .

Test 3.3
In one program this is line is executed:

```
0120 LONGSIDE:=30; SHORTSIDE:=20; HIGHT:=6
```

Later on in the program the following line is executed:

```
0130 PRINT "AREA OF TRAPEZIUM: ",LONGSIDE+SHORTSIDE*HIGHT/2
```

What value is returned by SHORTSIDE*HIGHT2?......... What value is returned by

LONGSIDE+SHORTSIDE*HIGHT/2?........ However, the correct value should be
150. The reason for the faulty value is that brackets are missing. Try to find out where
and insert them:

```
        LONGSIDE + SHORTSIDE * HIGHT/2
```

Test 3.4
Below is the listing of a program:

```
0010 INPUT NUMBER
0020 INPUT PRICE
0030 DISCOUNT:=50
0040 SALESPRICE:=NUMBER*PRICE
0050 TOTAL:=SALESPRICE-DISCOUNT
0060 PRINT
0070 PRINT "ODDINGTON PET SHOP,"
0080 PRINT
0090 PRINT "WE ARE HEREBY FORWARDING"
0100 PRINT NUMBER," STRIPED TOMCATS."
0110 PRINT
0120 PRINT "SINCE YOU ARE GRANTED A DISCOUNT,"
0130 PRINT "TOTAL, EXCLUSIVE OF VAT, IS: ",TOTAL
0140 PRINT
0150 PRINT "                    YOURS  TRULY"
0160 PRINT "                    OSCAR  WHISKERS"
0170 PRINT "                    CATS  WHOLESALE"
```

What are the names of the variables whose values are input from the keyboard?

.... and .... A numeric constant is found in

the program. Its value is........ and it is assigned to the variable....................

The program's output consists of some strings and two numeric values. What are the names of the two variables which hold the values? . . . . and . . . . Which variable is used for both input and output? . . . . In the program two assignments result from calculations. In what lines are they found? . . . . and . . . . In one of them the constant held in the program is used. In what line? . . . . During the execution of the program the values 35 and 10 are input in that order. What then is output from line 100?

. . . .
and from line 130?

. . . .

Test 3.5
A few strings are shown below. Some of them may be used as variable names, others may not. Tick the legal ones:

NUMBER . . . . , MAXVALUE . . . . , MAX67 . . . . , MAX7 . . . . ,

JOHN . . . . ,   PETER . . . . ,   67MAX . . . . ,   007 . . . . ,

AGENT007 . . . . , COCKLESANDMUSSELS . . . .

SELF-TEST FOR CHAPTER 4
Test 4.1
In a program this statement is found:

        INPUT ARTICLENO

When it is executed, the system displays the prompt . . . . and the user may type in a numeric value to be assigned to the variable . . . .

In an improved version of the program these statements are used:

        PRINT "ENTER ARTICLE NUMBER",
        INPUT ARTICLENO

When they are executed, the system outputs the prompt:

. . . .

and waits for the user to type in a value for . . . . How can you tell that

ARTICLENO is a variable name and not a string constant? . . . .

. . . .

Test 4.2
When the statement

INPUT MAXNUMBER

is executed, the system submits the prompt . . . . and waits for the user to type in
a numeric value. Instead of that, however, you want this prompt displayed:

HOW MANY EXERCISES?

What statement must be inserted before the INPUT statement in order to obtain that?

. . . .

Test 4.3
Look at the program:

```
0030 INPUT NUMBER
0040 NUMBER:=NUMBER+2
0050 PRINT NUMBER
```

What does the program display if you type in: 105? . . . ., 208? . . . ., 10.32?

. . . ., 15? . . . ., −27.5? . . . .

Test 4.4
Look at the program below:

```
0010 PRINT "HOW MUCH WOULD YOU LIKE TO BORROW",
0020 INPUT LOAN
0030 PRINT
0040 IF LOAN>1000 THEN
0050    INTEREST:=.25*LOAN
0060 ELSE
0070    INTEREST:=.3*LOAN
0080 ENDIF
0090 TOTAL:=LOAN+INTEREST
0100 PRINT "IN ONE YEAR YOU OWE ME ",TOTAL," POUNDS.'
```

What variable is used to obtain input from the keyboard? . . . ., In the program

three numeric constants are found. For each of them give its value and the number of

the line in which it is found: . . . . in line . . . ., ... in line . . . .,

and . . . ., in line . . . . One of the constants is part of a Boolean expression.

Copy the expression: . . . . During execution of the program the value

2000 is entered. Write down the printout from the program:

. . . .

The program may be split up in three segments:

1. Takein LOAN
2. Compute INTEREST
3. Printout TOTAL

The structure diagram below is to represent part 2. Complete it:

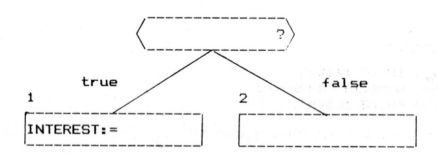

Test 4.5

A numeric expression returns a . . . . value and a Boolean expression

returns a . . . . value.

SELF-TEST FOR CHAPTER 5
Test 5.1
What do you call an area of an external device holding a program? . . . .

Test 5.2
What printout is produced by the following program?

```
0010 PRINT "GIVE ME 1 MINUTE MORE"
0020 FOR I:=2 TO 4 DO
0030   PRINT "GIVE ME ",I," MINUTES MORE"
0040 NEXT I
0050 PRINT "NO, I AM NOT WAITING ANY LONGER."
```

. . . .

. . . .

. . . .

. . . .

. . . .

Test 5.3
Four programs with a FOR loop are found below. For each program write down the number of times the block of statements in the range of the loop is executed.

```
0010 FOR I:=1 TO 10 DO
0020   PRINT
0030   PRINT "THIS PROGRAM MAKES ME DIZZY."
0040   PRINT
0050 NEXT
```

The block is executed . . . . times.

```
0010 FOR I:=6 TO 10 DO
0020   PRINT
0030   PRINT "THIS ONE IS NOT THAT BAD"
0040   PRINT
0050 NEXT I
```

The block is executed . . . . times.

```
0010 FOR TRICK:=-5 TO 5 DO
0020   PRINT
0030   PRINT "I THINK THIS PROGRAM IS"
0040   PRINT "MUCH TOO TRICKY."
0050 NEXT TRICK
```

The block is executed . . . . times.

```
0010 FOR C:=5 TO 3 DO
0020    PRINT
0030    PRINT "I DO NOT THINK IT IS NICE"
0040    PRINT "TO CHEAT ME THAT WAY"
0050 NEXT C
```

The block is executed . . . . times.

Test 5.4

What numbers are printed out by this program:

```
0010 FOR N:=1 TO 5 DO
0020    Y:=N*N+1
0030    PRINT Y
0040 NEXT N
```

. . . ., ..., ..., ..., ...

Test 5.5

The following program prints out simple exercises in arithmetic:

```
0010 PRINT "WHAT TABLE DO YOU WANT TO PRACTICE",
0020 INPUT T
0030 PRINT "FROM",
0040 INPUT FIRST
0050 PRINT "TO",
0060 INPUT LAST
0070 PRINT
0080 FOR A:=FIRST TO LAST DO
0090    PRINT T," + ",A," = . . . . . . . ."
0100    PRINT
0110 NEXT A
```

Write down the first input prompt from the program:

. . . .

What are the names of the variables that take their values from input?

. . . ., ..., and . . . .

Imagine T is set to 4, FIRST to 3, and LAST to 8. What printout is produced by the program?

. . . .

. . . .

. . . .

. . . .

. . . .

. . . .

Test 5.6
How many times is the block in the range of the FOR loop executed in the following program:

```
0030 FOR I:=1 TO 5 DO
0040    PRINT
0050    PRINT "BEWARE, THIS IS A TRICKY PROGRAM!"
0060    I:=5
0070 NEXT I
```

The block is executed . . . . times.

———————————

SELF-TEST FOR CHAPTER 6

Test 6.1
Use the listing in the program in Exercise 5.2 found in the program booklet. We would like to introduce some comments in the program. At the beginning of the program this comment should be inserted:

SMALL POEM ABOUT GIRLS WITH FRECKLES

and the following comment should terminate the program:

END OF POEM WRITING PROGRAM

These two comments need a program line each. Suggest them.

. . . .

. . . .

Test 6.2
Look at this program:

```
0010 FOR N:=1 TO 5 DO
0020    Y:=N*N+1
0030    PRINT Y
0040 NEXT N
```

A structure diagram below is shown to picture the program. Fill in the boxes:

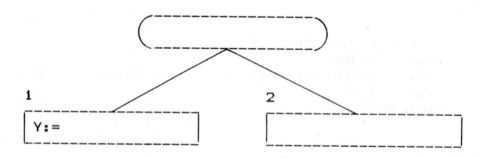

Test 6.3
In a program this line is found

    40 OUTCOME:=RND (5, 10)

What values may be assigned to OUTCOME when the line is executed?

. . . .

What are numbers generated by the RND function called?

. . . .

SELF-TEST FOR CHAPTER 7

Test 7.1

Use the listing in the program "TEST71" (in program booklet) with this test. We shall take a close look at the segment of the program holding lines 190–440. In what line is the statement

FOR GAME:=1 TO MAX DO

found? . . . . A statement like that cannot stand alone in a program. Its counterpart

is found in line . . . . and goes like this: . . . . Find all assignments in the segment and put them down on the lines below:

. . . . , ... ,

. . . .

Find all Boolean expressions in the segment and write them on the lines below:

. . . . , ... ,

. . . .

Imagine STAKED has been set to 4. What output is produced by the segment if GUESS is equal to 0 and the value of GAME is less than the value of MAX?

. . . .

. . . .

. . . .

. . . .

. . . .

With the same value of STAKED what is displayed by the segment if GUESS has a value of 1 and GAME is equal to MAX?

. . . .

. . . .

. . . .

. . . .

SELF-TEST FOR CHAPTER 8

Test 8.1
In some program this segment is found:

```
0030 PROC PRINTOUT
0040    PRINT
0050    PRINT "ON THE ",DATE," YOUR ACCOUNT"
0060    PRINT "SHOWED A BALANCE OF ",AMOUNT," POUNDS."
0070    PRINT
0080 ENDPROC PRINTOUT
```

What is a segment like that called? . . . . The statement in line 30 is

called its . . . ., and the statement in line 80 is called its

. . . . The block of statements held in the range between those two

statements is called its . . . . The segment in question is only executed

if it is called from somewhere else in the program. How does the statement to do this go?

. . . .

Test 8.2
Use the program "TEST82" in the program booklet with this exercise. The program

contains four procedures. What are their names? . . . .,

. . . ., ..., and . . . . The

first two of them are called from line . . . . and . . . ., respectively. The variable

LEVEL is assigned a value through input. What values may be given to LEVEL according

to the prompt from the program? . . . . and . . . . In what line is LEVEL used

after it has been assigned a value? . . . . The structure diagram below represents

PRINTOUT. Complete it:

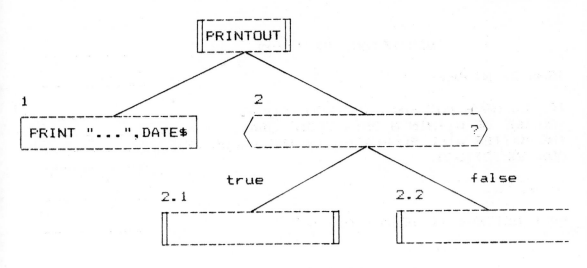

Test 8.3

Use a listing of "TEST82" with this exercise, too. Below is a dialog between a user and the program. On a line with each printout put down the numbers of the program lines that have displayed it. Also underline the numeric values typed in by the user.

```
ENTER DATE (YY/MM/DD)? 82/11/02        _____
WHO IS GOING TO BE PRESSED? SIMPLE SIMON  _____
HOW MUCH MONEY? 200                    _____
PRESSED HARD (1=YES/0=NO)? 0           _____



              ODDINGTON, 82/11/02      _____

DEAR SIMPLE SIMON                      _____

YOU ARE KINDLY ASKED TO PAY OUR        _____
OUTSTANDING ACCOUNT OF 200 POUNDS      _____
AT YOUR EARLIEST CONVENIENCE.          _____

SINCERELY,                             _____
ALFRED BACON.                          _____

MORE LETTERS (1=YES/0=NO)? 1           _____
WHO IS GOING TO BE PRESSED? JOHN S. WINDLER  _____
HOW MUCH MONEY? 800                    _____
PRESSED HARD (1=YES/0=NO)? 1           _____
```

```
            ODDINGTON,  82/11/02              _____

JOHN S. WINDLER                              _____

IF YOU HAVE NOT PAID THE 800 POUNDS          _____
YOU OWE US WITHIN 8 DAYS FROM TODAY,         _____
THE MATTER WILL BE PLACED IN THE HANDS OF    _____
OUR SOLICITORS.                              _____

A.  BACON.                                   _____

MORE LETTERS  (1=YES/0=NO)?  0               _____
```

SELF-TEST FOR CHAPTER 9

Test 9.1

The following program has been given:

```
0030 T:=1
0040 REPEAT
0050   PRINT "NOW T IS EQUAL TO ",T
0060   T:=T+1
0070 UNTIL T=5
0080 PRINT "NOW T IS EQUAL TO ",T
0090 PRINT
0100 PRINT "T TIME IS OUT."
```

What is the value of the variable **T** when the REPEAT loop has been executed? . . . .
What is the full printout of the program?

The program may be improved by giving **T** a different initial value, swap two statements and delete one. What initial value should **T** be given? .... Which lines should be swapped? .... and .... What line should be deleted? ....

Text 9.2
How many times is the PRINT statement in this program executed?

```
0030 FOR P:=1 TO 5 DO
0040    PRINT "NO PARKING ON THIS REFUGE."
0050    P:=P+1
0060 NEXT P
```

.... Rewrite the program to use a REPEAT loop instead of the FOR loop:

. . . .

. . . .

. . . .

. . . .

. . . .

. . . .

SELF-TEST FOR CHAPTER 10

Test 10.1
The following program has been given:

```
0010 ROOT:=5; POWER:=1; T:=0
0020 REPEAT
0030    T:=T+1
0040    POWER:=POWER*ROOT
0050    PRINT POWER
0060 UNTIL T=4
```

What numeric values are displayed by the program? ...., ..., ...,

and ....

Test 10.2
The following program has been given:

```
0010 INPUT X
0020 IF X>20 OR (X MOD 2)=0 THEN
0030    PRINT X
0040 ENDIF
```

During a series of runs the following are input to the program: 1, 10, 20, 19, 7, 25, 9, 18.

What numeric values are printed out by the program? ....

Test 10.3
The following program has been given:

```
0010 INPUT X
0020 IF X<21 AND (X MOD 5)=0 THEN
0030    PRINT X
0040 ENDIF
```

During a series of runs the following are input to the program: 5, 10, 12, 15, 18, 20, 21,

33. What numeric values are printed out by the program? ....

Test 10.4
This program segment has been loaded into workspace:

```
0200 //* MONITOR *//
0210 REPEAT
0220   REPEAT
0230     PRINT "1 = CREATE"
0240     PRINT "2 = CORRECT"
0250     INPUT JOBCODE
0260     IF JOBCODE=1 THEN EXEC CREATE
0270     IF JOBCODE=2 THEN EXEC CORRECT
0280   UNTIL JOBCODE=1 OR JOBCODE=2
0290   PRINT "MORE JOBS TO DO (1=YES/0=NO)",
0300   INPUT ANSW
0310 UNTIL ANSW=0
0320 EXEC STATE
```

Now someone uses the command

RENUM 2000,5

In what line is the statement

INPUT JOBCODE

held after the above command has been issued? . . . .

SELF-TEST FOR CHAPTER 11

Test 11.1
Look at this COMAL statement:

DIM NAME$ OF 30, ADR$ OF 20, TOWN$ of 20

What are variables referred to in the statement called? . . . . What is

the length of a string? . . . .

After the statement above has been executed, this statement is encountered:

INPUT NAME$

Someone types in the name: "PETER DAVID JOHN MARAMALADE-SPREADING-EQUIPMENT". Later on this statement is executed:

PRINT NAME$

What is printed out?

. . . .

Test 11.2
This is part of a COMAL program:

```
0010 PRINT "WHAT DATE IS TODAY (MM/DD/YY)",
0020 INPUT DATE$
```

In the two lines there is one string constant and one string variable. Put down the value

of the string constant:. . . . .

What is the name of the string variable? . . . . What is the length of

the string constant? . . . . How is a value assigned to the string variable? . . . .

. . . .

From the part of the program shown above, you cannot judge what the maximum length

of a string to be assigned to DATE$ would be. Why not? . . . .

. . . .

Test 11.3
When the following statement is executed

```
DIM A$ OF 3, DATE$ OF 10
```

place in the workspace is reserved for two strings of up to 3 and 10 characters, respectively.

The two variables are also said to be . . . .

SELF-TEST FOR SECTION 12

Test 12.1
In the following statement a string array is declared:

```
0030 DIM COLOUR$ (5) OF 10
```

How many strings can be held by the array? . . . . What is the maximum length of

each of these strings? . . . . Values are assigned to the entries of the array in the
following segment:

```
0040 COLOUR$(1):="RED"
0050 COLOUR$(2):="YELLOW"
0060 COLOUR$(3):="GREEN"
0070 COLOUR$(4):="BLUE"
0080 COLOUR$(5):="VIOLET"
```

COLOUR$(2) is an entry of the array. The quantity held in brackets is called the . . . .

of the entry. In this example it is given as a numeric constant. It may be given in two

other ways, namely as a . . . . or as an . . . . What printout results from executing the statement

        PRINT COLOUR$(I)

if I is equal to 2? . . . ., and if I is equal to 4? . . . .

What printout is produced by

        PRINT COLOUR$(N+1)

if N is equal to 0? . . . ., and if N is equal to 3? . . . .

What is the value of N if "GREEN" is displayed? . . . .

Test 12.2
What is the name of the string given as follows:

        " "

. . . . What is its length? . . . . In a program this statement is given:

        INPUT ANSW$

When the statement is executed the system as usual displays a prompt and waits for the user to enter some string. What must you do in order that ANSW$ gets the value " "

SELF-TEST FOR CHAPTER 13

Test 13.1
Here is a program:

```
0030 I:=0
0040 REPEAT
0050    GOTO SKIP
0060    I:=I+1
0070 SKIP:
0080    PRINT "THIS IS RUN NO. ",I
0090 UNTIL I=10
```

What printout is produced by the program when the loop is executed for the third time?

. . . .

Test 13.2
Look at this program segment:

```
0030 FOR J:=1 TO 100 DO
0040    EXEC PRINTOUT
0050    IF J=6 THEN STOP
0060 NEXT J
```

How many times is PRINTOUT called?. . . . .

SELF-TEST FOR CHAPTER 14

Test 14.1
Use the listing of the program "TEST141" from the program booklet with the following. In the program a READ statement and some DATA statements are found. In what line is

the READ statement found? . . . . What lines hold the DATA statements? . . . . ,

. . . . , and . . . . The set of data elements held in the three DATA statements is

also called a . . . . How many entries does the array NAME$ hold?

. . . . How many characters can be held in each entry? . . . . The statement

```
READ NAME$(I)
```

is in the range of a FOR loop. Put down the value of each of the following entries after the loop is finished:

NAME$(1):........................, NAME$(2):..........................,

NAME$(5):........................, NAME$(11):.......................,

NAME$(7):........................, NAME$(12):.......................

Test 14.2
Use the program listing of "TEST141" with the following, too. Copy the statement from line 280:

....

To the right of the sign of assignment a string variable, a string constant, and an entry of

an array are found. What is the name of the variable? .... What is

the value of the string constant? .... What is the array of string

called? ....

Test 14.3
Once again the listing of "TEST141" should be used. The procedure that "draws" the cards is FINDCARD. To pick up a name and a colour this procedure uses the RND function twice. Below is shown a set of printouts from the program. Next to each print-out put down the values that RND(1,13) and RND(1,4) must have returned in order to generate that specific "card".

	RND (1, 13)	RND (1, 4)
KNIGHT OF CLUBS	....	
FIVE OF CLUBS	....	
SEVEN OF HEARTS	....	
QUEEN OF HEARTS	....	
FIVE OF DIAMONDS	....	
ACE OF DIAMONDS	....	

And now a hard one: In line 290 an UNTIL statement is found that holds the Boolean expression:

      NOT CARD$ IN DRAWN$

The expression is TRUE if the string held by CARD$ is not found as a substring of the string presently held by DRAWN$. In line 300 you can see that each time a card has been drawn, its value is added to DRAWN$. Thus the present value of DRAWN$ is a string holding all the names of all the cards that have been drawn so far. Try to explain what the REPEAT loop in FINDCARD is used for.

· ·

· ·

Test 15.1

The procedure below is used to simulate a game involving a roulette wheel:

```
0120 PROC WHEEL
0130    OUTCOME:=RND(1,15)
0140    CASE OUTCOME OF
0150    WHEN 1,3,6,9,12,15
0160       COLOR$:="RED"
0170       FACTOR:=1.5
0180    WHEN 2,5,8,11,14
0190       COLOR$:="YELLOW"
0200       FACTOR:=2
0210    WHEN 4,10,13
0220       COLOR$:="GREEN"
0230       FACTOR:=3
0240    WHEN 7
0250       COLOR$:="BLUE"
0260       FACTOR:=9
0270    ENDCASE
0280    EXEC DISPLAY(COLOR$)
0290 ENDPROC WHEEL
```

The wheel has six red fields, five yellow fields, three green fields, and one blue field. The function RND(1,15) returns integers from 1 to 15 at random. Each time an integer is generated it is assigned as a value to the variable OUTCOME. In the table below some values of OUTCOME are suggested. Fill in the table with the corresponding values of COLOR$ and FACTOR:

OUTCOME	COLOR$	FACTOR
10		
8		
12		
13		
7		

Test 15.2
Havelock's uncle, Dr. David Harris, has come to the fair and is gambling at the electronic roulette wheel. In a certain game he stakes 10 pounds, and after the game is over he is

paid 30 pounds. What colour has come out? . . . .

Put down the values OUTCOME may have assumed in this case:

. . . .

Test 15.3
The structure diagram below pictures the procedure WHEEL from Test 15.1. Complete it.

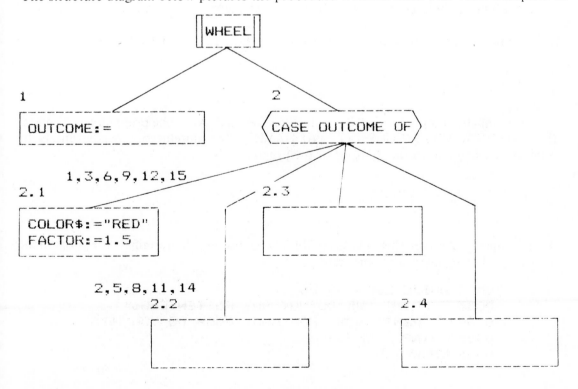

SELF-TEST FOR CHAPTER 16

Test 16.1
Look at this program segment:

```
0030 I:=1
0040 WHILE I<=5 DO
0050    PRINT I
0060    I:=I+1
0070 ENDWHILE
```

Copy the Boolean expression in the WHILE statement:.................... What is

the value of I after the execution of the loop is finished?........ What values are

printed out by the program?....................

Test 16.2
Look at this program segment:

```
0030 I:=1
0040 REPEAT
0050    PRINT I
0060    I:=I+1
0070 UNTIL I>5
```

Copy the Boolean expression in the REPEAT statement:.................... What

is the value of I after the loop has been executed?........ What values are printed out

by the program? ....

Test 16.3
A teaser runs the program "EGGS" from Exercise 16.3. After the program has displayed the text "HOW MANY EGGS DO YOU HAVE?", this mischievous person enters the number −8. Write down the printout of the program:

....

....

A programmer observes this, and after the teaser has left the terminal, the programmer adds the following lines to the program:

```
0052 WHILE EGGS<=0 DO
0053    PRINT "WE DO NOT BUY ROTTEN EGGS!"
0054    PRINT "NOW, HOW MANY EGGS DO YOU HAVE",
0055    INPUT EGGS
0056 ENDWHILE
```

The next time this same mischievous person runs the program, he tries to type in the number −10 but this time his enterprise is stopped by the WHILE loop above. After having considered the situation for a moment, he runs the program again and with a crafty smile on his face he types in a number that makes the program printout the following:

```
WE HAVE PACKED 3 EGG TRAY(S).
AND LEFT OVER 2.5 EGG(S).
```

What number has been entered by the teaser?. . . . . Why has this meaningless number not been stopped by the WHILE statement?

. . . .

Test 16.4

Use the listing of the program "WHEEL" found in the program booklet with this exercise. Below is shown a dialog between a user and the program. Against each line put down the number(s) of the line(s) that has produced the program's part. Also score the users replies.

```
WHAT COLOR? YELLOW              _____
HOW MUCH DO YOU WANT TO BET? 20 _____


****** RED WINS ******          _____


SORRY YOU HAVE LOST 20 PENCE.   _____
BETTER LUCK NEXT TIME.          _____


PLAY AGAIN (Y/N)? Y             _____
WHAT COLOR? YELLOW              _____
HOW MUCH DO YOU WANT TO BET? 20 _____


****** YELLOW WINS ******       _____


HURRAY, YOU WIN!!               _____
YOU HAVE STAKED 20 PENCE,       _____
SO YOU GET 40 PENCE.            _____
```

```
PLAY AGAIN (Y/N)? Y                          _____
WHAT COLOR? BLACK                            _____
ONLY (RED,YELLOW,GREEN,BLUE) ALLOWED!        _____
NOW, WHAT DO YOU PICK OUT? BLUE              _____
HOW MUCH DO YOU WANT TO BET? 5               _____
DON'T BE MEAN, MAN!                          _____
NOT LESS THEN 10 PENCE.                      _____
MAY WE ASK FOR YOUR BET? 15                  _____


******* BLUE WINS *******                    _____


HURRAY, YOU WIN!!                            _____
YOU HAVE STAKED 15 PENCE,                    _____
SO YOU GET 135 PENCE.                        _____


PLAY AGAIN (Y/N)? N                          _____
```

SELF-TEST FOR CHAPTER 17

Test 17.1

The program below generates exercises in fractions:

```
0030 FOR NO:=1 TO 5 DO
0040     NUMERATOR1:=1; DENOMINATOR1:=RND(2,5)
0050     NUMERATOR2:=1; DENOMINATOR2:=RND(2,5)
0060     EXEC DISPLAY
0070     PRINT
0080 NEXT NO
0090 //
0100 PROC DISPLAY
0110     EXEC PRINTOUT(NUMERATOR1,NUMERATOR2)
0120     PRINT "- + - ="
0130     EXEC PRINTOUT(DENOMINATOR1,DENOMINATOR2)
0140 ENDPROC DISPLAY
0150 //
0160 PROC PRINTOUT(A,B)
0170     PRINT A,"    ",B
0180 ENDPROC PRINTOUT
0190 //
```

Which lines hold calls to procedure PRINTOUT?........ and .... What are
the names of the parameters found in the first call?..................... and
.... What are the names of the parameters found in the second call?
.... and .... What are the names of the parameters found in the head of PRINTOUT?.................... and ....
Parameters that appear in procedure calls are also called .... parameters.
Below is shown an exercise produced by the program:

$$\frac{1}{4} + \frac{1}{2} =$$

How many exercises does the program produce during one run? .... What values
may the numerator assume? ....; and the denominator?

....

Test 17.2
Look at this program segment:

```
0030 MAX:=8
0040 DIM NAME$(MAX) OF 30
0050 DIM WANTED$ OF 30, ANSW$ OF 1
0060 FOR I:=1 TO MAX DO
0070    READ NAME$(I)
0080 NEXT I
0090 //
0100 REPEAT
0110    PRINT
0120    PRINT "WHOM ARE YOU LOOKING FOR",
0130    INPUT WANTED$
0140    NO:=0
0150    REPEAT
0160       NO:=NO+1
0170       FOUND:=(WANTED$=NAME$(NO))
0180    UNTIL FOUND OR NO=MAX
0190    IF FOUND THEN
0200       PRINT "FOUND AS NUMBER ",NO
0210    ELSE
0220       PRINT "PERSON NOT FOUND"
0230    ENDIF
0240    PRINT "MORE (Y/N)",
0250    INPUT ANSW$
0260 UNTIL ANSW$="N"
0270 //
0280 DATA "ALFRED","BARRY","MARY","PETER"
0290 DATA "ROY","ELIZA","HANNIBAL","LOUISE"
0300 //
```

What is the value of NAME$(3) when lines 30–80 have been executed?. . . . .,
and what is the value of NAME$(7)?. . . . . As line 130 is executed the
name "ELIZA" is entered. The variable NO is then set to zero and a REPEAT loop is
started. What is the value of NO after the loop is finished?. . . . ., and what is the
value of FOUND? . . . . What printout is produced by the program after that?

. . . .

. . . .

Some other time the name "CURT" is entered. What value does NO assume this time?

........., and FOUND?........ What printout is produced by the program in this case?

. . . .

. . . .

Below is displayed a dialog between some user and the program. Against each line put the number(s) of the line(s) that has/have produced the program's part. Also score the users replies.

```
WHOM ARE YOU LOOKING FOR? BARRY        _____
FOUND AS NUMBER 2                      _____
MORE (Y/N)? Y                          _____

WHOM ARE YOU LOOKING FOR? CURT         _____
PERSON NOT FOUND                       _____
MORE (Y/N)? Y                          _____

WHOM ARE YOU LOOKING FOR? ROY          _____
FOUND AS NUMBER 5                      _____
MORE (Y/N)? N                          _____
```

How many times is the four line REPEAT loop executed in the first case?........,

in the second one?........, and in the third?........

_____

SELF-TEST FOR CHAPTER 18

Test 18.1

Below is listing of a small program:

```
0030 DIM NAME$(5) OF 20
0040 DIM TRADE$(5) OF 10
0050 DIM ANSW$ OF 3
0060 NAME$(1):="PETER BROWN"; TRADE$(1):="JOINER"
0070 NAME$(2):="JOHN SMITH"; TRADE$(2):="ELECTRICIAN"
0080 NAME$(3):="ROY MANNING"; TRADE$(3):="MECHANIC"
0090 NAME$(4):="ELIZA MOOR"; TRADE$(4):="TEACHER"
0100 NAME$(5):="MINNA JACOBS"; TRADE$(5):="CAB DRIVER"
0110 //
0120 REPEAT   //REQUESTS
0130    PRINT CHR$(147) //CLEAR
0140    PRINT "ENTER NUMBER (1..5)",
0150    INPUT NO
0160    PRINT
0170    IF NO<6 THEN
0180       PRINT "PERSON NUMBER ",NO
0190       PRINT "IS CALLED ",NAME$(NO),""
0200       PRINT "AND IS A ",TRADE$(NO)
0210    ELSE
0220       PRINT "NO PERSON WITH THAT NUMBER"
0230    ENDIF
0240    PRINT
0250    PRINT "MORE (Y/N)",
0260    INPUT ANSW$
0270 UNTIL ANSW$="N"
```

In the program two arrays of texts are declared. The first one is . . . . ;
it can hold . . . . elements each of which may have a length of . . . . characters.
The second one is . . . . ; it can hold . . . . elements each of which
may have a length of . . . . characters. The two arrays are assigned values in line
. . . . - . . . . In the program a REPEAT loop is found that starts in line . . . .
and ends in line . . . . Copy the Boolean expression in the UNTIL statement:
. . . . In what line is a value assigned to ANSW$ . . . .

Test 18.2
Use the program from Test 18.1 with this test. The main lines of the program are held in a REPEAT loop. During execution of it stored data as well as input data are used to produce the output. Where are the stored data found?

. . . .

Input is captured when line 150 is executed. What is the name of the variable used to

capture the input?. Output to answer the request is produced by

line. . . . .-. . . . . or line . . . . In two of these lines stored data is output.

Which ones? . . . . and . . . . If the number 3 is input, the program produces the
following output:

. . . .

. . . .

. . . .

If the number 7 is input, the program outputs:

. . . .

Note. The main purpose of the program is to answer requests based on input (the request) and stored data (where the answer may be found). The answer entered when line 250–260 is executed is used to control the program, and has no impact on the output from it.

Test 18.3

Below is the printout of a dialog between the program and a user. Against each line put the number(s) of the line(s) that has/have produced the program's part. Also score the users replies.

```
ENTER NUMBER (1..5)? 3              _____

PERSON NUMBER 3                     _____
IS CALLED ROY MANNING              _____
AND IS A MECHANIC                  _____

MORE (Y/N)? Y                      _____

ENTER NUMBER (1..5)? 6             _____

NO PERSON WITH THAT NUMBER         _____

MORE (Y/N)? Y                      _____

ENTER NUMBER (1..5)? 1             _____

PERSON NUMBER 1                    _____
IS CALLED PETER BROWN              _____
AND IS A JOINER                    _____

MORE (Y/N)? N                      _____
```

SELF-TEST FOR CHAPTER 19

Test 19.1

The listing of a program is shown below:

```
0030 DIM NAME$(5) OF 20
0040 DIM TEL(5), N$ OF 20
0050 NAME$(1):="PETER BROWN"; TEL(1):=344567
0060 NAME$(2):="JOHN SMITH"; TEL(2):=342356
0070 NAME$(3):="ROY MANNING"; TEL(3):=346712
0080 NAME$(4):="ELIZA MOOR"; TEL(4):=341278
0090 NAME$(5):="MINNA JACOBS"; TEL(5):=347895
0100 //
0110 REPEAT   //REQUESTS
0120    PRINT
0130    INPUT "NAME: ": N$
0140    I:=0
0150    REPEAT
0160       I:=I+1
0170       FOUND:=N$=NAME$(I)
0180    UNTIL FOUND OR I=5
0190    PRINT
0200    IF FOUND THEN
0210       PRINT N$," HAS TELEPHONE NUMBER ",TEL(I)
0220    ELSE
0230       PRINT N$," HAS NO TELEPHONE."
0240    ENDIF
0250 UNTIL N$="NO TALK"
```

In the program, an array of strings, a numeric array and a string variable are declared. The array of strings NAME$ is declared to hold . . . . elements, each with a length of . . . . characters. The numeric array is called . . . . and has been declared to hold . . . . elements. The string variable is called . . . . and may hold up to . . . . characters. The user may type in a name and this name is assigned to the variable . . . . The program then tries to look the name up in an array. Which one? . . . . The result of the "lookup" determines which printout the program will produce. Copy the five lines responsible for the lookup:

. . . .

. . . .

. . . .

. . . .

. . . .

During a certain run the user enters the name "ROY MANNING", and the program starts

to look for it. Having found it the variable I has assumed a value of . . . ., and FOUND
has assumed a value of TRUE/FALSE (score correct). What printout is produced by the
program?

. . . .

Later, the user types in the name "BRIAN MEEK". After the lookup has been finished, I

has assumed the value . . . . and FOUND has assumed the value TRUE/FALSE (score

correct). What printout does the program produce this time? . . . .

. . . .

What "name" must be entered in order to stop the program? . . . .

What printout does the program produce before it stops?

. . . .

A string constant is held in the INPUT statement. How does it go? . . . .

What do you call a text used like that? . . . .

Test 19.2

The program below uses a quite different method to look something up in a telephone record.

```
0030 DIM N$ OF 20, NAME$ OF 20
0040 REPEAT
0050    PRINT
0060    INPUT "ENTER NAME: ": N$
0070    RESTORE
0080    REPEAT
0090       READ NAME$,TEL
0100    UNTIL N$=NAME$ OR EOD
0110    IF N$=NAME$ THEN
0120       PRINT N$," HAS TELEPHONE NO. ",TEL
0130    ELSE
0140       PRINT N$," HAS NO TELEPHONE"
0150    ENDIF
0160 UNTIL N$="NO TALK"
0170 //
0180 DATA "PETER BROWN",344567,"JOHN SMITH",342356
0190 DATA "ROY MANNING",346712,"ELIZA MOOR",341278
0200 DATA "MINNA JACOBS",347895
```

The stored data are found in the data queue in line . . . . – . . . . The lookup in the telephone record is done by the REPEAT loop in line 60–80. Put down the Boolean expression in the UNTIL statement:

. . . .

That means that execution of the loop is stopped if the name entered is found in the record (the data queue) or if . . . . In line 70 a RESTORE statement is found. What does it do?

. . . .

Test 19.3

Look at this program line:

```
PRINT INT (X)
```

What printout does the line produce if X has a value of 3.4? . . . ., 81.45? . . . ., 15? . . . ., −7? . . . ., −7.4? . . . ., −23.456? . . . . What does INT(X) mean? . . . .

Test 19.4

In a program this line is found:

```
PRINT NAME$, TAB (20), HIGHT
```

What printout is produced by the line if NAME$ has a value of "SIMON HARRIS" and HIGHT is equal to 179?

. . . .
     5   10   15   20   25   30   35

What printout does this line produce

```
PRINT TAB (5) ,NAME$,TAB (30) ,HIGHT
```

if NAME$ and HIGHT have the same values as before?

. . . .
     5   10   15   20   25   30   35

SELF-TEST FOR CHAPTER 20

Test 20.1
A listing of a program is shown below:

```
0030 DIM NAME$(10) OF 20
0040 DIM ANSW$ OF 1
0050 DIM PERSDATA(10,3)
0060 I:=0
0070 REPEAT
0080    I:=I+1
0090    READ NAME$(I)
0100    FOR J:=1 TO 3 DO READ PERSDATA(I,J)
0110 UNTIL EOD
0120 MAX:=I
0130 //
0140 REPEAT
0150    INPUT "ENTER NUMBER: ": NO
0160    WHILE NO<1 OR MAX<NO DO
0170       PRINT "ERROR! ONLY 1..",MAX," MAY BE USED"
0180       INPUT "ENTER NUMBER: ": NO
0190    ENDWHILE
0200    PRINT CHR$(147) //CLEAR
0210    PRINT NAME$(NO)
0220    PRINT "AGE:",TAB(20),PERSDATA(NO,1)
0230    PRINT "HIGHT:",TAB(20),PERSDATA(NO,2)
0240    PRINT "WEIGHT:",TAB(20),PERSDATA(NO,3)
0250    PRINT
0260    INPUT "MORE REQUESTS (Y/N)? ": ANSW$
0270 UNTIL ANSW$="N"
0280 //
0290 DATA "PETER BROWN",38,172,68,"JOHN SMITH",43,176,72
0300 DATA "ROY MANNING",45,176,75,"ELIZA MOOR",34,168,57
0310 DATA "MINNA JACOBS",26,168,55
```

In the program an array of strings, a string variable, and a two dimensional numeric array are declared. The name of the string array is . . . . and it has got

. . . . elements each of which may hold a string of up to . . . . characters. The

two dimensional numeric array is called . . . . It will hold . . . .

rows of . . . . elements each. The stored data used by the program are held in a data queue. When the program starts the arrays are filled in with the data in the queue. How

many names are given in the program above? . . . . What is the maximum number of names to be administered by the program?. . . . . Each name is followed by a set of

three numeric data elements, the first of which gives the person's age, the second one the

person's. . . . . and the third one the person's. . . . .

What are the values of the following elements after the first part of the program is executed?

NAME$ (3): . . . ., PERSDATA(3,1) . . . ., PERSDATA(3,2):

. . . ., PERSDATA(3,3): . . . ., NAME$ (5): . . . .,

PERSDATA(2,1): . . . ., PERSDATA(1,2): . . . ., PERSDATA (6,3): . . . .

Which element(s) of PERSDATA has/have assumed the value 168?

. . . .

and the value 34?

. . . .

and the value 75?

. . . .

Test 20.2
In the program from Test 20.1 a WHILE loop is found. It starts in line . . . .

and ends in line . . . . What is the purpose of the loop? . . . .

. . . .

What printout is produced by the program if the number 7 is entered as line 150 is
executed? . . . .

. . . .

What printout does the program produce if the number 5 is typed in as line 150 is executed?

. . . .

5   10   15   20   25   30   35

. . . .

. . . .

. . . .

. . . .

. . . .
    5   10   15   20   25   30   35

What printout does this line produce?

```
FOR I:=1 TO 5 DO PRINT I, " ",
```

. . . .
    5   10   15   20   25   30   35

What printout does this line produce?

```
FOR I:=1 TO 5 DO PRINT I, TAB(5*I),
```

. . . .
    5   10   15   20   25   30   35

Test 20.3
Below is shown the last part of a new version of the program from Test 19.1:

```
0110 REPEAT   //REQUESTS
0120    PRINT
0130    INPUT "NAME: ": N$
0140    I:=1
0150    WHILE NOT (N$=NAME$(I) OR I=5) DO I:=I+1
0160    PRINT
0170    IF N$=NAME$(I) THEN
0180       PRINT N$,"HAS TELEPHONE NUMBER ",TEL(I)
0190    ELSE
0200       PRINT N$," HAS NO TELEPHONE"
0210    ENDIF
0220 UNTIL N$="NO TALK"
```

The looking up in the array of names is done by a WHILE loop instead of a REPEAT loop. The program from Test 19.2 may be modified in a similar way. Put down below the lines to replace the REPEAT loop with a WHILE loop in the program (lines 80–100) from test 19.2:

. . . .

. . . .

Test 20.4

In a program a two dimensional numeric array has been declared using

> DIM TABLE (4,3)

and each element of the array has been assigned a value. Write a program segment using only three lines to produce a printout of the values stored in the array:

. . . .

. . . .

. . . .

(*Hint:* use two FOR loops).

SELF-TEST FOR CHAPTER 21

Test 21.1

What printout is produced by this line:

> PRINT 2,3,4

with ZONE set to zero?. . . . .
What printout is produced by this program;

```
0010 ZONE 15
0020 PRINT 2,3,4
```

. . . .
```
        5         10        15        20        25        30        35
```

What printout is produced by this program:

```
0010 FOR I:=5 TO 12 DO
0020    ZONE I
0030    PRINT I,
0040 NEXT I
```

. . . .
```
        5         10        15        20        25        30        35
```

Test 21.2

Here is a small program:

```
0010 SELECT OUTPUT "LP"
0020 PRINT "HERE I AM"
0030 PRINT "WHERE ARE YOU"
0040 SELECT OUTPUT "DS"
0050 PRINT "I AM HERE"
```

Where will the first text appear? . . . .

Where will the second text appear? . . . .

Where will the third text appear? . . . .

Test 21.3

With this test the program from Test 18.1 is going to be used. Fancy that the program lines 30–110 have been typed in. We now want to rewrite the last part of the program in order that it can be used to find a person with a given trade. Below is a suggested second part of the program written in pseudo code:

> *REPEAT*
>   *enter trade*
>   *look for trade in table*
>   *IF the trade has been found THEN*
>   *PRINT the name of the person*
>   *that exercises the trade*
>   *ELSE*
>   *PRINT that no person on our list*
>   *can carry out the trade*
>   *ENDIF*
>   *more requests?*
> *UNTIL no more requests*

Put down a COMAL program segment that will perform the specified process (the program from Test 19.1 may be used as a model):

. . . .

. . . .

. . . .

. . . .

. . . .

. . . .

SELF-TEST FOR CHAPTER 22

Test 22.1
Below is a listing of two segments which are both parts of a program used at Oldham's to administer pupil's options:

```
0010 //PROGRAM: EXHIBITOPTIONS//
0020 DIM NAME$(15) OF 20, OPTION(15,4)
0030 DIM SUBJECT$(4) OF 12, N$ OF 20, A$ OF 3
0040 DIM UP$ OF 1, DOWN$ OF 1, SPACES$ OF 40
0050 //
0060 UP$:=CHR$(145); DOWN$:=CHR$(17); SPACES$(1:40):=""
0070 SUBJECT$(1):="BIOLOGY"
0080 SUBJECT$(2):="GERMAN"
0090 SUBJECT$(3):="INFORMATICS"
0100 SUBJECT$(4):="MUSIC"
0110 //

  ...

0270 PROC OPTIONS
0280    EXEC WINDOW(8,20)
0290    INPUT "STUDENT'S NAME: ": N$
0300    I:=0; FOUND:=FALSE
0310    WHILE NOT (FOUND OR I=MAX) DO
0320       I:=I+1
0330       FOUND:=(N$=NAME$(I))
0340    ENDWHILE
0350    IF FOUND THEN
0360       PRINT
0370       PRINT N$,"'S OPTION:"
0380       PRINT
0390       FOR J:=1 TO 4 DO
0400          IF NOT OPTION(I,J)=-1 THEN
0410             PRINT SUBJECT$(J),TAB(15),"AT LEVEL ",OPTION(I,J
0420          ENDIF
0430       NEXT J
0440       EXEC WINDOW(18,18)
0450       INPUT "PRESS RETURN TO CONT. ": A$
0460    ELSE
0470       EXEC WINDOW(1,1)
0480       PRINT "NO STUDENT WITH THAT NAME"
0490       INPUT "DO YOU WANT A LIST (Y/N)? ": A$
0500       IF A$="Y" THEN EXEC DISPLAY
0510    ENDIF
0520 ENDPROC OPTIONS
```

The pupils may choose any of four optional subjects. The names of the subjects are held in

the array SUBJECT$. What are they? . . . ., ...,

. . . ., and . . . . The array OPTION is numeric. It

will hold . . . . elements arranged in . . . . rows of . . . . elements each.

Test 22.2

Use the program segments from Test 22.1 with this test. At Oldham's each pupil may choose freely whether he or she wants any one of the optional subjects at a basic level, at an advanced level, or not at all. A pupil's choice is stored in the table OPTION using the numbers 1, 2, or −1, respectively, to represent the options basic level, advanced level, or not at all. If for example OPTION(4,1) is equal to 2 this means that pupil no. 4 has chosen to have biology at an advanced level, and if OPTION(4,2) is equal to −1, the same pupil has decided not to do German at all. This is a picture of part of OPTION:

	1	2	3	4	
OPTION:	1	2	1	−1	1
	2	1	2	−1	2
	1	2	−1	2	3
	2	−1	−1	1	4

Which subjects at what levels has pupil no. 3 chosen to do?

. . . .

. . . .

From the above excerpt of the table you can also see that the following pupils (give

numbers) have chosen to do German at an advanced level: . . . .
We can also see that the following pupils have picked up Biology at one of the two levels:

. . . .

It is further to be seen from the table that the following pupils have chosen not to take the following subjects (give pupils' numbers and subjects − but not level):

. . . .

. . . .

Test 22.3
With this test we also use the program segments from Test 22.1. It is known that pupil no. 1 is called "PETER BARROW", pupil no. 2 is called "JOHN BROWN", and pupil no. 3 is called "ANNIE BURTON". Also the excerpt of OPTION from test 22.2 is known. As line 290 is executed, the name "ANNIE BURTON" is typed in by the user, and the program starts to look in the table of names. After the search has been finished what is the value

assumed by the variable I? . . . . and FOUND? . . . . What printout is produced by the program?

. . . .

. . . .

. . . .

. . . .

. . . .

. . . .

Test 22.4
Given the following statement:

OK:=FALSE; LACKING:=TRUE

What is the numeric value of OK after the statement has been executed? . . . ., and of

LACKING? . . . . What is a numeric variable used in this way called? . . . .

. . . .

Below are some Boolean expressions. OK and LACKING are supposed to have the values assigned to them in the statement above.
Against each expression put the word TRUE or FALSE to indicate its truth value:

NOT OK OR LACKING: . . . ., OK AND LACKING: . . . ., NOT OK=0:

. . . ., LACKING=1: . . . ., LACKING=OK: . . . ., NOT LACKING

AND NOT OK: . . . ., LACKING=0 AND NOT OK=1: . . . ., NOT OK=

FALSE: . . . ., (NOT LACKING AND OK)=TRUE: . . . ., NOT 0:

. . . ., NOT 1: . . . ., NOT TRUE: . . . ., TRUE=0: . . . .

SELF-TEST FOR CHAPTER 23

Test 23.1

The procedure below is part of the program "ENTEROPTIONS" (listing in program booklet):

```
0560 PROC STARTPROGRAM
0570    OPEN 2, "OPTIONS", READ
0580    READ FILE 2: MAX
0590    FOR I:=1 TO MAX DO
0600       READ FILE 2: NAME$(I)
0610       FOR J:=1 TO 4 DO READ FILE 2: OPTION(I,J)
0620    NEXT I
0630    CLOSE
0640 ENDPROC STARTPROGRAM
```

What is the name of the data file opened in the procedure?. What is the number of the channel opened to it?. . . . . Is it opened for data to be stored in it or retrieved from it?. . . . . How can you see that?. . . . . What lines hold the statements that are used to retrieve data from the file?. . . . ., ..., and . . . . What keyword is used to cut off the channel to the file? . . . .

Test 23.2

Below is depicted part of the file "OPTIONS":

OPTIONS: | 7 | PETER BARROW | 1 | 2 | 1 | −1 | JOHN BROWN | 2 | 1 | 2 | −1 |

Write down on the lines below the names of the variables that are assigned values when the part of the file shown above is read. Indices for array elements, if any, should be given using constants, such as OPTION(1, 3), etc.

. . . .

. . . .

. . . .

. . . .

Test 23.3

The procedure below does the same job as the one from Test 23.2 but uses a slightly different approach:

```
0560 PROC STARTPROGRAM
0570    OPEN 2,"OPTIONS",READ
0580    READ FILE 2: MAX
0585    I:=1
0590    WHILE NOT EOF(2) DO
0600       READ FILE 2: NAME$(I)
0610       FOR J:=1 TO 4 DO READ FILE 2: OPTION(I,J)
0620    ENDWHILE
0630    CLOSE
0640 ENDPROC STARTPROGRAM
```

Copy the Boolean expression in the WHILE statement:

. . . . What is EOF?

. . . .

. . . .

"Translate" the following into COMAL:
WHILE the file opened as no. 3 is not finished

. . . .

Test 23.4

Below is shown a procedure from "ENTEROPTIONS":

```
0660 PROC STOPPROGRAM
0670    OPEN 3,"90:OPTIONS",WRITE
0680    WRITE FILE 3: MAX
0690    FOR I:=1 TO MAX DO
0700       WRITE FILE 3: NAME$(I)
0710       FOR J:=1 TO 4 DO WRITE FILE 3: OPTION(I,J)
0720    NEXT I
0730    CLOSE 3
0740 ENDPROC STOPPROGRAM
```

What is the name of the file opened by the procedure?. What

channel number is used?. . . . . Is it opened for data to be stored in it or retrieved

from it?. In what line is the file signed off?. . . . . Explain the difference between the statement

CLOSE

and the statement:

CLOSE FILE 3

. . . .

. . . .

On a certain occasion MAX has a value of 10, and the first pupil to be entered is PETER HARROW who has chosen to do biology at a basic level, German and informatics at an advanced level, but no music at all. Fill in the picture of OPTIONS shown below supposing that the procedure STOPPROGRAM has been executed

OPTIONS:

SELF-TEST FOR CHAPTER 24

Test 24.1

The procedure below is from the program "EXHIBITOPTIONS" (listing in program booklet):

```
0850 PROC STARTPROGRAM
0860    OPEN 2,"OPTIONS",READ
0870    READ FILE 2: MAX
0880    FOR I:=1 TO MAX DO
0890      READ FILE 2: NAME$(I)
0900        FOR J:=1 TO 4 DO READ FILE 2: OPTION(I,J)
0910    NEXT I
0920    CLOSE
0930 ENDPROC STARTPROGRAM
```

Assume the first item in the file is the number 7. When it has been read and assigned as a value to MAX, a FOR − NEXT loop with a one-line FOR loop inside is executed. Each time the statements in the range of the FOR − NEXT loop are executed, data are retrieved from the file. What variables are assigned values as the loop is executed the first time?

. . . .

. . . .

What variables are assigned values as the loop is executed the last time?

. . . .

. . . .

The values stored in the file are retrieved in certain patterns. What do we call a set of data elements that belong together according to the way in which we use them?

. . . . What are the individual elements of such a set

called?. . . . .

Test 24.2

It is evident from the previous examples that the file "OPTIONS" has this structure: First a numeric appears that gives the number of records stored in the file. Then a name and four numerics follow, then another name with four numbers, etc. until the end of the file is reached. We would like to rearrange the information into a file with this structure:

MAX	here are all the names	here are all the options

We must of course set it up such that the first four numbers in the segment to hold the options go with the first name in the segment holding the names, the next four numbers belong to the second name, etc. Below is shown some of the statement it will take to modify the body of the procedure STOPPROGRAM – from program "ENTEROPTIONS" – such that it will create a file of the above structure. Complete it:

. . . . OPEN 3, "@0:OPTIONS",WRITE

. . . . WRITE FILE 3: MAX

. . . . FOR I:=1 TO MAX DO WRITE FILE 3: NAME$ (I)

. . . . FOR I:=1 TO MAX DO

. . . .

. . . .

. . . . CLOSE

Test 24.3
Having changed the procedure STOPPROGRAM to store data in a different way, we must
of course change STARTPROGRAM, too, in order to have data retrieved according to the
new structure of the file. If we still try to read a name and four numerics where only
names are found, we would of course mess up the whole business and most likely have
the program stopped with an error message. Below is suggested parts of a new body of
STARTPROGRAM. Complete it:

....   OPEN ....

....   READ FILE 2: MAX

....   FOR I:=1 TO MAX DO ....

....   FOR I:=1 TO MAX DO

....

....

....

....

(has anybody told you all the blank lines must be used?)

Test 24.4
The information about the pupils' options may also be stored in two different files, one of
which holds the names and the other one the numerics representing the options. We shall
call the former file "NAMES" and the latter one "THE'OPTIONS". Below are suggested
parts of new bodies of STOPPROGRAM and STARTPROGRAM. The value of MAX is
stored at the beginning of "NAMES". Complete the two sketches:

....   OPEN 2, "@0:NAMES", WRITE

....   OPEN 3, "@0:THE'OPTIONS", WRITE

....   WRITE FILE 2: MAX

....   FOR I:=1 TO MAX DO WRITE FILE 2: NAME$ (I)

....   FOR I:=1 TO MAX DO

....

....

```
........   CLOSE

........   OPEN 2, "NAMES", READ

.......    OPEN 3, "THE'OPTIONS", READ

.......    READ FILE 2: MAX

........   ................................................................

........   ................................................................

.......    ................................................................

.......    ................................................................

.......    ................................................................
```

An even better approach to an alternative body of STARTPROGRAM could be made if one uses the EOF (End-Of-File) function. Also, in that case you would not have to store the value of MAX. Delete the statement:

WRITE FILE 2: MAX

from the body of STOPPROGRAM as suggested above. Then rewrite the whole body of STARTPROGRAM to match the new approach using the EOF function. Write your suggestion on a separate piece of paper.

Note. Listings of the programs "ENTEROPTIONS" and "EXHIBITOPTIONS" are found in the program booklet and the programs are stored on the library diskette to accompany this book. It is suggested that you try to modify the two programs using the procedures set up in this test and run the new system thus designed.

Program listings

EXERCISE 1.7

```
0010 PRINT "XXXXXXXXXXXXXXXXXXXXXXXXXXXXXXXXX"
0020 PRINT "X                               X"
0030 PRINT "X                               X"
0040 PRINT "XXXXXXXXXXXXXXXXXXXXXXXXXXXXXXXXX"
```

EXERCISE 1.8

```
0010 PRINT "A PROGRAM LINE CAN WALK AWAY"
0020 PRINT "THAT IS - OF COURSE -"
0030 PRINT "IF YOU DON'T WANT IT TO STAY"
```

EXERCISE 1.9

```
0010 PRINT "BYE, BYE ONE LINE"
0020 PRINT "BYE, BYE TWO!"
0030 PRINT "THE NUMBER OF LINES TO GO"
0040 PRINT "IS UP TO YOU."
0050 PRINT "IF YOU USE THE"
0060 PRINT "DEL FIRST-LAST"
0070 PRINT "OFF THEY GO"
0080 PRINT "AND VERY FAST!"
```

EXERCISE 1.10

```
0010 PRINT "ALL THE KINGS MEN"
0020 PRINT "HEAVE THEIR HEAVY AXES!"
```

EXERCISE 2.2

```
0010 INPUT QUANT
0020 INPUT AMOUNT
0030 PRINT
0040 PRINT
0050 PRINT "QUANTITY:   ",QUANT
0060 PRINT "AMOUNT:     ",AMOUNT
```

EXERCISE 2.3

```
0010 PRINT "QUANTITY",
0020 INPUT QUANT
0030 PRINT "AMOUNT",
0040 INPUT AMOUNT
0050 PRINT
0060 PRINT
```

EXERCISE 3.1

```
0010 QUANTITY:=20; PRICE:=12.85
0020 PRINT "A TOTAL OF ",QUANTITY," ITEMS AT ",PRICE
```

EXERCISE 3.2

```
0010 LENGTH:=10; WIDTH:=35
0020 AREA:=LENGTH*WIDTH
0030 PRINT "THE AREA IS ",AREA
```

EXERCISE 3.4

```
0010 QUANTITY:=20; PRICE:=35
0020 PCTVAT:=25
0030 AMOUNT:=QUANTITY*PRICE
0040 VAT:=AMOUNT*PCTVAT/100
0050 TOTAL:=AMOUNT+VAT
```

EXERCISE 3.6

```
0010 INPUT QUANTITY
0020 INPUT PRICE
0030 AMOUNT:=QUANTITY*PRICE
0040 VAT:=AMOUNT*25/100
0050 TOTAL:=AMOUNT+VAT
0060 PRINT
0070 PRINT "YOU HAVE RECIEVED ",QUANTITY," PIECES"
0080 PRINT "AT ",PRICE," POUNDS A PIECE."
0090 PRINT "TOTAL INCL. VAT IS ",TOTAL," POUNDS,"
0100 PRINT "WHICH YOU ARE ASKED TO PAY"
0110 PRINT "AT YOUR EARLIEST CONVENIENCE."
```

EXERCISE 4.1

```
0010 INPUT QUANT
0020 INPUT PRICE
0030 PRINT "YOU HAVE ORDERED ",QUANT," LOOSE SCREWS"
0040 PRINT "TO REPLACE THE ONES YOU LOST DURING"
0050 PRINT "THE LAST ROCK FESTIVAL."
0060 PRINT
0070 PRINT "EACH SCREW COSTS ",PRICE," PENCE,"
0080 PRINT "SO TOTAL THE AMOUNT IS ",QUANT*PRICE/100," POUNDS.
```

EXERCISE 4.2

```
0010 INPUT NUMBER
0020 NUMBER:=NUMBER+1
0030 PRINT NUMBER
```

DISCOUNT

```
0010 PRINT "NUMBER OF UNITS     ",
0020 INPUT NUMBER
0030 PRINT "PRICE PER UNIT      ",
0040 INPUT PRICE
0050 TOTAL:=NUMBER*PRICE
0060 IF NUMBER>20 THEN
0070    TOTAL:=TOTAL*95/100
0080 ENDIF
0090 PRINT "TOTAL:              ",TOTAL," POUNDS."
```

EXERCISE 4.5

```
0010 PRINT "NUMBER OF UNITS     ",
0020 INPUT NUMBER
0030 PRINT "PRICE PER UNIT      ",
0040 INPUT PRICE
0050 PRINT
0060 PRINT
0070 AMOUNT:=NUMBER*PRICE
0080 IF NUMBER<20 THEN
0090    AMOUNT:=AMOUNT*105/100
0100    PRINT "A DELIVERY CHARGE HAS BEEN ADDED"
0110    PRINT "TO THE TOTAL PRICE. THIS CHARGE"
0120    PRINT "IS 5 PCT. OF THE SELLING PRICE."
0130    PRINT "IF YOU BUY AT LEAST 20 UNITS"
0140    PRINT "NO DELIVERY CHARGE IS MADE."
0150    PRINT
0160 ENDIF
0170 PRINT "TOTAL:              ",AMOUNT," POUNDS."
```

EXERCISE 4.6

```
0010 PRINT "ENTER NUMBER OF UNITS",
0020 INPUT NUMBER
0030 PRINT "ENTER PRICE PER UNIT",
0040 INPUT PRICE
0050 IF NUMBER<20 THEN
0060    AMOUNT:=NUMBER*PRICE+15
0070    PRINT "TOTAL PRICE PLUS DELIVERY CHARGE: ",AMOUNT
0080 ELSE
0090    AMOUNT:=NUMBER*PRICE
0100    PRINT "TOTAL PRICE: ",AMOUNT
0110 ENDIF
```

EXERCISE 5.1

```
0010 FOR NO:=1 TO 5 DO
0020    PRINT "THIS WAS TIME NO. ",NO
0030    PRINT
0040 NEXT NO
```

EXERCISE 5.2

```
0010 FOR VS:=1 TO 3 DO
0020    PRINT "OH, I LOVE GIRLS WITH FRECKLES,"
0030    PRINT "THEY'RE WHAT I LIKE TO SEE."
0040    PRINT "AND THOSE WHO ARE NOT FRECKLED"
0050    PRINT "ARE NOT THE KIND FOR ME."
0060    PRINT
0070    PRINT "THIS WAS THE ",VS,". VERS"
0080    PRINT
0090 NEXT VS
0100 PRINT "I THINK YOU KNOW WHAT APPEALS TO ME."
```

EXERCISE 5.3

```
0010 FOR TRIP:=1 TO 4 DO
0020    PRINT "CROSS THE ATLANTIC AND COME BACK AGAIN."
0030    PRINT
0040    PRINT "ANOTHER TRIP:"
0050    PRINT
0060 NEXT TRIP
0070 PRINT "NO, I AM SICK OF THE ATLANTIC."
```

ODDEVEN

```
0010 //* ODD OR EVEN *//
0020 //
0030 //PREPARE TO PLAY//
0040 PRINT "NOW WE ARE GOING TO PLAY 'ODD OR EVEN'"
0050 PRINT
0060 PRINT "HOW MANY GAMES DO YOU LIKE TO PLAY",
0070 INPUT NUMBER
0080 PRINT
0090 PRINT "OK, HERE WE GO."
0100 PRINT "IF YOUR GUESS IS 'ODD' THEN TYPE 1,"
0110 PRINT "BUT IF YOUR GUESS IS 'EVEN' THEN TYPE 0."
0120 PRINT
0130 COUNTWIN:=0
0140 //---------------//
0150 FOR I:=1 TO NUMBER DO
0160    //-GUESSING-//
0170    PRINT "WHAT IS YOUR GUESS (1,0)",
0180    INPUT GUESS
0190    OUTCOME:=RND(0,1)
0200    PRINT
0210    //-DISPLAY RESULT-//
0220    IF OUTCOME=0 THEN
0230      PRINT "THE RESULT WAS EVEN."
0240    ELSE
0250      PRINT "THE RESULT WAS ODD."
0260    ENDIF
0270    //-ANNOUNCE WINNER-//
0280    IF GUESS=OUTCOME THEN
0290      PRINT "CONGRATULATIONS, YOU WIN."
0300      COUNTWIN:=COUNTWIN+1
0310    ELSE
0320      PRINT "SORRY, YOU HAVE LOST."
0330    ENDIF
0340    PRINT
0350    PRINT "HERE IS ANOTHER ROUND:"
0360 NEXT I
0370 //---------------//
0380 //-GAME IS OVER-//
0390 PRINT
0400 PRINT "THANK'S FOR THE GAME"
0410 PRINT "YOU HAVE WON ",COUNTWIN," ROUND(S),"
0420 PRINT "AND I HAVE WON ",NUMBER-COUNTWIN," ROUND(S)."
0430 PRINT
0440 PRINT "GOODBYE."
0450 //---------------//
```

EXERCISE 7.1

```
0010 FOR I:=1 TO 12 DO
0020    OUTCOME:=RND(1,2)
0030    IF OUTCOME=2 THEN
0040      PRINT "HEADS"
0050    ELSE
0060      PRINT "TAILS"
0070    ENDIF
0080 NEXT I
0090 PRINT
0100 PRINT "END OF GAME."
```

EXERCISE 7.2

```
0010 FOR GAME:=1 TO 10 DO
0020    OUTCOME:=RND(1,6)
0030     PRINT "THE NUMBER SHOWN IS ",OUTCOME
0040 NEXT GAME
0050 PRINT
0060 PRINT "END OF GAME."
```

EXERCISE 7.3

```
0010 FOR NO:=1 TO 5 DO
0020    PRINT
0030    PRINT "DIVIDEND (INTEGER)",
0040    INPUT DIVIDEND
0050    PRINT "DIVISOR (POSITIVE INTEGER)",
0060    INPUT DIVISOR
0070    PRINT DIVIDEND," MOD ",DIVISOR," = ",
0080    PRINT DIVIDEND MOD DIVISOR
0090 NEXT NO
0100 PRINT
0110 PRINT "THE END"
0120 PRINT "IF YOU WANT SOME MORE"
0130 PRINT "THEN TYPE: RUN"
```

PEANUTS

```
0010 //* PROGRAM: PEANUTS *//
0020 //-PREPARE TO PLAY-//
0030 PRINT CHR$(147) //CLEAR SCREEN//
0040 PRINT "NOW WE ARE GOING TO PLAY"
0050 PRINT "'PEANUTS'."
0060 PRINT "HOW MANY GAMES SHOULD WE PLAY",
0070 INPUT MAX
0080 PRINT
0090 PRINT "OK, HERE WE GO:"
0100 PRINT "IF YOU THINK I AM HOLDING"
0110 PRINT "AN ODD NUMBER OF PEANUTS"
0120 PRINT "THEN ENTER 1;"
0130 PRINT "BUT IF YOU THINK I AM HOLDING"
0140 PRINT "AN EVEN NUMBER OF PEANUTS"
0150 PRINT "THEN ENTER 0"
0160 PRINT
0170 COUNTWIN:=0
0180 //
0190 FOR GAME:=1 TO MAX DO
0200    //-THIS IS THE GAME ITSELF-//
0210    PRINT "WELL, WHAT IS YOUR GUESS (0,1)",
0220    INPUT GUESS
0230    STAKED:=RND(1,8)
0240    PRINT
0250    //-ODD OR EVEN-//
0260    IF OUTCOME=0 THEN
0270      PRINT "I AM HOLDING ",STAKED," PEANUTS"
0280      PRINT "I.E. AN EVEN NUMBER, ",
0290    ELSE
0300      PRINT "I AM HOLDING ",STAKED," PEANUTS"
0310      PRINT "I.E. AN ODD NUMBER, ",
0320    ENDIF
0330    //-WHO WINS?-//
0340    IF OUTCOME=GUESS THEN
0350      PRINT "SO YOU WIN."
0360      PRINT "CONGRATULATIONS!"
0370      COUNTWIN:=COUNTWIN+STAKED
0380    ELSE
0390      PRINT "SO YOU LOSE."
0400      PRINT "I AM SORRY!"
0410    ENDIF
0420    PRINT
0430    IF GAME<MAX THEN PRINT "NEXT GAME:"
0440 NEXT GAME
```
Listing continued next page

PEANUTS   *Continued from previous page*

```
0450 //
0460 //-FINAL RESULT-//
0470 PRINT "THANKS FOR THE GAME!"
0480 IF COUNTWIN>0 THEN
0490    PRINT "YOU WIN ",COUNTWIN," PEANUT(S)."
0500 ELSE
0510    PRINT "YOU HAVE LOST ",-COUNTWIN," PEANUT(S)."
0520 ENDIF
0530 PRINT
0540 PRINT "COME AND PLAY SOME OTHER DAY."
0550 //-END OF PROGRAM: PEANUTS-//
```

See page 294 for TEST 7.1

BIGNUTS

```
0010 //* PROGRAM: BIGNUTS *//
0020 EXEC INTRODUCTION
0030 EXEC GAME
0040 EXEC FINITO
0050 //* END OF PROGRAM: BIGNUTS *//
0060 //
0070 PROC INTRODUCTION
0080    //-PREPARE TO PLAY-//
0090    PRINT CHR$(147) //CLEAR SCREEN//
0100    PRINT "NOW WE ARE GOING TO PLAY"
0110    PRINT "'PEANUTS'."
0120    PRINT "HOW MANY GAMES SHOULD WE PLAY",
0130    INPUT MAX
0140    PRINT
0150    PRINT "OK, HERE WE GO:"
0160    PRINT "IF YOU THINK I AM HOLDING"
0170    PRINT "AN ODD NUMBER OF PEANUTS"
0180    PRINT "THEN ENTER 1;"
0190    PRINT "BUT IF YOU THINK I AM HOLDING"
0200    PRINT "AN EVEN NUMBER OF PEANUTS"
0210    PRINT "THEN ENTER 0"
0220    PRINT
0230    COUNTWIN:=0
0240 ENDPROC INTRODUCTION
```

Listing continued next page

BIGNUTS *Continued from previous page*

```
0250 //
0260 PROC GAME
0270    FOR NO:=1 TO MAX DO
0280       //-THIS IS THE GAME ITSELF-//
0290       PRINT "WELL, WHAT IS YOUR GUESS (0,1)",
0300       INPUT GUESS
0310       STAKED:=RND(1,8)
0320       OUTCOME:=STAKED MOD 2
0330       PRINT
0340       EXEC RESULT
0350       EXEC WINNER
0360       PRINT
0370       IF NO<MAX THEN PRINT "NEXT GAME:"
0380    NEXT NO
0390 ENDPROC GAME
0400 //
0410 PROC FINITO
0420    //-FINAL RESULT-//
0430    PRINT "THANKS FOR THE GAME!"
0440    IF COUNTWIN>0 THEN
0450       PRINT "YOU HAVE WON ",COUNTWIN," PEANUT(S)."
0460    ELSE
0470       PRINT "YOU HAVE LOST ",-COUNTWIN," PEANUT(S)."
0480    ENDIF
0490    PRINT
0500    PRINT "COME AND PLAY SOME OTHER DAY."
0510 ENDPROC FINITO
0520 //
0530 PROC RESULT
0540    IF OUTCOME=0 THEN
0550       PRINT "I AM HOLDING ",STAKED," PEANUTS"
0560       PRINT "I.E. AN EVEN NUMBER, ",
0570    ELSE
0580       PRINT "I AM HOLDING ",STAKED," PEANUTS"
0590       PRINT "I.E. AN ODD NUMBER, ",
0600    ENDIF
0610 ENDPROC RESULT
0620 //
0630 PROC WINNER
0640    IF OUTCOME=GUESS THEN
0650       PRINT "SO YOU WIN."
0660       PRINT "CONGRATULATIONS!"
0670       COUNTWIN:=COUNTWIN+STAKED
0680    ELSE
0690       PRINT "SO YOU LOSE."
0700       PRINT "I AM SORRY!"
0710       COUNTWIN:=COUNTWIN-STAKED
0720    ENDIF
0730 ENDPROC WINNER
0740 //
```

TEST 8.2

```
0010 //* BUTCHER BACON'S PROGRAM *//
0020 //* WRITTEN BY CHRISTIAN BORGE *//
0030 //
0040 DIM NAME$ OF 30, DATE$ OF 10
0050 //-MAINLINES-//
0060 PRINT "ENTER DATE (YY/MM/DD)",
0070 INPUT DATE$
0080 REPEAT
0090    EXEC TAKEIN
0100    EXEC PRINTOUT
0110    PRINT
0120    PRINT "MORE LETTERS (1=YES/0=NO)",
0130    INPUT CODE
0140 UNTIL CODE=0
0150 //
0160 PROC TAKEIN
0170    PRINT "WHO IS GOING TO BE PRESSED",
0180    INPUT NAME$
0190    PRINT "HOW MUCH MONEY",
0200    INPUT AMOUNT
0210    PRINT "PRESSED HARD (1=YES/0=NO)",
0220    INPUT LEVEL
0230    FOR I:=1 TO 3 DO PRINT
0240 ENDPROC TAKEIN
0250 //
0260 PROC PRINTOUT
0270    PRINT CHR$(147) //CLEAR SCREEN
0280    PRINT "            ODDINGTON, ",DATE$
0290    PRINT
0300    IF LEVEL=1 THEN
0310       EXEC RUDELETTER
0320    ELSE
0330       EXEC KINDLETTER
0340    ENDIF
0350 ENDPROC PRINTOUT
0360 //
0370 PROC KINDLETTER
0380    PRINT "DEAR ",NAME$
0390    PRINT
0400    PRINT "YOU ARE KINDLY ASKED TO PAY OUR"
0410    PRINT "OUTSTANDING ACCOUNT OF ",AMOUNT," POUNDS"
0420    PRINT "AT YOUR EARLIEST CONVENIENCE."
0430    PRINT
0440    PRINT "SINCERELY,"
0450    PRINT "ALFRED BACON."
0460 ENDPROC KINDLETTER
```

Listing continued next page

TEST 8.2 *Continued from previous page*

```
0470 //
0480 PROC RUDELETTER
0490    PRINT NAME$
0500    PRINT
0510    PRINT "IF YOU HAVE NOT PAID THE ",AMOUNT," POUNDS"
0520    PRINT "YOU OWE US WITHIN 8 DAYS FROM TODAY,"
0530    PRINT "THE MATTER WILL BE PLACED IN THE HANDS OF"
0540    PRINT "OUR SOLICITORS."
0550    PRINT
0560    PRINT "A. BACON."
0570 ENDPROC RUDELETTER
```

EXERCISE 9.1

```
0010 PRINT CHR$(147) //CLEAR SCREEN//
0020 //
0030 FOR I:=1 TO 10 DO
0040    EXEC GAME
0050 NEXT I
0060 PRINT
0070 PRINT "NOW I'M TIRED OF THIS GAME!"
0080 //
0090 PROC GAME
0100    THINKOF:=RND(1,3)
0110    EXEC TRYGUESS
0120 ENDPROC GAME
0130 //
0140 PROC TRYGUESS
0150    PRINT
0160    PRINT "WHAT NUMBER DO I THINK OF (1,2,3)",
0170    INPUT GUESS
0180    PRINT
0190    IF GUESS=THINKOF THEN
0200      PRINT "BRAVO, THAT'S RIGHT,"
0210      PRINT "I LIKE YOU."
0220    ELSE
0230      PRINT "NO, THAT IS NOT RIGHT,"
0240      PRINT "I WAS THINKING OF ",THINKOF
0250    ENDIF
0260 ENDPROC TRYGUESS
0270 //
```

EXERCISE 9.4

```
0010 PRINT CHR$(147) //CLEAR SCREEN//
0020 //
0030 FOR NO:=1 TO 5 DO
0040    EXEC GAME
0050    PRINT
0060 NEXT NO
0070 PRINT
0080 PRINT "NOW I'M TIRED OF THIS GAME!"
0090 //
0100 PROC GAME
0110    THINKOF:=RND(1,6)
0120    EXEC TRYGUESS
0130 ENDPROC GAME
0140 //
0150 PROC TRYGUESS
0160    REPEAT
0170      PRINT "WHAT NUMBER DO I THINK OF (1..6)",
0180      INPUT GUESS
0190      PRINT
0200      IF GUESS=THINKOF THEN
0210        PRINT "YES, I WAS THINKING OF ",THINKOF
0220        PRINT "WAS IT HARD TO GUESS?"
0230        FOR I:=1 TO 3 DO PRINT
0240        PRINT "!-------------------------------!"
0250      ELSE
0260        PRINT "NO, THAT IS NOT RIGHT,"
0270        PRINT "TRY AGAIN!"
0280      ENDIF
0290    UNTIL GUESS=THINKOF
0300 ENDPROC TRYGUESS
0310 //
```

EXERCISE 10.1

```
0010 PRINT CHR$(147) //CLEAR SCREEN//
0020 //
0030 PRINT "HOW MANY EXERCISES",
0040 INPUT MAXNO
0050 FOR NO:=1 TO MAXNO DO
0060    A:=RND(1,5); B:=RND(1,5)
0070    RESULT:=A+B
0080    EXEC EXERCISE
0090    EXEC GETANSWER
0100    EXEC CONTROL
0110 NEXT NO
0120 //
0130 PROC EXERCISE
0140    FOR I:=1 TO 3 DO PRINT
0150    PRINT "-----------------------------"
0160    PRINT "EXERCISE NO. ",NO
0170    PRINT
0180 ENDPROC EXERCISE
0190 //
0200 PROC GETANSWER
0210    PRINT A," + ",B," = ",
0220    INPUT "": ANSWER
0230    PRINT
0240 ENDPROC GETANSWER
0250 //
0260 PROC CONTROL
0270 ENDPROC CONTROL
```

EXERCISE 10.5

```
0010 PRINT CHR$(147) //CLEAR SCREEN//
0020 //
0030 PRINT "HOW MANY EXERCISES",
0040 INPUT MAXNO
0050 FOR NO:=1 TO MAXNO DO
0060    A:=RND(1,5); B:=RND(1,5)
0070    RESULT:=A+B
0080    EXEC EXERCISE
0090    EXEC GETANSWER
0100    EXEC CONTROL
0110 NEXT NO
0120 //
0130 PROC EXERCISE
0140    FOR I:=1 TO 3 DO PRINT
0150    PRINT "----------------------------"
0160    PRINT "EXERCISE NO. ",NO
0170    PRINT
0180 ENDPROC EXERCISE
0190 //
0200 PROC GETANSWER
0210    PRINT A," + ",B," = ",
0220    INPUT "": ANSWER
0230    PRINT
0240 ENDPROC GETANSWER
0250 //
0260 PROC CONTROL
0270    IF ANSWER=RESULT THEN
0280      PRINT "THAT'S CORRECT!"
0290    ELSE
0300      PRINT "YOUR ANSWER IS NOT CORRECT;"
0310      PRINT
0320      PRINT A," + ",B," = ",RESULT
0330    ENDIF
0340 ENDPROC CONTROL
0350 //
```

ADDITION

```
0010 PRINT CHR$(147) //CLEAR SCREEN//
0020 //
0030 PRINT "HOW MANY EXERCISES",
0040 INPUT MAXNO
0050 FOR NO:=1 TO MAXNO DO
0060    A:=RND(1,5); B:=RND(1,5)
0070    RESULT:=A+B
0080    EXEC EXERCISE
0090    EXEC GETANSWER
0100    EXEC CONTROL
0110 NEXT NO
0120 //
0130 PROC EXERCISE
0140    FOR I:=1 TO 3 DO PRINT
0150    PRINT "------------------------------"
0160    PRINT "EXERCISE NO. ",NO
0170    PRINT
0180 ENDPROC EXERCISE
0190 //
0200 PROC GETANSWER
0210    C:=0
0220    REPEAT
0230      PRINT A," + ",B," = ",
0240      INPUT "": ANSWER
0250      C:=C+1
0260      PRINT
0270    UNTIL ANSWER=RESULT OR C=3
0280 ENDPROC GETANSWER
0290 //
0300 PROC CONTROL
0310    IF ANSWER=RESULT THEN
0320      PRINT "THAT'S CORRECT!"
0330    ELSE
0340      PRINT "YOUR ANSWER IS NOT CORRECT;"
0350      PRINT
0360      PRINT A," + ",B," = ",RESULT
0370    ENDIF
0380 ENDPROC CONTROL
0390 //
```

EXERCISE 11.2

```
0010 DIM NAME$ OF 25, STREET$ OF 20
0020 DIM TOWN$ OF 20, CODE$ OF 10
0030 PRINT CHR$(147) //CLEAR SCREEN
0040 FOR I:=1 TO 3 DO PRINT  //3 DOWN
0050 PRINT "NAME..............",
0060 INPUT NAME$
0070 PRINT "HOUSE NO..........",
0080 INPUT HOUSENO
0090 PRINT "STREET............",
0100 INPUT STREET$
0110 PRINT "TOWN..............",
0120 INPUT TOWN$
0130 PRINT "POST CODE.........",
0140 INPUT CODE$
0150 //
0160 PRINT CHR$(147) //CLEAR
0170 FOR I:=1 TO 3 DO PRINT  //3 DOWN
0180 PRINT "             READING, MAY 6 1981"
0190 PRINT
0200 PRINT NAME$
0210 PRINT HOUSENO," ",STREET$
0220 PRINT TOWN$," ",CODE$
0230 PRINT
0240 PRINT "DEAR SIR/MADAM,"
0250 PRINT
0260 PRINT "ALLOW US TO OFFER YOU OUR FINE"
0270 PRINT "SALT-CURED HAM AT THE VERY SPECIAL"
0280 PRINT "PRICE OF 4 POUNDS A KG."
0290 PRINT
0300 PRINT "             SINCERELY,"
0310 PRINT "             ALFRED BACON,"
0320 PRINT "             BUTCHER."
```

UNCLEXMAS

```
0010 DIM SENDER$ OF 30, DATE$ OF 20
0020 DIM RECIPIENT$ OF 30, ANSW$ OF 2
0030 //
0040 EXEC CLEAR(3)
0050 PRINT "WHAT DATE (E.G. NOV. 12 1979)",
0060 INPUT DATE$
0070 SENDER$:="HANNIBAL"
0080 //
0090 REPEAT
0100    EXEC CLEAR(3)
0110    PRINT "TO WHOM",
0120    INPUT RECIPIENT$
0130    EXEC PRINTOUT
0140    PRINT
0150    PRINT "MORE X-MAS CARDS (Y/N)",
0160    INPUT ANSW$
0170 UNTIL ANSW$="N"
0180 EXEC CLEAR(3)
0190 PRINT "OK, THAT'S IT. DON'T FORGET"
0200 PRINT "TO PUT THE STAMPS ON!"
0210 //
0220 PROC PRINTOUT
0230    EXEC CLEAR(2)
0240    PRINT "           ODDINGTON, ",DATE$
0250    PRINT
0260    PRINT "DEAR ",RECIPIENT$
0270    PRINT
0280    PRINT "I WISH YOU A MERRY CHRISTMAS AND"
0290    PRINT "A HAPPY AND PROFITABLE NEW YEAR."
0300    PRINT
0310    PRINT "                  LOVE FROM"
0320    PRINT "                  ",SENDER$
0330 ENDPROC PRINTOUT
0340 //
0350 PROC CLEAR(X)
0360    //THIS PROCEDURE
0370    PRINT CHR$(147) //CLEARS THE SCREEN
0380    FOR I:=1 TO X DO PRINT  //AND SENDS
0390    //THE CURSOR X LINES DOWN
0400 ENDPROC CLEAR
```

EXERCISE 12.2

```
0010 DIM ANSW$ OF 10, ART$(10) OF 20
0020 //
0030 EXEC SETUP
0040 EXEC REQUEST
0050 //
0060 PROC SETUP
0070    ART$(1):="BROWN SUGAR"
0080    ART$(2):=""
0090    ART$(3):="SOAP FLAKES"
0100    ART$(4):="RIPE CHEESE"
0110    ART$(5):="CINNAMON"
0120    ART$(6):=""
0130    ART$(7):="CARDAMOM"
0140    ART$(8):="CURLED PARSLEY"
0150    ART$(9):="LIVER SAUSAGE"
0160    ART$(10):=""
0170 ENDPROC SETUP
0180 //
0190 PROC REQUEST
0200    REPEAT
0210      PRINT CHR$(147) //CLEAR
0220      PRINT "ARTICLE NO.",
0230      INPUT NO
0240      PRINT
0250      IF ART$(NO)="" THEN
0260        PRINT "NO ARTICLE WITH THAT NUMBER!"
0270      ELSE
0280        PRINT "ARTICLE NO. ",NO,": ",ART$(NO)
0290      ENDIF
0300      PRINT
0310      PRINT "MORE REQUESTS (Y/N)",
0320      INPUT ANSW$
0330    UNTIL ANSW$="N"
0340 ENDPROC REQUEST
0350 //
```

EXERCISE 12.3

```
0010 DIM PUPIL$(10) OF 30, NAME$ OF 30
0020 DIM ANSW$ OF 10, JOB$ OF 5
0030 //
0040 REPEAT   //MAIN LOOP//
0050    CLEAR(5)
0060    PRINT "WHAT JOB (ENTRY,LIST,REQUEST)",
0070    INPUT JOB$
0080    //POINT OUT JOB//
0090    IF JOB$="ENTRY" THEN TAKEIN
0100    IF JOB$="LIST" THEN PRINTALL
0110    IF JOB$="REQUE" THEN PRINTONE
0120    PRINT CHR$(19) //HOME
0130    PRINT "MORE JOBS (Y/N)",
0140    INPUT ANSW$
0150 UNTIL ANSW$="N"
0160 //
0170 PROC TAKEIN
0180    CLEAR(5)
0190    REPEAT
0200      PRINT "NAME",
0210      INPUT NAME$
0220      IF NAME$<>"" THEN
0230        PRINT "NUMBER",
0240        INPUT NO
0250        PUPIL$(NO):=NAME$
0260      ENDIF
0270      PRINT
0280    UNTIL NAME$=""
0290 ENDPROC TAKEIN
0300 //
0310 PROC PRINTALL
0320    CLEAR(5) //CLEAR SCREEN
0330    FOR NO:=1 TO 10 DO
0340      PRINT NO,": ",PUPIL$(NO)
0350    NEXT NO
0360 ENDPROC PRINTALL
```

Listing continued next page

EXERCISE 12.3 *Continued from previous page*

```
0370 //
0380 PROC PRINTONE
0390    CLEAR(5)
0400    PRINT "NUMBER",
0410    INPUT NO
0420    IF PUPIL$(NO)<>"" THEN
0430       PRINT "THE PUPILS NAME IS ",PUPIL$(NO)
0440    ELSE
0450       PRINT "NO PUPIL WITH THAT NUMBER!"
0460       PRINT "HAVE A LIST PRINTED (LIST)."
0470    ENDIF
0480 ENDPROC PRINTONE
0490 //
0500 PROC CLEAR(X)
0510    PRINT CHR$(147), //CLEAR
0520    FOR I:=1 TO X DO PRINT  //X DOWN
0530 ENDPROC CLEAR
```

EXERCISE 13.1

```
0010 DIM FRUIT$(6) OF 10, TOKEN$ OF 1
0020 DIM F1$ OF 10, F2$ OF 10, F3$ OF 10
0030 WINNINGS:=0; STAKED:=0
0040 //
0050 FRUIT$(1):="APPLE"
0060 FRUIT$(2):="PEAR"
0070 FRUIT$(3):="PLUM"
0080 FRUIT$(4):="BANANA"
0090 FRUIT$(5):="LEMON"
0100 FRUIT$(6):="GRAPE"
0110 //
0120 EXEC CLEAR(4)
0130 PRINT "HERE WE GO! TO INSERT A COIN"
0140 PRINT "IN THE SLOT, PRESS 'RETURN'."
0150 PRINT "TO STOP, PRESS 'N' AND 'RETURN'."
0160 REPEAT
0170    PRINT
0180    PRINT "INSERT A COIN",
0190    INPUT TOKEN$
0200    IF TOKEN$="N" THEN EXEC ADIEU
0210    EXEC THE'GAME
0220 UNTIL FALSE //FOREVER//
0230 //
```

Listing continued next page

EXERCISE 13.1 *Continued from previous page*

```
0240 PROC THE'GAME
0250    STAKED:=STAKED+1
0260    F1$:=FRUIT$(RND(1,6))
0270    F2$:=FRUIT$(RND(1,6))
0280    F3$:=FRUIT$(RND(1,6))
0290    EXEC CLEAR(5)
0300    PRINT F1$,TAB(15),F2$,TAB(30),F3$
0310    EXEC RESULT
0320 ENDPROC THE'GAME
0330 //
0340 PROC RESULT
0350    FOR I:=1 TO 3 DO PRINT   //3 DOWN
0360    IF F1$=F2$ AND F2$=F3$ THEN
0370       EXEC BELL(7)
0380       PRINT "HURRAH! H U R R A H!  H  U  R  R  A  H!!"
0390       PRINT "YOU HAVE WON 20 COINS!!!"
0400       WINNINGS:=WINNINGS+20
0410    ELSE
0420       IF F1$=F2$ OR F2$=F3$ THEN
0430          EXEC BELL(2)
0440          PRINT "FINE!"
0450          PRINT "YOU HAVE WON 2 COINS!"
0460          WINNINGS:=WINNINGS+2
0470       ENDIF
0480    ENDIF
0490 ENDPROC RESULT
0500 //
0510 PROC ADIEU
0520    EXEC CLEAR(5)
0530    PRINT "IT WAS NICE TO PLAY WITH YOU."
0540    PRINT "ASK OUR CASHIER TO EXCHANGE"
0550    PRINT "YOUR WINNINGS INTO REAL MONEY"
0560    PRINT "- IF HE HAS ANY - AS A RULE HE HASN'T,"
0570    PRINT "BUT WE HOPE YOU HAD SOME FUN."
0580    STOP   //STOP THE PROGRAM
0590 ENDPROC ADIEU
0600 //
0610 PROC CLEAR(X)
0620    PRINT CHR$(147), //CLEAR
0630    FOR I:=1 TO X DO PRINT   //X DOWN
0640 ENDPROC CLEAR
0650 //
0660 PROC BELL(X)
0670    FOR I:=1 TO X DO PRINT CHR$(7),
0680 ENDPROC BELL
```

EXERCISE 14.1

```
0010 DIM TEXT$ OF 70, WORD$ OF 10
0020 DIM ANSW$ OF 10, HINT$ OF 2
0030 EXEC CLEAR(5)
0040 PRINT "HOW MANY EXERCISES (MAX. 6)",
0050 INPUT MAXNO
0060 FOR NO:=1 TO MAXNO DO EXEC EXERCISE
0070 //
0080 PROC EXERCISE
0090    ATTEMPTS:=0
0100    READ TEXT$,WORD$
0110    REPEAT
0120       EXEC DISPLAY
0130       EXEC GETANSWER
0140       EXEC CONTROL
0150    UNTIL ANSW$=WORD$ OR ATTEMPTS=3
0160 ENDPROC EXERCISE
0170 //
0180 PROC DISPLAY
0190    EXEC CLEAR(2)
0200    PRINT "------- EXERCISE NO. ",NO," --------"
0210    PRINT
0220    PRINT TAB(2),TEXT$
0230    PRINT
0240    PRINT "-------------------------------"
0250 ENDPROC DISPLAY
0260 //
0270 PROC GETANSWER
0280    PRINT
0290    PRINT "VERB IN PAST TENSE",
0300    INPUT ANSW$
0310 ENDPROC GETANSWER
0320 //
0330 PROC CONTROL
0340    ATTEMPTS:=ATTEMPTS+1
0350    IF ANSW$<>WORD$ THEN
0360       PRINT
0370       PRINT "NO - ",ANSW$," - IS NOT CORRECT."
0380       EXEC HELP
0390    ELSE
0400       PRINT
0410       PRINT "YES, THAT IS CORRECT!"
0420    ENDIF
0430    EXEC WAIT(3)
0440 ENDPROC CONTROL
```

Listing continued next page

EXERCISE 14.1   *Continued from previous page*

```
0450 //
0460 PROC HELP
0470    IF ATTEMPTS=1 THEN
0480      HINT$:=WORD$
0490      PRINT "TRY TO START LIKE THIS :- ",HINT$
0500      PRINT
0510    ELSE
0520      IF ATTEMPTS=2 THEN
0530        PRINT "TRY THIS ONE:- ",WORD$
0540      ELSE
0550        PRINT "THE CORRECT PAST TENSE IS"
0560        PRINT "         - ",WORD$," -"
0570        PRINT "TRY TO REMEMBER!"
0580        EXEC WAIT(2)
0590      ENDIF
0600    ENDIF
0610    EXEC WAIT(4)
0620 ENDPROC HELP
0630 //
0640 //*DATA QUEUE OF TEXTS AND ANSWERS*//
0650 DATA "BACH *GOES* TO TOWN","WENT"
0660 DATA "LOTTIE *WINS* THE GAME","WON"
0670 DATA "THEY *SIT* BY THE FIRE","SAT"
0680 DATA "WE *TELL* THE TRUTH","TOLD"
0690 DATA "YOU *SING* IN THE CHOIR","SANG"
0700 DATA "THEY *RUN* TO SEE THE FIRE","RAN"
0710 DATA "FRANK *CHOOSES* THE BLUE JACKET","CHOSE"
0720 //
0730 PROC CLEAR(X)
0740    PRINT CHR$(147), //CLEAR SCREEN
0750    FOR I:=1 TO X DO PRINT   //X DOWN
0760 ENDPROC CLEAR
0770 //
0780 PROC WAIT(X)
0790    FOR I:=1 TO X*500 DO
0800    NEXT I //WAIT APPROX. X SEC.//
0810 ENDPROC WAIT
```

TEST 14.1

```
0030 DIM COLOUR$(4) OF 10, NAME$(13) OF 10
0040 DIM CARD$ OF 20, HAND$(6) OF 20
0050 DIM DRAWN$ OF 300
0060 //
0070 COLOUR$(1):="DIAMONDS"
0080 COLOUR$(2):="CLUBS"
0090 COLOUR$(3):="SPADES"
0100 COLOUR$(4):="HEARTS"
0110 //
0120 FOR I:=1 TO 13 DO
0130    READ NAME$(I)
0140 NEXT I
0150 DATA "ACE","TWO","THREE","FOUR"
0160 DATA "FIVE","SIX","SEVEN","EIGHT"
0170 DATA "NINE","TEN","KNIGHT","QUEEN","KING"
0180 //
0190 FOR DRAW:=1 TO 6 DO
0200    EXEC FINDCARD
0210    HAND$(DRAW):=CARD$
0220 NEXT DRAW
0230 EXEC DISPLAY
0240 //
0250 PROC FINDCARD
0260    REPEAT
0270       CARD$:=NAME$(RND(1,13))
0280       CARD$:=CARD$+" OF "+COLOUR$(RND(1,4))
0290    UNTIL NOT CARD$ IN DRAWN$
0300    DRAWN$:=DRAWN$+CARD$
0310 ENDPROC FINDCARD
0320 //
0330 PROC DISPLAY
0340    FOR I:=1 TO 6 DO
0350       PRINT HAND$(I)
0360    NEXT I
0370 ENDPROC DISPLAY
```

AUNTIE

```
0010 //* AUNT LOUISE'S PROGRAM *//
0020 //* WRITTEN BY ELISABETH OLDHAM *//
0030 //* IN COOPERATION WITH LOUISE OLSEN *//
0040 //* THIS VERSION: 9. JAN. 1981 *//
0050 //*
0060 //DECLARATION OF STRINGS//
0070 DIM NAME$ OF 30, TYPE$ OF 3, SIGN$ OF 1
0080 DIM SPACES$ OF 70
0100 //*
0110 //SET UP SOME CONSTANTS//
0140 MAXNO:=10; BASE:=30
0150 THISNAME:=1; THISTYPE:=2; THISLEVEL:=3
0160 SPACES$(1:70):=""
0170 //*
0180 //MAINLINES//
0190 PRINT CHR$(147) //CLEAR SCREEN
0200 EXEC TAKEIN(THISNAME)
0210 EXEC REGISTER
0220 EXEC TAKEIN(THISTYPE)
0230 EXEC TAKEIN(THISLEVEL)
0240 EXEC EXERCISES
0250 EXEC RECORD
0260 //*
0270 PROC EXERCISES
0280    FOR EXERCISENO:=1 TO MAXNO DO
0290       EXEC WORKSHOP
0300       EXEC WRITEEXERCISE
0310       EXEC GETANSWER
0320    NEXT EXERCISENO
0330 ENDPROC EXERCISES
0340 //
0350 PROC RECORD
0360    //
0370    //STUD//
0380    //
0390 ENDPROC RECORD
0400 //
0410 PROC TAKEIN(MATTER)
0420    EXEC ENTRY
0430    WHILE NOT OK DO
0440       EXEC ERROR
0450       EXEC ENTRY
0460    ENDWHILE
0470 ENDPROC TAKEIN
```

Listing continued next page

AUNTIE   *Continued from previous page*

```
0480 //
0490 PROC ENTRY
0500    EXEC WINDOW(8,12)
0510    CASE MATTER OF
0520    WHEN 1
0530      PRINT "WHAT IS YOUR NAME",
0540      INPUT NAME$
0550    WHEN 2
0560      PRINT "ENTER TYPE (ADD, SUB, MUL, DIV)",
0570      INPUT TYPE$
0580    WHEN 3
0590      PRINT "ENTER LEVEL (1, 2, 3)",
0600      INPUT LEVEL
0610    ENDCASE
0620    PRINT CHR$(147) //CLEAR SCREEN
0630    EXEC CONTROL
0640 ENDPROC ENTRY
0650 //
0660 PROC CONTROL
0670    CASE MATTER OF
0680    WHEN 1
0690      OK:=(" " IN NAME$)
0700    WHEN 2
0710      OK:=(TYPE$="ADD" OR TYPE$="SUB")
0720      LACKS:=(TYPE$="MUL" OR TYPE$="DIV")
0730    WHEN 3
0740      OK:=(LEVEL=1 OR LEVEL=2 OR LEVEL=3)
0750    ENDCASE
0760 ENDPROC CONTROL
0770 //
0780 PROC ERROR
0790    EXEC WINDOW(1,2)
0800    CASE MATTER OF
0810    WHEN 1
0820      PRINT "MOST PEOPLE HAVE BOTH A FIRST NAME"
0830      PRINT "AND A SURNAME. PLEASE GIVE BOTH!"
0840    WHEN 2
0850      PRINT "NO SUCH TYPE OF EXERCISE!"
0860      IF LACKS THEN
0870        PRINT "MUL AND DIV ARE NOT YET INSERTED"
0880        PRINT "PLEASE PICK OUT ADD OR SUB"
0890      ENDIF
0900    WHEN 3
0910      PRINT "NO SUCH LEVEL OF EXERCISES!"
0920    ENDCASE
0930 ENDPROC ERROR
```

Listing continued next page

AUNTIE   *Continued from previous page*

```
0940 //
0950 PROC REGISTER
0960    //
0970    //STUD//
0980    //
0990 ENDPROC REGISTER
1000 //
1010 PROC WORKSHOP
1020    CASE TYPE$ OF
1030    WHEN "ADD"
1040       EXEC ADDITION
1050    WHEN "SUB"
1060       EXEC SUBTRACTION
1070    WHEN "MUL"
1080       EXEC MULTIPLICATION
1090    WHEN "DIV"
1100       EXEC DIVISION
1110    ENDCASE
1120 ENDPROC WORKSHOP
1130 //
1140 PROC ADDITION
1150    CASE LEVEL OF
1160    WHEN 1
1170      N1:=RND(0,5); N2:=RND(0,5)
1180    WHEN 2
1190      N1:=RND(0,9); N2:=RND(0,9)
1200    WHEN 3
1210      N1:=RND(40,50); N2:=RND(1,10)
1220    ENDCASE
1230    RESULT:=N1+N2
1240    SIGN$:="+"
1250 ENDPROC ADDITION
1260 //
1270 PROC SUBTRACTION
1280    CASE LEVEL OF
1290    WHEN 1
1300      N1:=RND(5,9); N2:=RND(1,5)
1310    WHEN 2
1320      N1:=RND(10,19); N2:=RND(1,10)
1330    WHEN 3
1340      N1:=RND(50,89); N2:=RND(10,19)
1350    ENDCASE
1360    RESULT:=N1-N2
1370    SIGN$:="-"
1380 ENDPROC SUBTRACTION
```

Listing continued next page

AUNTIE   *Continued from previous page*

```
1390 //
1400 PROC MULTIPLICATION
1410    //
1420    //STUD//
1430    //
1440 ENDPROC MULTIPLICATION
1450 //
1460 PROC DIVISION
1470    //
1480    //STUD//
1490    //
1500 ENDPROC DIVISION
1510 //
1520 PROC GETANSWER
1530    TRY:=1
1540    EXEC ENTERANSWER
1550    WHILE NOT OK DO
1560       EXEC HELP
1570       EXEC WRITEEXERCISE
1580       EXEC ENTERANSWER
1590       TRY:+1
1600    ENDWHILE
1610 ENDPROC GETANSWER
1620 //
1630 PROC ENTERANSWER
1640    EXEC TABULATOR(RESULT)
1650    INPUT "": ANSWER
1660    OK:=(ANSWER=RESULT)
1670    PRINT CHR$(147) //CLEAR SCREEN
1680 ENDPROC ENTERANSWER
1690 //
1700 PROC WRITEEXERCISE
1710    EXEC WINDOW(7,15)
1720    CASE TYPE$ OF
1730    WHEN "ADD","SUB"
1740       EXEC TABULATOR(N1)
1750       PRINT N1
1760       PRINT TAB(BASE-3),SIGN$,
1770       EXEC TABULATOR(N2)
1780       PRINT N2
1790       PRINT TAB(BASE-3),"====="
1800    WHEN "MUL","DIV"
1810       //
1820       //STUD//
1830       //
1840    ENDCASE
1850 ENDPROC WRITEEXERCISE
```

Listing continued next page

AUNTIE　*Continued from previous page*

```
1860 //
1870 PROC HELP
1880    EXEC WINDOW(1,2)
1890    IF TRY<3 THEN
1900       PRINT "NO, TRY AGAIN"
1910    ELSE
1920       PRINT "NO, THE CORRECT ANSWER IS ",RESULT
1930       PRINT "TYPE THAT."
1940    ENDIF
1950 ENDPROC HELP
1960 //
1970 PROC TABULATOR(T)
1980    POSITION:=BASE-(T>=10)-(T>=100)
1990    PRINT TAB(POSITION),
2000 ENDPROC TABULATOR
2010 //
2020 PROC WINDOW(FIRST,LAST)
2030    EXEC SCREEN(FIRST,1)
2040    FOR I:=1 TO LAST-FIRST+1 DO PRINT SPACES$
2050    EXEC SCREEN(FIRST,1)
2060 ENDPROC WINDOW
2070 //
2080 PROC SCREEN(ROW,COL) CLOSED
2090    PRINT CHR$(19) //CURSOR HOME
2100    FOR I:=1 TO ROW DO PRINT   //CURSOR DOWN
2105    FOR I:=1 TO COL-1 DO PRINT CHR$(29), //CURSOR RIGHT
2110 ENDPROC SCREEN
2120 //
```

FESTIVALS

```
0010 //DECLARATIONS
0020 DIM SENDER$ OF 30, DATE$ OF 20
0030 DIM RECIPIENT$ OF 30, ANSW$ OF 3
0040 //*
0050 //MAINLINES//
0060 PRINT CHR$(147) //CLEAR SCREEN//
0070 PRINT "FROM WHOM",
0080 INPUT SENDER$
0090 REPEAT  //WRITING LETTERS//
0100    PRINT "TO WHOM",
0110    INPUT RECIPIENT$
0120    PRINT
0130    PRINT "1=XMAS / 2=EASTER / 3=WHITSUN ",
0140    INPUT FESTIVAL
0150    EXEC WRITELETTER
0160    PRINT CHR$(19) //HOME//
0170    PRINT "MORE LETTERS (YES/NO)",
0180    INPUT ANSW$
0190    PRINT CHR$(147)
0200 UNTIL ANSW$="NO"
0210 //*
0220 PROC WRITELETTER
0230    PRINT CHR$(147) //CLEAR SCREEN//
0240    FOR I:=1 TO 8 DO PRINT  //8 DOWN//
0250    PRINT "DEAR ",RECIPIENT$
0260    PRINT
0270    CASE FESTIVAL OF
0280    WHEN 1
0290      PRINT "A VERY MERRY CHRISTMAS"
0300      PRINT "AND A MOST HAPPY NEW YEAR"
0310    WHEN 2
0320      PRINT "I WISH YOU A HAPPY EASTER"
0330      PRINT "WITH A JOLLY GOOD PARADE."
0340    WHEN 3
0350      PRINT "MAY YOU WHITSUN BE GAY AND FAIR."
0360      PRINT "I HOPE LAST YEARS SPRING SUIT"
0370      PRINT "STILL FITS YOU."
0380    ENDCASE
0390    PRINT
0400    PRINT "         LOVE FROM"
0410    PRINT "           ",SENDER$
0420 ENDPROC WRITELETTER
0430 //
```

DOCTOR

```
0010 //DOCTOR WILLIAM OLDHAM'S PROGRAM//
0020 //WRITTEN BY ELISABETH OLDHAM//
0030 //THIS VERSION: OCTOBER 2, 1981//
0040 //*
0050 //DECLARATIONS//
0060 DIM COLOUR$ OF 10, ANSW$ OF 10
0070 //*
0080 //MAINLINES//
0090 PRINT CHR$(147) //CLEAR SCREEN//
0100 REPEAT
0110    FOR I:=1 TO 8 DO PRINT   //8 DOWN
0120    PRINT "WHAT IS THE COLOUR OF YOU FACE"
0130    PRINT "(PALE/PINK/BLUE/YELLOW)",
0140    INPUT COLOUR$
0150    EXEC DIAGNOSIS
0160    PRINT CHR$(19) //HOME
0170    PRINT "MORE PATIENTS (Y/N)",
0180    INPUT ANSW$
0190    PRINT CHR$(147) //CLEAR SCREEN//
0200 UNTIL ANSW$="N"
0210 //*
0220 PROC DIAGNOSIS
0230    PRINT
0240    CASE COLOUR$ OF
0250    WHEN "PALE"
0260      PRINT "YOU SUFFER FROM ANAMEIA AND NEED SOME IRON."
0270      PRINT "GO HOME AND MAKE SOUP FROM YOUR BICYCLE."
0280    WHEN "PINK"
0290      PRINT "YOU ARE JUST FINE. PLEASE DO NOT WASTE MY TIME."
0300      PRINT "DID YOU NOT KNOW THAT MONEY IS VERY TIGHT IN"
0310      PRINT "THE NATIONAL HEALTH SERVICE THESE DAYS."
0320    WHEN "BLUE"
0330      PRINT "YOU HAVE BEEN DRINKING FAR TOO MUCH."
0340      PRINT "YOU ARE HEREBY FORBIDDEN TO TAKE ANY"
0350      PRINT "BEVERAGES FOR THE NEXT 30 YEAR - IF"
0360      PRINT "YOU GET THAT OLD!"
0370    WHEN "YELLOW"
0380      PRINT "ARE YOU A CHINESE (Y/N)",
0390      INPUT ANSW$
0400      IF ANSW$="Y" THEN
0410        PRINT
0420        PRINT "THERE IS NOTHING THE MATTER WITH YOU."
0430        PRINT "THE COLOUR OF YOUR SKIN IS NORMAL."
0440      ELSE
0450        PRINT "YOU HAVE GOT THE YELLOW FEVER, AND YOU"
0460        PRINT "SHOULD NOT GO TO AFRICA ANY MORE."
0470        PRINT "YOU MAY TRY TO PAINT YOUR SKIN TO"
0480        PRINT "LOOK A BIT MORE ATTRACTIVE."
0490      ENDIF
0500    ENDCASE
0510 ENDPROC DIAGNOSIS
0520 //
```

EGGS

```
0010 // THE WOMAN WITH THE EGGS //
0020 PRINT CHR$(147) //CLEAR SCREEN
0030 FOR I:=1 TO 8 DO PRINT   //8 DOWN
0040 PRINT "HOW MANY EGGS DO YOU HAVE",
0050 INPUT EGGS
0060 TRAYS:=0
0070 WHILE EGGS>=6 DO
0080    EGGS:=EGGS-6
0090    TRAYS:=TRAYS+1
0100 ENDWHILE
0110 PRINT CHR$(147) //CLEAR
0120 FOR I:=1 TO 8 DO PRINT   //8 DOWN
0130 PRINT "WE HAVE PACKED ",TRAYS," EGG TRAY(S),"
0140 PRINT "AND LEFT OVER ",EGGS," EGG(S)."
0150 END
```

WHEEL

```
0010 //PROGRAM: WHEEL//
0020 //
0030 DIM COLOR$ OF 10, GUESS$ OF 10
0040 DIM ANSW$ OF 3, LEGAL$ OF 30
0050 LEGAL$:=".RED.YELLOW.GREEN.BLUE."
0060 REPEAT
0070    EXEC BET
0080    EXEC WHEEL
0090    EXEC RESULT
0100 UNTIL HALT
```

Listing continued next page

WHEEL   *Continued from previous page*

```
0110 //
0120 PROC WHEEL
0130    OUTCOME:=RND(1,15)
0140    CASE OUTCOME OF
0150    WHEN 1,3,6,9,12,15
0160       COLOR$:="RED"
0170       FACTOR:=1.5
0180    WHEN 2,5,8,11,14
0190       COLOR$:="YELLOW"
0200       FACTOR:=2
0210    WHEN 4,10,13
0220       COLOR$:="GREEN"
0230       FACTOR:=3
0240    WHEN 7
0250       COLOR$:="BLUE"
0260       FACTOR:=9
0270    ENDCASE
0280    EXEC DISPLAY(COLOR$)
0290 ENDPROC WHEEL
0300 //
0310 PROC BET
0320    EXEC WRITEFROM(8)
0330    PRINT "WHAT COLOR",
0340    INPUT GUESS$
0350    WHILE NOT ("."+GUESS$+".") IN LEGAL$ DO
0360       EXEC WRITEFROM(8)
0370       PRINT "ONLY (RED,YELLOW,GREEN,BLUE) ALLOWED!"
0380       PRINT "NOW, WHAT DO YOU PICK OUT",
0390       INPUT GUESS$
0400    ENDWHILE
0410    EXEC WRITEFROM(8)
0420    PRINT "HOW MUCH DO YOU WANT TO BET",
0430    INPUT STAKE
0440    WHILE STAKE<10 DO
0450       EXEC WRITEFROM(8)
0460       PRINT "DON'T BE MEAN, MAN!"
0470       PRINT "NOT LESS THEN 10 PENCE."
0480       PRINT "MAY WE ASK FOR YOUR BET",
0490       INPUT STAKE
0500    ENDWHILE
0510 ENDPROC BET
```

Listing continued next page

WHEEL *Continued from previous page*

```
0520 //
0530 PROC RESULT
0540    EXEC WRITEFROM(8)
0550    IF GUESS$=COLOR$ THEN
0560       PRINT "HURRAY, YOU WIN!!"
0570       PRINT "YOU HAVE STAKED ",STAKE," PENCE,"
0580       PRINT "SO YOU GET ",STAKE*FACTOR," PENCE."
0590    ELSE
0600       PRINT "SORRY YOU HAVE LOST ",STAKE," PENCE."
0610       PRINT "BETTER LUCK NEXT TIME."
0620    ENDIF
0630    FOR I:=1 TO 5 DO PRINT   //5 DOWN
0640    INPUT "PLAY AGAIN (Y/N)? ": ANSW$
0650    HALT:=ANSW$="N"
0660 ENDPROC RESULT
0670 //
0680 PROC DISPLAY(C$)
0690    FOR I:=1 TO 5 DO
0700       EXEC WRITEFROM(8)
0710       PRINT "******* ",C$," WINS *******"
0720       FOR T:=1 TO 100 DO DUMMY:=0 //WAIT
0730    NEXT I
0740 ENDPROC DISPLAY
0750 //
0760 PROC WRITEFROM(LN) CLOSED
0770    PRINT CHR$(147), //CLEAR SCREEN
0780    FOR I:=1 TO LN DO PRINT   //LN DOWN
0790 ENDPROC WRITEFROM
0800 //
```

ENROL

```
0010 //OLDHAM'S GRAMMAR SCHOOL//
0020 //PROGRAM TO ADMINISTER PUPILS' MARKS//
0030 //WRITTEN BY CHRIS BORGE IN CBM COMAL-80//
0040 //THIS VERSION: JAN. 1981//
0050 //THIS PART: TO ENROL PUPILS//
0060 //
0070 MAX:=8
0080 DIM NAME$(MAX) OF 20, ANSW$ OF 10
0090 DIM THISNAME$ OF 20
0100 DIM MARK(MAX,3), SUBJ$(3) OF 11, KEY(MAX)
0110 DIM SPACES$ OF 70
0120 //*
0130 SUBJ$(1):="ENGLISH"
0140 SUBJ$(2):="MATHEMATICS"
0150 SUBJ$(3):="FRENCH"
0160 SPACES$(1:70):=""
0190 //
0200 EXEC STARTSYSTEM
0210 //
0220 //* MAINLINES *//
0230 REPEAT
0240    PRINT CHR$(147) //CLEAR SCREEN
0250    EXEC FIELD(8,15)
0260    PRINT "1=ENROLL"
0270    PRINT "2=LIST"
0280    PRINT "3=STOP"
0290    PRINT
0300    INPUT "> ": JOBCODE
0310    IF JOBCODE=1 THEN EXEC ENROL
0320    IF JOBCODE=2 THEN EXEC PRINTOUT
0330    IF JOBCODE=3 THEN EXEC STOPSYSTEM
0340 UNTIL FALSE
0350 //
0360 PROC ENROL
0370    PRINT CHR$(147) //CLEAR//
0380    EXEC FIELD(8,20)
0390    INPUT "NEW CLASS (YES/RETURN): ": ANSW$
0400    IF ANSW$="YES" THEN
0410       EXEC NEWCLASS
0420    ELSE
0430       EXEC TAKEIN("PUPILNO")
0440       WHILE MORE DO
0450          IF NAME$(PUPILNO)<>"" THEN
0460             EXEC ERROR(3)
0470          ELSE
0480             EXEC TAKEIN("PUPILNAME")
0490             NAME$(PUPILNO):=THISNAME$
0500             FOR SUBJNO:=1 TO 3 DO MARK(PUPILNO,SUBJNO):=-1
0510          ENDIF
0520          EXEC TAKEIN("PUPILNO")
0530       ENDWHILE
0540    ENDIF
0550 ENDPROC ENROL
```

Listing continued next page

ENROL   *Continued from previous page*

```
0560 //
0570 PROC NEWCLASS
0580    EXEC TAKEIN("CLASS")
0590    EXEC INITCLASS
0600    PRINT CHR$(147) //CLEAR SCREEN//
0610    PUPILNO:=1
0620    EXEC TAKEIN("PUPILNAME")
0630    WHILE NOT (THISNAME$="" OR PUPILNO=MAX) DO
0640       NAME$(PUPILNO):=THISNAME$
0650       PUPILNO:=PUPILNO+1
0660       EXEC TAKEIN("PUPILNAME")
0670    ENDWHILE
0680    PRINT CHR$(147)
0690 ENDPROC NEWCLASS
0700 //
0710 PROC INITCLASS
0720    FOR PUPILNO:=1 TO MAX DO
0730       NAME$(PUPILNO):=""
0740       FOR SUBJNO:=1 TO 3 DO MARK(PUPILNO,SUBJNO):=-1
0750    NEXT PUPILNO
0760 ENDPROC INITCLASS
0770 //
0780 PROC TAKEIN(MATTER$)
0790    REPEAT
0800       EXEC FIELD(8,10)
0810       CASE MATTER$ OF
0820       WHEN "PUPILNO"
0830          INPUT "PUPIL NUMBER (0 TO STOP): ": PUPILNO
0840       WHEN "PUPILNAME"
0850          PRINT "PUPIL NUMBER ",PUPILNO,
0860          INPUT " : ": THISNAME$
0870       WHEN "CLASS"
0880          INPUT "CLASS (8,9,10): ": CLASS
0890       ENDCASE
0900       EXEC CONTROL
0910    UNTIL OK
0920    PRINT CHR$(147) //CLEAR SCREEN
0930 ENDPROC TAKEIN
0940 //
0950 PROC CONTROL
0960    CASE MATTER$ OF
0970    WHEN "PUPILNO"
0980       Ok:=(0<=PUPILNO AND PUPILNO<=MAX)
0990       MORE:=(PUPILNO>0)
1000    WHEN "PUPILNAME"
1010       Ok:=TRUE //NO TEST//
1020    WHEN "CLASS"
1030       OK:=(CLASS=8)
1040       LACKING:=(CLASS=9 OR CLASS=10)
1050    ENDCASE
1060    IF NOT OK THEN EXEC ERROR(10)
1070 ENDPROC CONTROL
```

Listing continued next page

ENROL   *Continued from previous page*

```
1080 //
1090 PROC ERROR(NO)
1100    EXEC FIELD(1,3)
1110    PRINT "ERROR!"
1120    //
1130    //NOT FINISHED//
1140    //
1150 ENDPROC ERROR
1160 //
1170 //
1180 PROC FIELD(L1,L2)
1190    EXEC SCREEN(L1,1)
1200    FOR I:=1 TO L2-L1+1 DO PRINT SPACES$
1210    EXEC SCREEN(L1,1)
1220    PRINT
1230 ENDPROC FIELD
1240 //
1250 PROC SCREEN(ROW,COL) CLOSED
1260    PRINT CHR$(19) //HOME
1270    FOR I:=1 TO ROW DO PRINT   //DOWN
1275    FOR I:=1 TO COL-1 DO PRINT CHR$(29), //RIGHT
1280 ENDPROC SCREEN
1290 //
1300 PROC STARTSYSTEM
1310    OPEN FILE 2,"MARKBOOKS",READ
1320    FOR PUPILNO:=1 TO MAX DO
1330      READ FILE 2: NAME$(PUPILNO)
1340      FOR SUBJNO:=1 TO 3 DO READ FILE 2: MARK(PUPILNO,SUBJNO)
1350    NEXT PUPILNO
1360    CLOSE
1370 ENDPROC STARTSYSTEM
1380 //
1390 PROC STOPSYSTEM
1400    OPEN FILE 2,"@0:MARKBOOKS",WRITE
1410    FOR PUPILNO:=1 TO MAX DO
1420      WRITE FILE 2: NAME$(PUPILNO)
1430      FOR SUBJNO:=1 TO 3 DO WRITE FILE 2: MARK(PUPILNO,SUBJNO)
1440    NEXT PUPILNO
1450    CLOSE
1460    STOP
1470 ENDPROC STOPSYSTEM
```

Listing continued next page

ENROL   *Continued from previous page*

```
1480 //
1490 PROC PRINTOUT
1500    PRINT CHR$(147) //CLEAR
1510    FOR PUPILNO:=1 TO MAX DO
1520       EXEC FIELD(8,9)
1530       IF NAME$(PUPILNO)<>"" THEN
1540          THISNAME$:=NAME$(PUPILNO)
1550          PRINT "STUDENT NUMBER ",PUPILNO,",  ",THISNAME$
1560          PRINT "HAS ACHIEVED THE FOLLOWING RESULTS:"
1570          PRINT
1580          FOR SUBJNO:=1 TO 3 DO
1590             PRINT SUBJ$(SUBJNO),": ",TAB(25),MARK(PUPILNO,SUBJNO)
1600          NEXT SUBJNO
1610          PRINT
1620          INPUT "PRESS RETURN-KEY: ": ANSW$
1630       ENDIF
1640    NEXT PUPILNO
1650 ENDPROC PRINTOUT
```

HANNIBAL

```
0010 //UNCLE HANNIBAL'S BACK SHOP//
0020 //WRITTEN BY CHRISTIAN BORGE//
0030 //THIS VERSION: OCT. 1981//
0040 //
0050 DIM NAME$ OF 30, ADRESS$ OF 20
0060 DIM TOWN$ OF 20, CODE$ OF 10
0070 DIM ARTICLE$(10) OF 20, PRICE(10)
0080 DIM TEXT$(10) OF 20, AMOUNT(10)
0090 DIM SPACES$ OF 40, QUANTITY(10)
0095 SPACES$(1:40):=""
0100 //*
0110 EXEC INITIALIZE
0120 REPEAT
0130    EXEC CUSTOMER
0140    EXEC GETORDER
0150    IF LINE<>0 THEN EXEC WRITEBILL
0160    INPUT "TYPE RETURN ": CODE$
0170 UNTIL THECOWSCOMEIN
0180 //*
0190 PROC INITIALIZE
0200    PRINT CHR$(147) //CLEAR SCREEN
0210    THECOWSCOMEIN:=FALSE
0220    I:=0
0230    REPEAT
0240      I:=I+1
0250      READ ARTICLE$(I),PRICE(I)
0260    UNTIL EOD //END OF DATA//
0270    MAX:=I
0280 ENDPROC INITIALIZE
0290 //
0300 PROC CUSTOMER
0310    TOTAL:=0; LINE:=0
0320    //
0330    //STUD
0340    //
0350 ENDPROC CUSTOMER
0360 //
0370 PROC GETORDER
0380    EXEC MENU
0390    EXEC TAKEIN("ARTNO")
0400    WHILE NOT FINISHED DO
0410      LINE:=LINE+1
0420      EXEC TAKEIN("QUANTITY")
0430      EXEC INVOICELINE
0440      EXEC TAKEIN("ARTNO")
0450    ENDWHILE
0460 ENDPROC GETORDER
```

Listing continued next page

HANNIBAL   *Continued from previous page*

```
0470 //
0480 PROC INVOICELINE
0490    TEXT$(LINE):=ARTICLE$(ARTNO)
0500    AMOUNT(LINE):=PRICE(ARTNO)*QUANTITY(LINE)
0510    TOTAL:=TOTAL+AMOUNT(LINE)
0520 ENDPROC INVOICELINE
0530 //
0540 PROC WRITEBILL
0550    PRINT CHR$(147) //CLEAR SCREEN
0560    EXEC SCREEN(4,1)
0570    PRINT NAME$
0580    PRINT ADRESS$
0590    PRINT TOWN$," ",CODE$
0600    PRINT
0610    PRINT "QUANT.",TAB(10),"ARTICLE",TAB(30),"AMOUNT"
0620    PRINT "----------------------------------------"
0630    FOR I:=1 TO LINE DO
0640       PRINT TAB(2),QUANTITY(I)," LB",
0650       PRINT TAB(9),TEXT$(I),
0660       PRINT TAB(32-LGTH(AMOUNT(I))),AMOUNT(I)
0670    NEXT I
0680    PRINT TAB(28),"--------"
0690    PRINT TAB(22),"TOTAL:",TAB(32-LGTH(TOTAL)),TOTAL
0700 ENDPROC WRITEBILL
0710 //
0720 PROC TAKEIN(KINDOF$)
0730    EXEC WINDOW(10,15)
0740    CASE KINDOF$ OF
0750    WHEN "ARTNO"
0760       REPEAT
0770          EXEC WINDOW(10,15)
0780          INPUT "> ": ARTNO
0790          OK:=(0<=ARTNO AND ARTNO<=MAX)
0800       UNTIL OK
0810       FINISHED:=(ARTNO=0)
0820    WHEN "QUANTITY"
0830       REPEAT
0840          EXEC SCREEN(ARTNO,20)
0850          INPUT QUANT
0860       UNTIL 0<QUANT AND INT(QUANT)=QUANT
0870       QUANTITY(LINE):=QUANT
0880    ENDCASE
0890 ENDPROC TAKEIN
```

Listing continued next page

HANNIBAL   *Continued from previous page*

```
0900 //
0910 PROC MENU
0920    PRINT CHR$(147)
0930    FOR I:=1 TO MAX DO
0940       PRINT I,". ",ARTICLE$(I)
0950    NEXT I
0960    PRINT "0. STOP"
0970 ENDPROC MENU
0980 //
0990 PROC WINDOW(X,Y)
1000    EXEC SCREEN(X,1)
1010    FOR LN:=1 TO Y-X+1 DO PRINT SPACES$
1020    EXEC SCREEN(X,1)
1030 ENDPROC WINDOW
1040 //
1050 PROC SCREEN(X,Y)
1060    PRINT CHR$(19),
1070    FOR LN:=1 TO X DO PRINT CHR$(17),
1080    FOR CH:=1 TO Y DO PRINT CHR$(29),
1090 ENDPROC SCREEN
1100 //
1110 FUNC LGTH(X)
1120    ETURN )(X>1)+(X>10)+(X>100)+(X>1000)
1130 ENDFUNC LGTH
1140 //
```

WORDGAME

```
0010 DIM MYWORD$(5) OF 20, YOURWORD$ OF 20
0020 DIM SPACES$ OF 40, CH$ OF 1, CATCH$ OF 100
0030 SPACES$(1:40):=" "
0040 PRINT CHR$(147) //CLEAR SCREEN
0050 //
0060 EXEC INTRODUCTION
0070 EXEC WORDGAME
0080 EXEC RESULT
0090 //
0100 PROC INTRODUCTION
0110    EXEC WINDOW(8,20)
0120    PRINT "IN THIS GAME FIVE WORDS"
0130    PRINT "ARE DISPLAYED. THEY WILL BE"
0140    PRINT "ON THE SCREEN FOR ABOUT FIVE SECONDS."
0150    PRINT "THEN THEY DISSAPEAR, AND YOU ARE"
0160    PRINT "ASKED TO TYPE IN AS MANY OF THEM"
0170    PRINT "AS YOU CAN REMEMBER."
0180    PRINT
0190    INPUT "PRESS RETURN KEY TO CONTINUE: ": CH$
0200    EXEC WINDOW(8,20)
0210    PRINT "---------------------------"
0220    FOR I:=1 TO 5 DO
0230      READ MYWORD$(I)
0240      PRINT TAB(5),MYWORD$(I)
0250    NEXT I
0260    PRINT "---------------------------"
0270 ENDPROC INTRODUCTION
0280 //
0290 PROC WORDGAME
0300    EXEC WAIT(5)
0310    FOR NO:=1 TO 5 DO
0320      EXEC WINDOW(8,15)
0330      PRINT "TYPE IN YOUR ",NO,". WORD: ",
0340      INPUT "": YOURWORD$
0350      I:=1
0360      WHILE YOURWORD$<>MYWORD$(I) AND I<5 DO
0364        I:=I+1
0368      ENDWHILE
0370      PRINT
0380      IF YOURWORD$=MYWORD$(I) THEN
0390        CATCH$:=CATCH$+YOURWORD$+" "
0400      ENDIF
0410    NEXT NO
0420 ENDPROC WORDGAME
```

Listing continued next page

WORDGAME   *Continued from previous page*

```
0430 //
0440 PROC RESULT
0450    EXEC WINDOW(8,15)
0460    PRINT "MINE: ",
0470    FOR NO:=1 TO 5 DO PRINT MYWORD$(NO);
0480    FOR I:=1 TO 2 DO PRINT
0490    PRINT "YOURS: ",
0500    PRINT CATCH$
0510 ENDPROC RESULT
0520 //
0530 PROC WINDOW(X,Y)
0540    PRINT CHR$(19), //HOME
0550    FOR I:=1 TO X DO PRINT   //DOWN X LINES
0560    FOR I:=1 TO Y-X+1 DO PRINT SPACES$ //CLEAR LINES
0570    PRINT CHR$(19) //HOME AGAIN
0580    FOR I:=1 TO X DO PRINT   //DOWN TO START
0590 ENDPROC WINDOW
0600 //
0610 PROC WAIT(T)
0620    FOR I:=1 TO 900*T DO
0630    NEXT I
0640 ENDPROC WAIT
0650 //
0660 DATA "FISH","DOVE","HORSE","CAT","OWL"
```

ENTERMARKS

```
0010 //OLDHAM'S GRAMMAR SCHOOL//
0020 //PROGRAM TO ADMINISTER PUPILS' MARKS//
0030 //WRITTEN BY CHRIS BORGE IN CBM COMAL-80//
0040 //THIS VERSION: OCT. 1981//
0050 //THIS PART: TO ENTER PUPILS' MARKS//
0060 //
0070 MAX:=8
0080 DIM NAME$(MAX) OF 20, ANSW$ OF 11
0090 DIM MARK(MAX,3), SUBJ$(3) OF 11, KEY(MAX)
0100 DIM SPACES$ OF 70
0105 //*
0110 SUBJ$(1):="ENGLISH"
0130 SUBJ$(2):="MATHEMATICS"
0140 SUBJ$(3):="FRENCH"
0150 SPACES$(1:70):=""
```

Listing continued next page

ENTERMARKS
Continued from previous page

```
0180 //
0190 EXEC STARTSYSTEM
0200 //
0210 //* MAINLINES *//
0220 SUBJNO:=0
0230 REPEAT
0240    PRINT CHR$(147) //CLEAR SCREEN
0250    EXEC FIELD(8,15)
0260    PRINT "1=ENTER MARKS"
0270    PRINT "2=LIST MARKS"
0280    PRINT "3=STOP PROGRAM"
0290    PRINT
0300    INPUT "> ": JOBCODE
0310    IF JOBCODE=1 THEN EXEC ENTERMARKS
0320    IF JOBCODE=2 THEN EXEC PRINTOUT
0330    IF JOBCODE=3 THEN EXEC STOPSYSTEM
0340 UNTIL FALSE //FOREVER
0350 //
0360 PROC ENTERMARKS
0370    EXEC TAKEIN("CLASS")
0380    EXEC TAKEIN("SUBJECT")
0390    PRINT CHR$(147) //CLEAR SCREEN
0400    PRINT "YOU MAY NOW ENTER PUPILS' MARKS IN ",SUBJ$(SUBJNO)
0410    PRINT
0420    FOR PUPILNO:=1 TO MAX DO
0430       IF NAME$(PUPILNO)<>"" THEN
0440          EXEC TAKEIN("MARK")
0450       ENDIF
0460    NEXT PUPILNO
0470 ENDPROC ENTERMARKS
0480 //
0490 PROC TAKEIN(MATTER$)
0500    REPEAT
0510       EXEC FIELD(8,15)
0520       CASE MATTER$ OF
0530       WHEN "CLASS"
0540          INPUT "CLASS (8,9,10): ": CLASS
0550       WHEN "SUBJECT"
0560          PRINT "ENTER NAME OF SUBJECT:"
0570          PRINT "(ENGLISH, MATHEMATICS, FRENCH)",
0580          INPUT "> ": ANSW$
0590       WHEN "MARK"
0600          PRINT NAME$(PUPILNO),TAB(30),": ",
0610          INPUT "": THISMARK
0620       ENDCASE
0630       EXEC CONTROL
0640    UNTIL OK
0650    PRINT CHR$(147)
0660 ENDPROC TAKEIN
```

Listing continued next page

ENTERMARKS *Continued from previous page*

```
0670 //
0680 PROC CONTROL
0690    CASE MATTER$ OF
0700    WHEN "CLASS"
0710       OK:=(CLASS=8)
0720       LACKING:=(CLASS=9 OR CLASS=10)
0730    WHEN "SUBJECT"
0740       I:=1
0750       WHILE ANSW$<>SUBJ$(I) AND I<3 DO
0754          I:=I+1
0758       ENDWHILE
0760       OK:=ANSW$=SUBJ$(I); SUBJNO:=I
0770    WHEN "MARK"
0780       OK:=(0<=THISMARK AND THISMARK<=5)
0790       IF OK THEN MARK(PUPILNO,SUBJNO):=THISMARK
0800    ENDCASE
0810    IF NOT OK THEN EXEC ERROR(4)
0820 ENDPROC CONTROL
0830 //
0840 //
0850 PROC ERROR(NO)
0860    EXEC FIELD(1,3)
0870    PRINT "ERROR!"
0880    //
0890    //NOT FINISHED//
0900    //
0910 ENDPROC ERROR
0920 //
0930 //
0940 PROC FIELD(L1,L2)
0950    EXEC SCREEN(L1,1)
0960    FOR I:=1 TO L2-L1+1 DO PRINT SPACES$
0970    EXEC SCREEN(L1,1)
0980    PRINT
0990 ENDPROC FIELD
1000 //
1010 PROC SCREEN(ROW,COL)
1020    PRINT CHR$(19) //CURSOR HOME
1030    FOR I:=1 TO ROW DO PRINT   //DOWN
1035    FOR I:=1 TO COL-1 DO PRINT CHR$(29), //RIGHT
1040 ENDPROC SCREEN
1050 //
1060 PROC STARTSYSTEM
1070    OPEN FILE 2,"MARKBOOKS",READ
1080    FOR PUPILNO:=1 TO MAX DO
1090       READ FILE 2: NAME$(PUPILNO)
1100       FOR SUBJNO:=1 TO 3 DO READ FILE 2: MARK(PUPILNO,SUBJNO)
1110    NEXT PUPILNO
1120    CLOSE
1130 ENDPROC STARTSYSTEM
```

Listing continued next page

ENTERMARKS *Continued from previous page*

```
1140 //
1150 PROC STOPSYSTEM
1160    OPEN FILE 2,"ɔ0:MARKBOOKS",WRITE
1170    FOR PUPILNO:=1 TO MAX DO
1180      WRITE FILE 2: NAME$(PUPILNO)
1190      FOR SUBJNO:=1 TO 3 DO WRITE FILE 2: MARK(PUPILNO,SUBJNO)
1200    NEXT PUPILNO
1210    CLOSE
1220    STOP
1230 ENDPROC STOPSYSTEM
1240 //
1250 PROC PRINTOUT
1260    IF SUBJNO=0 THEN EXEC TAKEIN("SUBJECT")
1270    PRINT CHR$(147) //CLEAR
1280    PRINT "MARKS IN ",SUBJ$(SUBJNO),":"
1290    PRINT
1300    FOR PUPILNO:=1 TO MAX DO
1310      IF NAME$(PUPILNO)<>"" THEN
1320        PRINT PUPILNO,". ",NAME$(PUPILNO),":",TAB(25),
1330        PRINT MARK(PUPILNO,SUBJNO)
1340      ENDIF
1350    NEXT PUPILNO
1360    PRINT
1370    INPUT "TYPE RETURN TO CONTINUE ": ANSW$
1380 ENDPROC PRINTOUT
```

CORRECT

```
0010 //OLDHAM'S GRAMMAR SCHOOL//
0020 //PROGRAM TO ADMINISTER PUPILS' MARKS//
0030 //WRITTEN BY CHRIS BORGE IN CBM COMAL-80//
0040 //THIS VERSION: OCT. 1981//
0050 //THIS PART: TO MAKE CORRECTIONS //
0060 //
0070 MAX:=8
0080 DIM NAME$(MAX) OF 20, ANSW$ OF 10
0090 DIM THISNAME$ OF 20
0100 DIM MARK(MAX,3), SUBJ$(3) OF 10, KEY(MAX)
0110 DIM SPACES$ OF 70
0120 //*
0130 SUBJ$(1):="ENGLISH"
0140 SUBJ$(2):="MATH"
0150 SUBJ$(3):="FRENCH"
0160 SPACES$(1:70):=""
0190 //
0200 EXEC STARTSYSTEM
0210 //
0220 //* MAINLINES *//
0230 REPEAT
0240   EXEC CLEAR'SCREEN
0250   EXEC FIELD(8,15)
0260   PRINT "1=CORRECTIONS"
0270   PRINT "2=DELETE"
0280   PRINT "3=LOOKUP"
0290   PRINT "4=STOP"
0300   PRINT
0310   INPUT "> ": JOBCODE
0320   IF JOBCODE=1 THEN EXEC CORRECTIONS
0330   IF JOBCODE=2 THEN EXEC ERASE
0340   IF JOBCODE=3 THEN EXEC LOOKUP
0350   IF JOBCODE=4 THEN EXEC STOPSYSTEM
0360 UNTIL FALSE
0370 //
0380 PROC CORRECTIONS
0390   EXEC CLEAR'SCREEN
0400   EXEC TAKEIN("PUPILNO")
0410   EXEC DISPLAY
0420   INPUT "CORRECTIONS (YES/NO)? ": ANSW$
0430   IF ANSW$="YES" THEN
0440     EXEC TAKEIN("SUBJECT")
0450     EXEC TAKEIN("MARK")
0460   ENDIF
0470 ENDPROC CORRECTIONS
```

Listing continued next page

CORRECT   *Continued from previous page*

```
0480 //
0490 PROC ERASE
0500    EXEC CLEAR'SCREEN
0510    EXEC TAKEIN("PUPILNO")
0520    EXEC DISPLAY
0530    PRINT
0540    PRINT "DO YOU WANT TO DELETE THE RECORD"
0550    PRINT "DISPLAYED ABOVE (YES/RETURN)",
0560    INPUT ANSW$
0570    IF ANSW$="YES" THEN NAME$(PUPILNO):=""
0580 ENDPROC ERASE
0590 //
0600 PROC TAKEIN(MATTER$)
0610    REPEAT
0620       EXEC FIELD(8,10)
0630       CASE MATTER$ OF
0640       WHEN "PUPILNO"
0650          INPUT "PUPIL NUMBER: ": PUPILNO
0660       WHEN "SUBJECT"
0670          PRINT "ENGLISH, MATH, FRENCH",
0680          INPUT ANSW$
0690       WHEN "MARK"
0700          PRINT "THE CORRECT MARK IN ",SUBJ$(SUBJNO)
0710          PRINT "FOR THE PUPIL ",NAME$(PUPILNO)," IS:",
0720          INPUT " ": THISMARK
0730       ENDCASE
0740       EXEC CONTROL
0750    UNTIL OK
0760    EXEC CLEAR'SCREEN
0770 ENDPROC TAKEIN
0780 //
0790 PROC CONTROL
0800    CASE MATTER$ OF
0810    WHEN "PUPILNO"
0820       EXISTS:=FALSE
0830       OK:=(0<PUPILNO AND PUPILNO<=MAX)
0840       IF OK THEN EXISTS:=(NAME$(PUPILNO)<>"")
0850       OK:=OK AND EXISTS
0860    WHEN "SUBJECT"
0870       I:=1
0880       WHILE ANSW$<>SUBJ$(I) AND I<3 DO I:=I+1
0890       OK:=(ANSW$=SUBJ$(I)); SUBJNO:=I
0900    WHEN "MARK"
0910       OK:=(0<=THISMARK AND THISMARK<=5)
0920       IF OK THEN MARK(PUPILNO,SUBJNO):=THISMARK
0930    ENDCASE
0940    IF NOT OK THEN EXEC ERROR(4)
0950 ENDPROC CONTROL
```

CORRECT   *Continued from previous page*

```
0960 //
0970 PROC ERROR(NO)
0980    EXEC FIELD(1,3)
0990    PRINT "ERROR!"
1000    //
1010    //NOT FINISHED//
1020    //
1030 ENDPROC ERROR
1040 //
1050 //
1060 PROC FIELD(L1,L2)
1070    EXEC SCREEN(L1,1)
1080    FOR I:=1 TO L2-L1+1 DO PRINT SPACES$
1090    EXEC SCREEN(L1,1)
1100    PRINT
1110 ENDPROC FIELD
1120 //
1130 PROC SCREEN(ROW,COL) CLOSED
1140    PRINT CHR$(19) //HOME
1150    FOR I:=1 TO ROW DO PRINT   //DOWN
1155    FOR I:=1 TO COL-1 DO PRINT CHR$(29),  //RIGHT
1160 ENDPROC SCREEN
1170 //
1180 PROC STARTSYSTEM
1190    OPEN FILE 2,"MARKBOOKS",READ
1200    FOR PUPILNO:=1 TO MAX DO
1210      READ FILE 2: NAME$(PUPILNO)
1220      FOR SUBJNO:=1 TO 3 DO READ FILE 2: MARK(PUPILNO,SUBJNO)
1230    NEXT PUPILNO
1240    CLOSE
1250 ENDPROC STARTSYSTEM
1260 //
1270 PROC STOPSYSTEM
1280    OPEN FILE 2,"ව0:MARKBOOKS",WRITE
1290    FOR PUPILNO:=1 TO MAX DO
1300      WRITE FILE 2: NAME$(PUPILNO)
1310      FOR SUBJNO:=1 TO 3 DO WRITE FILE 2: MARK(PUPILNO,SUBJNO)
1320    NEXT PUPILNO
1330    CLOSE
1340    STOP
1350 ENDPROC STOPSYSTEM
1360 //
1370 PROC LOOKUP
1380    EXEC CLEAR'SCREEN
1390    EXEC TAKEIN("PUPILNO")
1400    EXEC DISPLAY
1410    PRINT
1420    INPUT "PRESS RETURN-KEY: ": ANSW$
1430 ENDPROC LOOKUP
```

Listing continued next page

CORRECT   *Continued from previous page*

```
1440 //
1450 PROC DISPLAY
1460    EXEC CLEAR'SCREEN
1470    EXEC FIELD(8,20)
1480    IF NAME$(PUPILNO)<>"" THEN
1490      THISNAME$:=NAME$(PUPILNO)
1500      PRINT "PUPIL NUMBER ",PUPILNO,", ",THISNAME$
1510      PRINT "HAS ACHIEVED THE FOLLOWING RESULTS:"
1520      PRINT
1530      FOR SUBJNO:=1 TO 3 DO
1540        PRINT SUBJ$(SUBJNO),": ",
1550        PRINT TAB(25),MARK(PUPILNO,SUBJNO)
1560      NEXT SUBJNO
1570    ENDIF
1580    PRINT
1590 ENDPROC DISPLAY
1600 //
1610 PROC CLEAR'SCREEN
1620    PRINT CHR$(147),
1630 ENDPROC CLEAR'SCREEN
1640 //
```

REPORT

```
0010 //OLDHAM'S GRAMMAR SCHOOL//
0020 //PROGRAM TO ADMINISTER PUPILS' MARKS//
0030 //WRITTEN IN CBM COMAL-80//
0040 //THIS VERSION: OCT. 1981//
0050 //THIS PART: TO PRINT REPORTS//
0060 //
0070 MAX:=8
0080 DIM NAME$(MAX) OF 20, ANSW$ OF 10
0090 DIM THISNAME$ OF 20
0100 DIM MARK(MAX,3), SUBJ$(3) OF 11, KEY(MAX)
0110 DIM SPACES$ OF 70
0120 //*
0130 SUBJ$(1):="ENGLISH"
0140 SUBJ$(2):="MATHEMATICS"
0150 SUBJ$(3):="FRENCH"
0160 SPACES$(1:70):=""
0190 //
0200 EXEC STARTSYSTEM
0210 //
0220 //* MAINLINES *//
0230 PRINT CHR$(147) //CLEAR SCREEN
0240 EXEC FIELD(8,15)
0250 PRINT "1=SCREEN"
0260 PRINT "2=PRINTER"
0270 PRINT
0280 INPUT "> ": DEVICE
0290 EXEC GETPERIOD
0300 IF DEVICE=2 THEN SELECT OUTPUT "LP"
0310 EXEC PRINTOUT
0320 IF DEVICE=2 THEN SELECT OUTPUT "DS"
0330 PRINT "END OF PROGRAM: REPORT"
0340 //
0350 PROC FIELD(L1,L2)
0360    EXEC CURSOR(L1,1)
0370    FOR I:=1 TO L2-L1+1 DO PRINT SPACES$
0380    EXEC CURSOR(L1,1)
0390    PRINT
0400 ENDPROC FIELD
0410 //
0420 PROC CURSOR(ROW,COL) CLOSED
0430    PRINT CHR$(19) //HOME
0440    FOR I:=1 TO ROW DO PRINT   //DOWN
0445    FOR I:=1 TO COL-1 DO PRINT CHR$(29) //DOWN
0450 ENDPROC CURSOR
```

Listing continued next page

REPORT   *Continued from previous page*

```
0460 //
0470 PROC STARTSYSTEM
0480    OPEN FILE 2,"MARKBOOKS",READ
0490    FOR PUPILNO:=1 TO MAX DO
0500      READ FILE 2: NAME$(PUPILNO)
0510      FOR SUBJNO:=1 TO 3 DO
0520        READ FILE 2: MARK(PUPILNO,SUBJNO)
0530      NEXT SUBJNO
0540    NEXT PUPILNO
0550    CLOSE
0560 ENDPROC STARTSYSTEM
0570 //
0580 PROC GETPERIOD
0590    PRINT CHR$(147)
0600    EXEC FIELD(8,10)
0610    REPEAT
0620      REPEAT
0630        INPUT "WHAT TERM: ": TERM;
0640      UNTIL 0<TERM AND TERM<5
0650      TERM:=INT(TERM)
0660      REPEAT
0670        INPUT "WHAT YEAR: ": YEAR
0680      UNTIL 0<YEAR AND YEAR<99
0690      YEAR:=INT(YEAR)
0700      EXEC FIELD(8,15)
0710      PRINT "YOU HAVE ENTERED: ",
0720      PRINT TERM,". TERM, 19",YEAR
0730      INPUT "OK (YES/NO)? ": ANSW$
0740    UNTIL ANSW$="YES"
0750 ENDPROC GETPERIOD
0760 //
0770 PROC PRINTOUT
0780    PRINT CHR$(147)
0790    FOR PUPILNO:=1 TO MAX DO
0800      IF NAME$(PUPILNO)<>"" THEN
0810        THISNAME$:=NAME$(PUPILNO)
0820        IF DEVICE=1 THEN
0830          EXEC FIELD(8,20)
0840        ELSE
0850          FOR I:=1 TO 8 DO PRINT
0860        ENDIF
0870        EXEC REPORT
0880      ENDIF
0890      PRINT
0900    NEXT PUPILNO
0910    PRINT CHR$(147)
0920 ENDPROC PRINTOUT
```

Listing continued next page

REPORT   *Continued from previous page*

```
0930 //
0940 PROC REPORT
0950    PRINT "O L D H A M' S  G R A M M A R  S C H O O L"
0960    PRINT "----------------------------------------"
0970    PRINT "    IN THE ",TERM,". TERM OF 19",YEAR
0980    PRINT "PUPIL NUMBER ",PUPILNO,", ",THISNAME$
0990    PRINT "HAS ACHIEVED THE FOLLOWING RESULTS:"
1000    PRINT
1010    ZONE 30
1020    FOR SUBJNO:=1 TO 3 DO
1030      PRINT SUBJ$(SUBJNO),
1040      PRINT MARK(PUPILNO,SUBJNO)
1050    NEXT SUBJNO
1060    IF DEVICE=1 THEN
1070      EXEC FIELD(18,18)
1080      INPUT "PRESS RETURN ": ANSW$
1090    ENDIF
1100    ZONE 0
1110 ENDPROC REPORT
```

XMASCARDS

```
0010 DIM RECIPIENT$ OF 30, SENDER$ OF 30
0020 DIM DATE$ OF 20, ANSW$ OF 10
0030 //
0040 EXEC WRITEFROM(5)
0050 INPUT "WHAT DATE (E.G. 12 DECEMBER 1980)? ": DATE$
0060 SENDER$:="HANNIBAL"
0070 //
0080 REPEAT
0090    READ RECIPIENT$
0100    EXEC WRITECARD
0110    FOR I:=1 TO 3 DO PRINT   //3 DOWN
0120    INPUT "PRESS THE RETURN-KEY: ": ANSW$
0130 UNTIL EOD //END-OF-DATA//
0140 EXEC WRITEFROM(5)
0150 PRINT "NO MORE XMAS CARDS."
0160 PRINT "DON'T FORGET TO STAMP THEM."
0170 END
0180 //
0190 PROC WRITECARD
0200    EXEC WRITEFROM(5)
0210    PRINT "            ODDINGTON, ",DATE$
0220    PRINT
0230    PRINT "DEAR ",RECIPIENT$
0240    PRINT
0250    PRINT "I WISH YOU A MERRY CHRISTMAS AND"
0260    PRINT "A HAPPY AND PROFITABLE NEW YEAR."
0270    PRINT "                    LOVE FROM"
0280    PRINT "                    ",SENDER$
0290 ENDPROC WRITECARD
0300 //
0310 PROC WRITEFROM(LINE)
0320    PRINT CHR$(147) //CLEAR//
0330    FOR I:=1 TO LINE DO PRINT   //CURSOR DOWN
0340 ENDPROC WRITEFROM
0350 //
0360 DATA "ELIZA","LOUISE","ROY","LITTLE JOHN"
0370 DATA "AGATHE","PETER","CURT HUGO","MAX"
```

XMASFILE

```
0010 DIM RECIPIENT$ OF 30, SENDER$ OF 30
0020 DIM DATE$ OF 20, ANSW$ OF 10
0030 //
0040 EXEC WRITEFROM(5)
0050 INPUT "WHAT DATE (E.G. 12 DECEMBER 1980)? ": DATE$
0060 SENDER$:="HANNIBAL"
0070 //
0080 OPEN FILE 2,"XMAS",READ
0090 REPEAT
0100    READ FILE 2: RECIPIENT$
0110    EXEC WRITECARD
0120    FOR LN:=1 TO 3 DO PRINT
0130    INPUT "PRESS THE RETURN-KEY: ": ANSW$
0140 UNTIL EOF(2) //END-OF-FILE//
0150 CLOSE
0160 EXEC WRITEFROM(5)
0170 PRINT "NO MORE XMAS CARDS."
0180 PRINT "DON'T FORGET TO STAMP THEM."
0190 END
0200 //
0210 PROC WRITECARD
0220    EXEC WRITEFROM(5)
0230    PRINT "            ODDINGTON, ",DATE$
0240    PRINT
0250    PRINT "DEAR ",RECIPIENT$
0260    PRINT
0270    PRINT "I WISH YOU A MERRY CHRISTMAS AND"
0280    PRINT "A HAPPY AND PROFITABLE NEW YEAR."
0290    PRINT "                    LOVE FROM"
0300    PRINT "                    ",SENDER$
0310 ENDPROC WRITECARD
0320 //
0330 PROC WRITEFROM(LINE)
0340    PRINT CHR$(147) //CLEAR//
0350    FOR I:=1 TO LINE DO PRINT   //CURSOR DOWN
0360 ENDPROC
```

ENTERNAMES

```
0010 DIM RECIPIENT$ OF 30
0020 OPEN 3,"ĐO:XMAS",WRITE
0030 INPUT RECIPIENT$
0040 WHILE RECIPIENT$<>"" DO
0050   WRITE FILE 3: RECIPIENT$
0060    INPUT RECIPIENT$
0070 ENDWHILE
0080 CLOSE
```

ENTEROPTIONS

```
0010 //PROGRAM: ENTEROPTIONS//
0020 DIM NAME$(15) OF 20, OPTION(15,4)
0030 DIM SUBJECT$(4) OF 12, N$ OF 20, A$ OF 3
0040 DIM SPACES$ OF 40
0050 //
0060 SPACES$(1:40):=""
0070 SUBJECT$(1):="BIOLOGY"
0080 SUBJECT$(2):="GERMAN"
0090 SUBJECT$(3):="INFORMATICS"
0100 SUBJECT$(4):="MUSIC"
0110 //
0120 EXEC STARTPROGRAM
0130 PRINT CHR$(147) //CLEAR SCREEN
0140 REPEAT
0150   EXEC WINDOW(8,15)
0160   OK:=FALSE
0170   PRINT "1 = NEW CLASS"
0180   PRINT "2 = ENTER INDIVIDUALS"
0190   PRINT
0200   INPUT "> ": JOB
0210   CASE JOB OF
0220   WHEN 1
0230     EXEC WINDOW(8,12)
0240     INPUT "DO YOU WANT TO DELETE OLD (Y/N)? ": A$
0250     IF A$="Y" THEN MAX:=0; OK:=TRUE
0260   WHEN 2
0270     OK:=TRUE
0280   ENDCASE
0290 UNTIL OK
0300 EXEC GETOPTIONS
0310 EXEC STOPPROGRAM
```

Listing continued next page

ENTEROPTIONS   *Continued from previous page*

```
0320 //
0330 PROC GETOPTIONS
0340    PRINT CHR$(147) //CLEAR
0350    EXEC WINDOW(8,9)
0360    INPUT "FIRST STUDENT'S NAME: ": N$
0370    WHILE NOT (N$="" OR MAX=15) DO
0380      MAX:=MAX+1
0390      NAME$(MAX):=N$
0400      EXEC WINDOW(5,5)
0410      PRINT N$,"'S OPTIONS ARE:"
0420      FOR J:=1 TO 4 DO
0430        REPEAT
0440          EXEC WINDOW(8,10)
0450          PRINT SUBJECT$(J)," AT LEVEL",
0460          INPUT ": ": LEVEL
0470        UNTIL LEVEL=-1 OR LEVEL=1 OR LEVEL=2
0480        OPTION(MAX,J):=LEVEL
0490      NEXT J
0500      PRINT CHR$(147) //CLEAR
0510      EXEC WINDOW(8,10)
0520      INPUT "NEXT STUDENT'S NAME: ": N$
0530    ENDWHILE
0540 ENDPROC GETOPTIONS
0550 //
0560 PROC STARTPROGRAM
0570    OPEN FILE 2,"OPTIONS",READ
0580    READ FILE 2: MAX
0590    FOR I:=1 TO MAX DO
0600      READ FILE 2: NAME$(I)
0610      FOR J:=1 TO 4 DO READ FILE 2: OPTION(I,J)
0620    NEXT I
0630    CLOSE
0640 ENDPROC STARTPROGRAM
0650 //
0660 PROC STOPPROGRAM
0670    OPEN FILE 3,"@0:OPTIONS",WRITE
0680    WRITE FILE 3: MAX
0690    FOR I:=1 TO MAX DO
0700      WRITE FILE 3: NAME$(I)
0710      FOR J:=1 TO 4 DO WRITE FILE 3: OPTION(I,J)
0720    NEXT I
0730    CLOSE FILE 3
0740 ENDPROC STOPPROGRAM
```

Listing continued next page

ENTEROPTIONS *Continued from previous page*

```
0750 //
0760 PROC WINDOW(X,Y)
0780    EXEC SCREEN(X,1)
0790    FOR I:=1 TO Y-X+1 DO PRINT SPACES$
0800    EXEC SCREEN(X,1)
0810 ENDPROC WINDOW
0820 //
0830 PROC SCREEN(ROW,COL) CLOSED
0840    PRINT CHR$(19), //HOME
0850    FOR I:=1 TO ROW DO PRINT   //DOWN
0860    FOR I:=1 TO COL-1 DO PRINT CHR$(29), //RIGHT
0870 ENDPROC SCREEN
0880 //
```

NEWSHOP

```
0010 //UNCLE HANNIBAL'S NEW SHOP//
0020 //WRITTEN BY CHRIS BORGE//
0030 //FILE VERSION: NOV. 1981//
0040 //
0050 DIM NAME$ OF 30, ADRESS$ OF 20
0060 DIM TOWN$ OF 20, CODE$ OF 10
0070 DIM ARTICLE$(10) OF 20, PRICE(10)
0080 DIM TEXT$(10) OF 20, AMOUNT(10)
0090 DIM SPACES$ OF 40, QUANTITY(10)
0100 //*
0110 EXEC INITIALIZE
0120 REPEAT
0130    EXEC CUSTOMER
0140    EXEC GETORDER
0150    IF LINE<>0 THEN EXEC WRITEBILL
0160    INPUT "TYPE RETURN ": CODE$
0170 UNTIL THECOWSCOMEIN
0180 //*
0190 PROC INITIALIZE
0200    PRINT CHR$(147) //CLEAR SCREEN
0210    THECOWSCOMEIN:=FALSE
0220    I:=0; SPACES$(1:40):=""
0230    OPEN 2,"OFFER",READ
0240    REPEAT
0250       I:=I+1
0260       READ FILE 2: ARTICLE$(I),PRICE(I)
0270    UNTIL EOF(2) //END-OF-FILE//
0280    MAX:=I
0290    CLOSE
0300 ENDPROC INITIALIZE
```

Listing continued next page

NEWSHOP *Continued from previous page*

```
0310  //
0320  PROC CUSTOMER
0330     TOTAL:=0; LINE:=0
0340     //
0350     //STUD
0360     //
0370  ENDPROC CUSTOMER
0380  //
0390  PROC GETORDER
0400     EXEC MENU
0410     EXEC TAKEIN("ARTNO")
0420     WHILE NOT FINISHED DO
0430        LINE:=LINE+1
0440        EXEC TAKEIN("QUANTITY")
0450        EXEC INVOICELINE
0460        EXEC TAKEIN("ARTNO")
0470     ENDWHILE
0480  ENDPROC GETORDER
0490  //
0500  PROC INVOICELINE
0510     TEXT$(LINE):=ARTICLE$(ARTNO)
0520     AMOUNT(LINE):=PRICE(ARTNO)*QUANTITY(LINE)
0530     TOTAL:+AMOUNT(LINE)
0540  ENDPROC INVOICELINE
0550  //
0560  PROC WRITEBILL
0570     PRINT CHR$(147) //CLEAR SCREEN
0580     EXEC SCREEN(4,1)
0590     PRINT NAME$
0600     PRINT ADRESS$
0610     PRINT TOWN$," ",CODE$
0620     PRINT
0630     PRINT "QUANT.",TAB(10),"ARTICLE",TAB(30),"AMOUNT"
0640     PRINT "-------------------------------------------"
0650     FOR I:=1 TO LINE DO
0660        PRINT TAB(2),QUANTITY(I),
0670        PRINT TAB(9),TEXT$(I),
0680        PRINT TAB(32-LGTH(AMOUNT(I))),AMOUNT(I)
0690     NEXT I
0700     PRINT TAB(28),"---------"
0710     PRINT TAB(22),"TOTAL:",TAB(32-LGTH(TOTAL)),TOTAL
0720  ENDPROC WRITEBILL
0730  //
```

Listing continued next page

NEWSHOP   *Continued from previous page*

```
0740 PROC TAKEIN(KINDOF$)
0750    EXEC WINDOW(10,15)
0760    CASE KINDOF$ OF
0770    WHEN "ARTNO"
0780      REPEAT
0790        EXEC WINDOW(10,15)
0800        INPUT "> ": ARTNO
0810        OK:=(0<=ARTNO AND ARTNO<=MAX)
0820      UNTIL OK
0830      FINISHED:=(ARTNO=0)
0840    WHEN "QUANTITY"
0850      REPEAT
0860        EXEC SCREEN(ARTNO,20)
0870        INPUT QUANT
0880      UNTIL 0<QUANT AND INT(QUANT)=QUANT
0890      QUANTITY(LINE):=QUANT
0900    ENDCASE
0910 ENDPROC TAKEIN
0920 //
0930 PROC MENU
0940    PRINT CHR$(147)
0950    FOR I:=1 TO MAX DO
0960      PRINT I,". ",ARTICLE$(I)
0970    NEXT I
0980    PRINT "0. STOP"
0990 ENDPROC MENU
1000 //
1010 PROC WINDOW(X,Y)
1020    EXEC SCREEN(X,1)
1030    FOR LN:=1 TO Y-X+1 DO PRINT SPACES$
1040    EXEC SCREEN(X,1)
1050 ENDPROC WINDOW
1060 //
1070 PROC SCREEN(X,Y)
1080    PRINT CHR$(19),
1090    FOR LN:=1 TO X DO PRINT CHR$(17),
1100    FOR CH:=1 TO Y DO PRINT CHR$(29),
1110 ENDPROC SCREEN
1120 //
1130 FUNC LGTH(X)
1140    RETURN (X>1)+(X>10)+(X>100)+(X>1000)
1150 ENDFUNC LGTH
1160 //
```

ADDRPGR

```
0010 DIM NAME$ OF 30
0020 DIM ADDR$(2) OF 30
0030 DIM ANSW$ OF 10
0040 //
0050 PRINT CHR$(147) //CLEAR
0060 EXEC SCREEN(8,0)
0070 PRINT "1=ENTER ADDRESSES"
0080 PRINT "2=PRINT ADDRESSES"
0090 PRINT "3=STOP"
0100 PRINT
0110 INPUT "> ": JOB
0120 IF JOB=1 THEN EXEC ENTERADDR
0130 IF JOB=2 THEN EXEC PRINTADDR
0140 END
0150 //
0160 PROC ENTERADDR
0170    MORE:=TRUE
0180    OPEN 3,"@0:ADDRESSES",WRITE
0190    WHILE MORE DO EXEC TAKEIN
0200    CLOSE
0210 ENDPROC ENTERADDR
0220 //
0230 PROC TAKEIN
0240    PRINT CHR$(147) //CLEAR
0250    EXEC SCREEN(8,0)
0260    PRINT "NAME      :"
0270    PRINT "            _____"
0280    PRINT "ADDRESS   :"
0290    PRINT "            _____"
0300    PRINT "          :"
0310    PRINT "            _____"
0320    EXEC SCREEN(8,11)
0330    INPUT "": NAME$
0340    MORE:=(NAME$<>"")
0350    IF MORE THEN
0360      FOR J:=1 TO 2 DO
0370        EXEC SCREEN(8+2*J,11)
0380        INPUT "": ADDR$(J)
0390      NEXT J
0400      WRITE FILE 3: NAME$,ADDR$(1),ADDR$(2)
0410    ENDIF
0420 ENDPROC TAKEIN
```

Listing continued next page

ADDRPGR   *Continued from previous page*

```
0430 //
0440 PROC PRINTADDR
0450   OPEN 2,"ADDRESSES",READ
0460   REPEAT
0470     READ FILE 2: NAME$,ADDR$(1),ADDR$(2)
0480     PRINT CHR$(147)
0490     EXEC SCREEN(8,0)
0500     PRINT NAME$
0510     PRINT ADDR$(1)
0520     PRINT ADDR$(2)
0530     EXEC SCREEN(15,0)
0540     INPUT "PRESS RETURN ": ANSW$
0550   UNTIL EOF(2)
0560   CLOSE
0570   PRINT CHR$(147) //CLEAR
0580 ENDPROC PRINTADDR
0590 //
0600 PROC SCREEN(L,C)
0610   PRINT CHR$(19), //HOME
0620   FOR I:=1 TO L DO PRINT CHR$(17),
0630   FOR I:=1 TO C DO PRINT CHR$(29),
0640 ENDPROC SCREEN
0650 //
```

EXHIBITOPTIONS

```
0010 //PROGRAM: EXHIBITOPTIONS//
0020 DIM NAME$(15) OF 20, OPTION(15,4)
0030 DIM SUBJECT$(4) OF 12, N$ OF 20, A$ OF 3
0040 DIM SPACES$ OF 40
0050 //
0060 SPACES$(1:40):=""
0070 SUBJECT$(1):="BIOLOGY"
0080 SUBJECT$(2):="GERMAN"
0090 SUBJECT$(3):="INFORMATICS"
0100 SUBJECT$(4):="MUSIC"
0110 //
0120 EXEC STARTPROGRAM
0130 REPEAT
0140    PRINT CHR$(147) //CLEAR
0150    EXEC WINDOW(8,15)
0160    PRINT "1 = A STUDENT'S OPTIONS"
0170    PRINT "2 = DISTRIBUTION OF SUBJECTS"
0180    PRINT "3 = STOP PROGRAM"
0190    PRINT
0200    INPUT "ENTER JOB: ": JOB
0210    //
0220    IF JOB=1 THEN EXEC OPTIONS
0230    IF JOB=2 THEN EXEC DISTRIBUTION
0240    IF JOB=3 THEN STOP
0250 UNTIL FALSE
0260 //
0270 PROC OPTIONS
0280    EXEC WINDOW(8,20)
0290    INPUT "STUDENT'S NAME: ": N$
0300    I:=0; FOUND:=FALSE
0310    WHILE NOT (FOUND OR I=MAX) DO
0320      I:=I+1
0330      FOUND:=(N$=NAME$(I))
0340    ENDWHILE
0350    IF FOUND THEN
0360      PRINT
0370      PRINT N$,"'S OPTION:"
0380      PRINT
0390      FOR J:=1 TO 4 DO
0400        IF NOT OPTION(I,J)=-1 THEN
0410          PRINT SUBJECT$(J),TAB(15),"AT LEVEL ",OPTION(I,J)
0420        ENDIF
0430      NEXT J
0440      EXEC WINDOW(18,18)
0450      INPUT "PRESS RETURN TO CONT. ": A$
0460    ELSE
0470      EXEC WINDOW(1,1)
0480      PRINT "NO STUDENT WITH THAT NAME"
0490      INPUT "DO YOU WANT A LIST (Y/N)? ": A$
0500      IF A$="Y" THEN EXEC DISPLAY
0510    ENDIF
0520 ENDPROC OPTIONS
```

Listing continued next page

EXHIBIT OPTIONS *Continued from previous page*

```
0530 //
0540 PROC DISTRIBUTION
0550   REPEAT
0560     EXEC WINDOW(8,15)
0570     INPUT "ENTER SUBJECT: ": N$
0580     I:=0; OK:=FALSE
0590     WHILE NOT OK AND I<4 DO
0600       I:=I+1
0610       OK:=(N$=SUBJECT$(I))
0620     ENDWHILE
0630   UNTIL OK
0640   REPEAT
0650     INPUT "ENTER LEVEL: ": LEVEL
0660   UNTIL LEVEL=1 OR LEVEL=2
0670   PRINT CHR$(147) //CLEAR
0680   PRINT "THE FOLLOWING STUDENTS TAKE"
0690   PRINT N$," AT LEVEL ",LEVEL,":"
0700   PRINT
0710   FOR STNO:=1 TO MAX DO
0720     IF OPTION(STNO,I)=LEVEL THEN PRINT NAME$(STNO)
0730   NEXT STNO
0740   EXEC WINDOW(18,18)
0750   INPUT "PRESS RETURN TO CONT. ": A$
0760 ENDPROC DISTRIBUTION
0770 //
0780 PROC DISPLAY
0790   PRINT CHR$(147) //CLEAR
0800   FOR STNO:=1 TO MAX DO PRINT NAME$(STNO)
0810   EXEC WINDOW(18,18)
0820   INPUT "PRESS RETURN TO CONT. ": A$
0830 ENDPROC DISPLAY
0840 //
0850 PROC STARTPROGRAM
0860   OPEN FILE 2,"OPTIONS",READ
0870   READ FILE 2: MAX
0880   FOR I:=1 TO MAX DO
0890     READ FILE 2: NAME$(I)
0900     FOR J:=1 TO 4 DO READ FILE 2: OPTION(I,J)
0910   NEXT I
0920   CLOSE
0930 ENDPROC STARTPROGRAM
0940 //
0950 PROC WINDOW(X,Y)
0970   EXEC SCREEN(X,1)
0980   FOR I:=1 TO Y-X+1 DO PRINT SPACES$
0990   EXEC SCREEN(X,1)
1000 ENDPROC WINDOW
1010 //
1020 PROC SCREEN(ROW,COL) CLOSED
1030   PRINT CHR$(19), //HOME
1040   FOR I:=1 TO ROW DO PRINT  //DOWN
1050   FOR I:=1 TO COL-1 DO PRINT CHR$(29), //RIGHT
1060 ENDPROC SCREEN
1070 //
```

TEST 7.1

```
0010 //* PROGRAM: PEANUTS *//
0020 //-PREPARE TO PLAY-//
0030 PRINT CHR$(147) //CLEAR SCREEN//
0040 PRINT "NOW WE ARE GOING TO PLAY"
0050 PRINT "'PEANUTS'."
0060 PRINT "HOW MANY GAMES SHOULD WE PLAY",
0070 INPUT MAX
0080 PRINT
0090 PRINT "OK, HERE WE GO:"
0100 PRINT "IF YOU THINK I AM HOLDING"
0110 PRINT "AN ODD NUMBER OF PEANUTS"
0120 PRINT "THEN ENTER 1;"
0130 PRINT "BUT IF YOU THINK I AM HOLDING"
0140 PRINT "AN EVEN NUMBER OF PEANUTS"
0150 PRINT "THEN ENTER 0"
0160 PRINT
0170 COUNTWIN:=0
0180 //
0190 FOR GAME:=1 TO MAX DO
0200    //-THIS IS THE GAME ITSELF-//
0210    PRINT "WELL, WHAT IS YOUR GUESS (0,1)",
0220    INPUT GUESS
0230    STAKED:=RND(1,8)
0235    OUTCOME:=STAKED MOD 2
0240    PRINT
0250    //-ODD OR EVEN-//
0260    IF OUTCOME=0 THEN
0270      PRINT "I AM HOLDING ",STAKED," PEANUTS"
0280      PRINT "I.E. AN EVEN NUMBER, ",
0290    ELSE
0300      PRINT "I AM HOLDING ",STAKED," PEANUTS"
0310      PRINT "I.E. AN ODD NUMBER, ",
0320    ENDIF
0330    //-WHO WINS?-//
0340    IF OUTCOME=GUESS THEN
0350      PRINT "SO YOU WIN."
0360      PRINT "CONGRATULATIONS!"
0370      COUNTWIN:=COUNTWIN+STAKED
0380    ELSE
0390      PRINT "SO YOU LOOSE."
0400      PRINT "I AM SORRY!"
0405      COUNTWIN:=COUNTWIN-STAKED
0410    ENDIF
0420    PRINT
0430    IF GAME<MAX THEN PRINT "NEXT GAME:"
0440 NEXT GAME
```

Listing continued on next page

TEST 7.1   *Continued from previous page*

```
0450 //
0460 //-FINAL RESULT-//
0470 PRINT "THANKS FOR THE GAME!"
0480 IF COUNTWIN>0 THEN
0490   PRINT "YOU WIN ",COUNTWIN," PEANUT(S)."
0500 ELSE
0510   PRINT "YOU HAVE LOST ",-COUNTWIN," PEANUT(S)."
0520 ENDIF
0530 PRINT
0540 PRINT "COME AND PLAY SOME OTHER DAY."
0550 //-END OF PROGRAM: PEANUTS-//
```

Answers to selected exercises

Exercise 1.11

```
0010  PRINT  "XXXXXXXXXXXXXXXXXXXXXXXXXXXXXXXXXXXXXXXXXXXXXXXXXX"
0020  PRINT  "X                                                X"
0030  PRINT  "X   IT IS HEREBY ANNOUNCED THAT FOURTH FORM      X"
0040  PRINT  "X   PUPILS ARE NO LONGER PERMITTED TO EAT        X"
0050  PRINT  "X   CARROTS IN MY GARDEN DURING LUNCH HOUR.      X"
0060  PRINT  "X                                                X"
0070  PRINT  "X                            HEADMASTER.         X"
0080  PRINT  "X                                                X"
0090  PRINT  "XXXXXXXXXXXXXXXXXXXXXXXXXXXXXXXXXXXXXXXXXXXXXXXXXX"
```

Exercise 2.4

"PLEASE PAY"   AMOUNT   PLEASE PAY 35.95
"PLEASE PAY"   "POUNDS TO COVER EXPENSES."   AMOUNT
PLEASE PAY 34.55 POUNDS TO COVER EXPENSES.

Exercise 2.5

YOU MUST PAY 14.25 POUNDS INTO OUR ACCOUNT BEFORE 800301

Exercise 2.6

```
0010 INPUT AMOUNT
0020 INPUT DATE
0030 PRINT "PLEASE PAY ",AMOUNT," POUNDS BEFORE"
0040 PRINT "THE DATE ",DATE,". FAILURE TO DO SO"
0050 PRINT "WILL MEAN THAT YOUR BARROW WILL BE"
0060 PRINT "REMOVED WITHOUT FUTHER NOTICE."
0070 PRINT
0080 PRINT "                    A. MEANY,"
0090 PRINT "                    BARROW FACTORY, LTD."
0100 PRINT "                    WHEELEY."
```

Exercise 3.1

A TOTAL OF 20 ITEMS AT 12.85

Exercise 3.2

THE AREA IS 350

Exercise 3.4

700   175   875

Exercise 4.1

5 PRINT   "NUMBER OF LOOSE SCREWS",

Exercise 4.2

35   46   101
Its value is increased by 1.

Exercise 4.3

80   400   4   800   40

Exercise 4.5

NUMBER<20   Increased   300   1050

Exercises 4.5 *continued*

```
0010 PRINT "NUMBER OF UNITS    ",
0020 INPUT NUMBER
0030 PRINT "PRICE PER UNIT      ",
0040 INPUT PRICE
0050 PRINT
0060 PRINT
0070 AMOUNT:=NUMBER*PRICE
0080 IF AMOUNT<30 THEN
0090    AMOUNT:=AMOUNT*105/100
0100    PRINT "A DELIVERY CHARGE HAS BEEN ADDED"
0110    PRINT "TO THE TOTAL PRICE. THIS CHARGE"
0120    PRINT "IS 5 PCT. OF THE SELLING PRICE."
0130    PRINT "IF THE SELLING PRICE IS 30 POUNDS"
0140    PRINT "OR MORE, NO DELIVERY CHARGE IS MADE."
0150    PRINT
0160 ENDIF
0170 PRINT "TOTAL:            ",AMOUNT," POUNDS."
```

Exercise 4.6

15 is added to AMOUNT
70   100   70   100   70
60 and 70   90 and 100

Exercise 4.7

False   True   True   True   False   True   True

Exercise 4.9

```
0010 PRINT "ENTER TOTAL AMOUNT",
0020 INPUT TOTAL
0030 PRINT
0040 IF TOTAL<10 THEN
0050    PRINT "GRAND TOTAL:              ",TOTAL
0060    TOTAL:=TOTAL+.75
0070    PRINT "INCLUDING DELIVERY FEE:    ",TOTAL
0080    PRINT
0090    PRINT "SINCE THE GRAND TOTAL OF YOUR ORDER"
0100    PRINT "IS LESS THAN 10 POUNDS, A DELIVERY"
0110    PRINT "CHARGE OF 0.75 IS ADDED."
0120 ELSE
0130    PRINT "GRAND TOTAL:              ",TOTAL
0140    PRINT
0150    PRINT "DELIVERY FREE BY COURTESY OF ATHERTON & BRAMER.
0160 ENDIF
```

Exercise 5.1
5   10

Exercise 5.2
3   7
10 FOR VS:=1 TO 10 DO

Exercise 5.3
3   8   0   0
3   2   0   4   7
LASTTRIP–FIRSTTRIP+1

Exercise 5.4

```
0005 PRINT "LAST NUMBER, PLEASE",
0006 INPUT LAST
0010 FOR NO:=1 TO LAST DO
0020   PRINT "COUNT TO ",NO
0030 NEXT NO
0040 PRINT "DO NOT COUNT ON ME ANY MORE"
```

Exercise 5.5

```
0010 FOR I:=1 TO 5 DO PRINT "THIS WAS RUN NO. ",I
0020 PRINT "WHICH WAS THE FINAL RUN!"
```

Exercise 6.2
The line with the empty comment is 20.

Exercise 6.3
150   360   I   NUMBER   70
HOW MANY GAMES DO YOU LIKE TO PLAY?

Exercise 6.4
220–260   280–330   GUESS   0   190
OUTCOME:=RND(0, 1)   NUMBER   COUNTWIN

Exercise 6.5
1, 2, 3, 4, 5   10   10   1, 2, . . . , 12

Exercise 6.6

"THE RESULT WAS EVEN."
"THE RESULT WAS ODD."

"CONGRATULATIONS, YOU WIN."
"SORRY, YOU HAVE LOST."

Exercise 6.7

After the last round.
IF I<NUMBER THEN PRINT "HERE IS ANOTHER ROUND"

Exercise 6.8

0   increased by 1   GUESS=OUTCOME
It counts how many times you win.
AND I HAVE WON 2 ROUND(S).

Exercise 7.1

TAILS   HEADS   Heads or Tails.   12

Exercise 7.2

1, 2, 3, 4, 5, 6   Throwing a dice.   10

```
0005 SIXES:=0
0010 FOR GAME:=1 TO 10 DO
0020    OUTCOME:=RND(1,6)
0025    IF OUTCOME=6 THEN SIXES:=SIXES+1
0030    PRINT "THE NUMBER SHOWN IS ",OUTCOME
0040 NEXT GAME
0050 PRINT
0060 PRINT "END OF GAME."
0070 PRINT "NUMBER OF SIXES: ",SIXES
```

Exercise 7.4

1   0   0   1
If X MOD 2 is equal to 0, X is even, but if X MOD 2 is equal to 1, X is odd.

Exercise 7.5

25   5
55 PRINT "AN EVEN NUMBER CAME OUT ",COUNTEVEN," TIMES."

Exercise 7.7

MAX
STAKED:=RND (1,8)   8
235 OUTCOME:=STAKED MOD 2
405 COUNTWIN:=COUNTWIN−STAKED

I AM HOLDING 5 PEANUTS
I.E. AN ODD NUMBER,
SO YOU LOOSE.
I AM SORRY!

I AM HOLDING 3 PEANUTS
I.E. AN ODD NUMBER,
SO YOU WIN.
CONGRATULATIONS!

Exercise 7.9

3   4   −1   −3   3
False
YOU HAVE LOST 9 PEANUT(S).
COME AND PLAY SOME OTHER DAY.

Exercise 7.10

```
0010 PRINT "ENTER·X (INTEGER ONLY)       ",
0020 INPUT X
0030 PRINT "ENTER Y (POSITIVE INTEGER) ",
0040 INPUT Y
0050 Q:=X DIV Y; R:=X MOD Y
0060 PRINT X," = ",Y,"*",Q," + ",R
```


```
0010 PRINT "ENTER X (INTEGER ONLY)       ",
0020 INPUT X
0030 PRINT "ENTER Y (POSITIVE INTEGER) ",
0040 INPUT Y
0050 Q:=X DIV Y; R:=X MOD Y
0055 IF Q>=0 THEN
0060    PRINT X," = ",Y,"*",Q," + ",R
0070 ELSE
0080    PRINT X," = ",Y,"*(",Q,") + ",R
0090 ENDIF
```

Exercise 8.1

140, 370, and 450

Exercise 8.2

PROC INTRODUCTION   ENDPROC INTRODUCTION
260, 390.   410, 510.

Exercise 8.3

EXEC GAME   EXEC FINITO

Exercise 8.4

70–240   260–390   410–510

Exercise 8.5

RESULT and WINNER   340 and 350.

Exercise 9.1

10   1, 2, 3

Exercise 9.2

100   170   GUESS   90   120   140   110
TRYGUESS
NO, THAT IS NOT RIGHT,
I WAS THINKING OF 2
215
25 HITS:=0
70 PRINT "YOU HAVE MADE ",HITS," CORRECT GUESSES."

Exercise 9.4

160 and 290.

Exercise 9.5

180

IF GUESS=THINKOF THEN
UNTIL GUESS=THINKOF

NO, THAT IS NOT RIGHT,
TRY AGAIN!
WHAT NUMBER DO I THINK OF (1 . . 6)?

Exercise 9.5 *continued*

```
0010 PRINT CHR$(147) //CLEAR SCREEN//
0020 //
0030 FOR NO:=1 TO 5 DO
0040    GAME
0050    PRINT
0060 NEXT NO
0070 PRINT
0080 PRINT "NOW I'M TIRED OF THIS GAME!"
0090 //
0100 PROC GAME
0110    THINKOF:=RND(1,6)
0120    TRYGUESS
0130 ENDPROC GAME
0140 //
0150 PROC TRYGUESS
0160    REPEAT
0170      PRINT "WHAT NUMBER DO I THINK OF (1..6)",
0180      INPUT GUESS
0190      PRINT
0200      CONTROL
0290    UNTIL GUESS=THINKOF
0300 ENDPROC TRYGUESS
0310 //
0320 PROC CONTROL
0340    IF GUESS=THINKOF THEN
0350      PRINT "YES, I WAS THINKING OF ",THINKOF
0360      PRINT "WAS IT HARD TO GUESS?"
0370      FOR I:=1 TO 3 DO PRINT
0380      PRINT "!------------------------------------!"
0390    ELSE
0400      PRINT "NO, THAT IS NOT RIGHT,"
0410      PRINT "TRY AGAIN!"
0420    ENDIF
0430 ENDPROC CONTROL
0440 //
```

Exercise 9.7

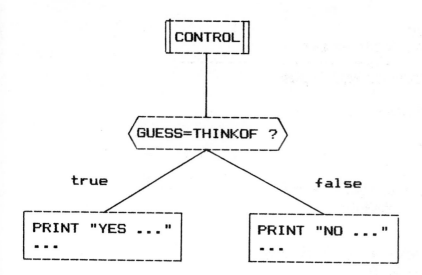

Exercise 10.1

A:=RND(1,5);   B:=RND(1,5)
70   8

Exercise 10.2

130 and 180   200 and 240   260 and 270
CONTROL

Exercise 10.6

```
0010 PRINT CHR$(147) //CLEAR SCREEN//
0020 //
0030 PRINT "HOW MANY EXERCISES",
0040 INPUT MAXNO
0042 PRINT "WHAT SHOULD LARGEST FACTOR BE",
0044 INPUT MAXFAC
0050 FOR NO:=1 TO MAXNO DO
0060    A:=RND(1,MAXFAC); B:=RND(1,MAXFAC)
0070    RESULT:=A*B
0080    EXERCISE
0090    GETANSWER
0100    CONTROL
0110 NEXT NO
```
Listing continued on next page

Exercise 10.6 *continued*

```
0120 //
0130 PROC EXERCISE
0140    FOR I:=1 TO 3 DO PRINT
0150    PRINT "----------------------------"
0160    PRINT "EXERCISE NO. ",NO
0170    PRINT
0180 ENDPROC EXERCISE
0190 //
0200 PROC GETANSWER
0210    C:=0
0220    REPEAT
0230      PRINT A," * ",B," = ",
0240      INPUT "": ANSWER
0250      C:=C+1
0260      PRINT
0270    UNTIL ANSWER=RESULT OR C=3
0280 ENDPROC GETANSWER
0290 //
0300 PROC CONTROL
0310    IF ANSWER=RESULT THEN
0320      PRINT "THAT'S CORRECT!"
0330    ELSE
0340      PRINT "YOUR ANSWER IS NOT CORRECT;"
0350      PRINT
0360      PRINT A," * ",B," = ",RESULT
0370    ENDIF
0380 ENDPROC CONTROL
0390 //
```

Exercise 10.7

1000, 1010, 1020, 1030, etc.
15, 17, 19, 21, etc.

Exercise 11.1

Name, Street, and Town.

Exercise 11.2

60, 100, 120, and 140   80

Exercise 11.3

20   15

Exercise 11.4

33   25

The string variable NAME$ cannot hold more than 25 characters at most.

Exercise 11.5

The string variables have been declared to hold more characters.
4   210   HOUSENO   STREET$

Exercise 11.6

SENDER$, DATE$, RECIPIENT$, and ANSW$
The three last should be marked.
"HANNIBAL"   220 and 330   130

Exercise 12.1

16   Lorentsen, Hans Joergen   Hansen, Pia
12   13   1, 10, 18, and 20.
ENOKSEN, HANS HENRIK   RIEMKE, BJARNE

Exercise 12.2

10   320   "N"
ARTICLE NO. 3: SOAP FLAKES
ARTICLE NO. 9: LIVER SAUSAGE
NO ARTICLE WITH THAT NUMBER!

Exercise 12.3

PUPIL$ 10   30
NAME$ ANSW$ JOB$
170 and 290   310 and 360   380 and 480
90   100   110   JOB$
"ENTRY", "LIST", and "REQUEST"
"N"   MORE JOBS (Y/N)?
220   NAME$<>" "

Exercise 12.4

PUPIL$(NO):=" "   PUPIL$(NO):=NAME$

```
0010 DIM PUPIL$(10) OF 30, NAME$ OF 30
0020 DIM ANSW$ OF 10, JOB$ OF 5
0030 //
0040 REPEAT   //MAIN LOOP//
0050    CLEAR(5)
0060    PRINT "WHAT JOB (ENTRY,LIST,REQUEST,ERASE)",
0070    INPUT JOB$
0080    //POINT OUT JOB//
0090    IF JOB$="ENTRY" THEN TAKEIN
0100    IF JOB$="LIST" THEN PRINTALL
0110    IF JOB$="REQUE" THEN PRINTONE
0115    IF JOB$="ERASE" THEN ERASE
0120    PRINT CHR$(19) //HOME
0130    PRINT "MORE JOBS (Y/N)",
0140    INPUT ANSW$
0150 UNTIL ANSW$="N"
0160 //
0170 PROC TAKEIN
0180    CLEAR(5)
0190    REPEAT
0200      PRINT "NAME",
0210      INPUT NAME$
0220      IF NAME$<>"" THEN
0230        PRINT "NUMBER",
0240        INPUT NO
0250        CONTROL
0260      ENDIF
0270      PRINT
0280    UNTIL NAME$=""
0290 ENDPROC TAKEIN
0300 //
0310 PROC PRINTALL
0320    CLEAR(5) //CLEAR SCREEN
0330    FOR NO:=1 TO 10 DO
0340      PRINT NO,": ",PUPIL$(NO)
0350    NEXT NO
0360 ENDPROC PRINTALL
```

Listing continued on next page

Exercise 12.4 *continued*

```
0370 //
0380 PROC PRINTONE
0390    CLEAR(5)
0400    PRINT "NUMBER",
0410    INPUT NO
0420    IF PUPIL$(NO)<>"" THEN
0430      PRINT "THE PUPILS NAME IS ",PUPIL$(NO)
0440    ELSE
0450      PRINT "NO PUPIL WITH THAT NUMBER!"
0460      PRINT "HAVE A LIST PRINTED (LIST)."
0470    ENDIF
0480 ENDPROC PRINTONE
0490 //
0500 PROC CLEAR(X)
0510    PRINT CHR$(147), //CLEAR
0520    FOR I:=1 TO X DO PRINT   //X DOWN
0530 ENDPROC CLEAR
0540 //
0550 PROC CONTROL
0560    IF PUPIL$(NO)="" THEN
0570      PUPIL$(NO):=NAME$
0580    ELSE   //THE ELEMENT IS IN USE
0590      PRINT "THAT NUMBER IS OCCUPIED!"
0600    ENDIF
0610 ENDPROC CONTROL
0620 //
0630 PROC ERASE
0640    PRINT "PUPILS NUMBER",
0650    INPUT NO
0660    IF PUPIL$(NO)="" THEN
0670      PRINT "NO PUPIL WITH THAT NUMBER!"
0680    ELSE
0690      PRINT "YOU ASK ME TO ERASE ",PUPIL$(NO)
0700      PRINT "IS THAT CORRECT (Y/N)",
0710      INPUT ANSW$
0720      IF ANSW$="Y" THEN PUPIL$(NO):=""
0730    ENDIF
0740 ENDPROC ERASE
0750 //
```

Exercise 12.5

See program listing for 12.4

Exercise 13.2

FRUIT$ 6   10
TOKEN$, F1$, F2$, and F3$
240, 320   340, 490
F1$:=FRUIT$(RND(1,6))   No
"PLUM"   "PEAR"   "LEMON"   "APPLE"
PEAR   BANANA   PLUM
All three   Two of them
TOKEN$="N"

Exercise 13.3

30   250   400   460
32   30   2   580   405

Exercise 13.4

```
0010 DIM FRUIT$(8) OF 10, TOKEN$ OF 1
0020 DIM F1$ OF 10, F2$ OF 10, F3$ OF 10
0025 DIM NAME$ OF 30
0030 WINNINGS:=0; STAKED:=0
0040 //
0050 FRUIT$(1):="APPLE"
0060 FRUIT$(2):="PEAR"
0070 FRUIT$(3):="PLUM"
0080 FRUIT$(4):="BANANA"
0090 FRUIT$(5):="LEMON"
0100 FRUIT$(6):="GRAPE"
0102 FRUIT$(7):="STRAWBERRY"
0104 FRUIT$(8):="BLACKBERRY"
0110 //
0120 CLEAR(4)
0121 PRINT "WHAT IS YOUR NAME",
0122 INPUT NAME$
0123 CLEAR(4)
0130 PRINT "HERE WE GO! TO INSERT A COIN"
0140 PRINT "IN THE SLOT, PRESS 'RETURN'."
0150 PRINT "TO STOP, PRESS 'N' AND 'RETURN'."
0160 REPEAT
0170    PRINT
0180    PRINT "INSERT A COIN",
0190    INPUT TOKEN$
0200    IF TOKEN$="N" THEN ADIEU
0210    THE'GAME
0220 UNTIL FALSE //FOREVER//
```

Listing continued on next page

Exercise 13.4 *continued*

```
0230 //
0240 PROC THE'GAME
0250    STAKED:=STAKED+1
0260    F1$:=FRUIT$(RND(1,8))
0270    F2$:=FRUIT$(RND(1,8))
0280    F3$:=FRUIT$(RND(1,8))
0290    CLEAR(5)
0300    PRINT F1$,TAB(15),F2$,TAB(30),F3$
0310    RESULT
0320 ENDPROC THE'GAME
0330 //
0340 PROC RESULT
0350    FOR I:=1 TO 3 DO PRINT   //3 DOWN
0360    IF F1$=F2$ AND F2$=F3$ THEN
0370       BELL(7)
0380       PRINT "HURRAH! H U R R A H!  H  U  R  R  A  H!!"
0390       PRINT "YOU HAVE WON 50 COINS!!!"
0400       WINNINGS:=WINNINGS+50
0410    ELSE
0420       IF F1$=F2$ OR F2$=F3$ THEN
0430          BELL(2)
0440          PRINT "FINE!"
0450          PRINT "YOU HAVE WON 2 COINS!"
0460          WINNINGS:=WINNINGS+2
0470       ENDIF
0480    ENDIF
0490 ENDPROC RESULT
0500 //
0510 PROC ADIEU
0520    CLEAR(5)
0530    PROFIT:=WINNINGS-STAKED
0531    PRINT "DEAR ",NAME$
0532    PRINT
0533    PRINT "THANKS FOR THE GAME."
0534    PRINT "YOU STAKED ",STAKED," COINS, BUT YOU WON ",WINNINGS,","
0535    IF PROFIT>=0 THEN
0540       PRINT "SO YOU HAVE MADE ",PROFIT," COINS PROFIT ON THIS GAME."
0545       PRINT "CONGRATULATIONS!"
0550    ELSE
0555       PRINT "SO YOU HAVE LOST ",-PROFIT," COINS ON THIS GAME."
0560       PRINT "BETTER LUCK NEXT TIME."
0565    ENDIF
0580    STOP   //STOP THE PROGRAM
0590 ENDPROC ADIEU
0600 //
0610 PROC CLEAR(X)
0620    PRINT CHR$(147),  //CLEAR
0630    FOR I:=1 TO X DO PRINT   //X DOWN
0640 ENDPROC CLEAR
0650 //
0660 PROC BELL(X)
0670    FOR I:=1 TO X DO PRINT CHR$(7),
0680 ENDPROC BELL
0690 //
```

Exercise 14.1

7   650–710   100
READ TEXT$,WORD$

Exercise 14.2

READ TEXT$,WORD$
EXEC DISPLAY (or simply: DISPLAY)
EXEC GETANSWER (or simply: GETANSWER)
EXEC CONTROL (or simply: CONTROL)
ANSW$=WORD$ OR ATTEMPTS=3
480   "WE"
TRY TO START LIKE THIS: – SA

THE CORRECT PAST TENSE IS

          –SANG–

TRY TO REMEMBER!

Exercise 15.1

WHAT IS YOUR NAME?
ENTER TYPE (ADD,SUB,MUL,DIV)?
ENTER LEVEL (1,2,3)?

Exercise 15.2

490, 640   530, 560, and 590
540   30   570 and 600.
TYPE$ and LEVEL   3

Exercise 15.3

By entering a 1, 2, or 3.

Exercise 15.4

220   270
280, 310, and 340   380

Exercise 15.6

670   680, 700, and 730   750
NO SUCH LEVEL OF EXERCISES!
MOST PEOPLE HAVE BOTH A FIRST NAME
AND A SURNAME. PLEASE GIVE BOTH!

Exercise 15.7

240   500   COLOUR$ String variable
250, 280, 320, and 370
"PINK"   "PALE", "BLUE", and "YELLOW"   "YELLOW"

Exercise 15.8

1020, 1110   TYPE$
"ADD", "SUB", "MUL", and "DIV"
WHEN "ADD", "SUB"
WHEN "MUL", "DIV"

Exercise 16.1

The program is stopped, and an error message is displayed.
An error message is displayed, but then the request for an input is repeated.

Exercise 16.3

70, 100   1, 3, 1, 0, 0, 1

Exercise 16.4

The error message is system dependent

Exercise 16.5

The first and the last part of a letter is not controlled by the CASE structure.

Exercise 17.1

Press the fire alarm.
The hour of the day.

Exercise 17.2

TYPE$ and SIGN$ 30   3   1
MAXNO:=10, BASE:=30, THISNAME:=1, THISTYPE:=2, THISLEVEL:=3
PROC TAKEIN(MATTER)
[EXEC] TAKEIN(THISNAME)
[EXEC] TAKEIN(THISTYPE)
[EXEC] TAKEIN(THISLEVEL)
490   780   630   660
510, 670, and 800
530–540, 620–630
560–570, 620–630
590–600, 620–630

Exercise 17.3

T   RESULT, N1, and N2

Exercise 17.4

N   NUMBER
After the procedure is finished, the parameter NUMBER is not known anymore.

Exercise 17.5

6, 7, and 9	FIRST and LAST
500: 8 and 12	790: 1 and 2 1710: 7 and 15
FIRST and 1	ROW and COL

Exercise 17.6

False, False, False, True, True

Exercise 17.7

ENTER TYPE (ADD,SUB,MUL,DIV)?
TYPE$ 0   False   0   False
430   False   True
NO SUCH TYPE OF EXERCISE!   ENTRY

Exercise 17.8

530–540, 820, 830, 530–540, 560–570, 850, 560–570, 850,
870, 880, 560–570, 590–600, 910, 590–600
ENTRY, CONTROL, ERROR, WINDOW, TAKEIN

Exercise 18.2

Is used as case-selector   900
"PUPILNO", "PUPILNAME", and "CLASS"
OK and LACKING   False, True   610
NOT (THISNAME$=" " OR PUPILNO=MAX)
THISNAME$=" "   PUPILNO=MAX

```
0610    PUPILNO:=0
0620    TAKEIN("PUPILNAME")
0625    REPEAT
0627      PUPILNO:=PUPILNO+1
0630      IF NOT (THISNAME$="" OR PUPILNO>MAX) THEN
0640        NAME$(PUPILNO):=THISNAME$
0660        TAKEIN("PUPILNAME")
0665      ENDIF
0670    UNTIL THISNAME$="" OR PUPILNO=MAX
```

Exercise 19.2

ARTICLE$ – string – 10	PRICE – numeric –10
TEXT$ – string – 10	AMOUNT – numeric – 10
QUANTITY – numeric – 10	

Exercise 19.3

3   1, 2, 3   1, 3, 6
"HONEY ROAST HAM", "DANISH BACON", "CREAM CHEESE"
2.29, 1.99, and 1.38   2, 1, and 2
4.58, 1.99, and 2.76   4.58, 6.57, and 9.33
4   "ARTNO" and "QUANTITY"
[EXEC] WINDOW(10,15)
INPUT "> ": ARTNO
OK:=(0<=ARTNO AND ARTNO<=MAX)

Exercise 19.5

QUANT   ARTICLE   AMOUNT

. . . . .10 . . . . .30. . . . .
2, 1, 3, and 0   31, 30, and 32

Exercise 20.1

4, 2, 0   0, 4, 2   1, 3, 4   2, 4   3
1 – Math,   3 – French,   4 – English

Exercise 20.2

100   SUBJ$ 3   11
"ENGLISH", "MATHEMATICS", and "FRENCH"
710, 760   PUPILNO and SUBJNO   −1 and " "
ENGLISH: 3
MATHEMATICS: 4
FRENCH: 2

Exercise 20.4

"FISH", "DOVE", "HORSE"
YOURWORD$<>MYWORD$(I) AND I<5
True, True, True, False   True, False   True, True, False

Exercise 20.5

1   "ENGLISH"   1, 0, 3, 3, 2   3, 1, 4, 4   1, 1, 0
WHILE ANSW$<>SUBJ$(I) AND I<3 DO I:=I+1

Exercise 20.7

The empty string
IF NAME$(PUPILNO)<>" "   600

Exercise 21.1

```
25      NAME$(PUPILNO)<>" "
FOR SUBJNO:=1 TO 3 DO
   PRINT SUBJ$(SUBJNO),":",
   PRINT TAB(25) ,MARK(PUPILNO,SUBJNO)
NEXT SUBJNO
```

Exercise 22.1

It has been replaced by the empty string
Nothing has happened to the marks

Exercise 22.3

```
[EXEC] TAKEIN("PUPILNO")
[EXEC] DISPLAY
INPUT "CORRECTIONS (YES/NO)? ":ANSW$
ANSW$="YES"
385, 464 468
```

Exercise 22.6

Otherwise you cannot get out of TAKEIN
KEYOK:=(KEY=725070)

Exercise 23.1

RECIPIENT$, 30	SENDER$, 30	DATE$, 20	ANSW$, 10
80 130 90			
RECIPIENT$ 360 and 370			
"ELIZA" False "MAX" True 230 4			

Exercise 23.5

```
OPEN FILE 3, "@0:XMAS",WRITE
WRITE FILE 3: RECIPIENT$
```
The empty string   3

Exercise 23.7

READ ARTICLE$ (I),PRICE(I)

```
0225 OPEN FILE 2,"OFFER",READ
0250 READ FILE 2: ARTICLE$(I),PRICE(I)
0260 UNTIL EOF(2)
0265 CLOSE
```

Exercise 23.7 *continued*

```
DIM ARTICLE$ OF 20
OPEN FILE 3,"@0:OFFER",WRITE
INPUT "NAME OF ARTICLE: ": ARTICLE$
WHILE ARTICLE$<>"" DO
   INPUT "PRICE:              ": PRICE
   WRITE FILE 3: ARTICLE$,PRICE
   INPUT "NAME OF ARTICLE: ": ARTICLE$
ENDWHILE
CLOSE
```

Exercise 24.1

230, 290
"MINCHED PORK", 1.22, "METTWURST", 1.56   No

Exercise 24.2

80, 150   90, 140   WRITECARD
Each time a name has been picked up
In "NEWSHOP" you do not know in what order the items are going to be used.
In "XMASFILE", however, names are used in the same order in which they are retrieved.

Exercise 24.3

NAME$ and ADDR$

```
0010 DIM NAME$ OF 30
0020 DIM ADDR$(2) OF 30
0030 DIM ANSW$ OF 10
0040 //
0050 PRINT CHR$(147) //CLEAR
0060 SCREEN(8,0)
0070 PRINT "1=ENTER ADDRESSES"
0080 PRINT "2=PRINT ADDRESSES"
0090 PRINT "3=STOP"
0100 PRINT
0110 INPUT "> ": JOB
0120 IF JOB=1 THEN ENTERADDR
0130 IF JOB=2 THEN PRINTADDR
0140 END
0150 //
0160 PROC ENTERADDR
0170    MORE:=TRUE
0180    OPEN FILE 3,"@0:ADDRESSES",WRITE
0190    WHILE MORE DO TAKEIN
0200    CLOSE
0210 ENDPROC ENTERADDR
0220 //
0230 PROC TAKEIN
0240    PRINT CHR$(147) //CLEAR
0250    SCREEN(8,0)
0260    PRINT "NAME      : "
0270    PRINT "          ------------------------------"
0280    PRINT "ADDRESS   : "
0290    PRINT "          ------------------------------"
0300    PRINT "          : "
0310    PRINT "          ------------------------------"
0320    SCREEN(8,11)
0330    INPUT "": NAME$
0340    MORE:=(NAME$<>"")
0350    IF MORE THEN
0360      FOR J:=1 TO 2 DO
0370        SCREEN(8+2*J,11)
0380        INPUT "": ADDR$(J)
0390      NEXT J
0400      WRITE FILE 3: NAME$,ADDR$(1),ADDR$(2)
0410    ENDIF
0420 ENDPROC TAKEIN
```

Listing continued next page

Exercise 24.3 *continued*

```
0430 //
0440 PROC PRINTADDR
0450    OPEN FILE 2,"ADDRESSES",READ
0451    INPUT "ADDRESS NO? ": NO
0452    I:=0
0460    REPEAT
0461       I:=I+1
0470       READ FILE 2: NAME$,ADDR$(1),ADDR$(2)
0471    UNTIL I=NO OR EOF(2)
0472    IF I=NO THEN
0480       PRINT CHR$(147)
0490       SCREEN(8,0)
0500       PRINT NAME$
0510       PRINT ADDR$(1)
0520       PRINT ADDR$(2)
0530       SCREEN(15,0)
0540       INPUT "PRESS RETURN ": ANSW$
0550    ENDIF
0560    CLOSE
0570    PRINT CHR$(147) //CLEAR
0580 ENDPROC PRINTADDR
0590 //
0600 PROC SCREEN(L,C)
0610    PRINT CHR$(19), //HOME
0620    FOR I:=1 TO L DO PRINT CHR$(17),
0630    FOR I:=1 TO C DO PRINT CHR$(29),
0640 ENDPROC SCREEN
0650 //
```

Exercise 24.4

NAME$ and MARK   2
NAME$(3), "MAX BRAMER"   MARK(3,1), 5
MARK(3,2) , 5   MARK(3,3) , 2

Exercise 24.5

```
1320 FOR I:=1 TO MAX DO READ FILE 2: NAME$(I)
1330 FOR I:=1 TO MAX DO
1340    FOR J:=1 TO 3 DO READ FILE 2: MARK(I,J)
1350 NEXT I
```

Exercise 24.7

```
0010 OPEN FILE 2,"ᗱO:PUPILS",WRITE
0015 WRITE FILE 2: MAX
0020 FOR I:=1 TO MAX DO WRITE FILE 2: NAME$(I)
0030 CLOSE
0040 OPEN FILE 2,"ᗱO:MARKS",WRITE
0050 FOR I:=1 TO MAX DO
0060    FOR J:=1 TO 3 DO WRITE FILE 2: MARK(I,J)
0070 NEXT I
0080 CLOSE
```

```
0010 OPEN FILE 2,"PUPILS",READ
0015 READ FILE 2: MAX
0020 FOR I:=1 TO MAX DO READ FILE 2: NAME$(I)
0030 CLOSE
0040 OPEN FILE 2,"MARKS",READ
0050 FOR I:=1 TO MAX DO
0060    FOR J:=1 TO 3 DO READ FILE 2: MARK(I,J)
0070 NEXT I
0080 CLOSE
```

Answers to self-tests

Test 1.1

Line number, statement   PRINT
"HE CAME ROLLING HOME."   no

Test 1.2

RUN   LIST   NEW
LOAD "JACOB"

Test 1.3

15 PRINT
24 PRINT "SHE SAYS SHE IS FINE."
28 PRINT
DEL 30–40

Test 2.1

INPUT   SIZE   ?
Type in a number and then press the RETURN-key.

Test 2.2

DATE   ACCOUNT   10 and 20
791501   65.75
40, 90   25   2
30, 50, 70, and 110

Test 2.3

INPUT   PRINT   overwritten

Test 2.4

10

Test 3.1

50   assignments   QUANTITY, TYPE, and PRICE
34.85

Test 3.2

assignment sign   expression   +, −, *, /

Test 3.3

60   90   (LONGSIDE + SHORTSIDE) * HIGHT/2

Test 3.4

NUMBER and PRICE   50   DISCOUNT
NUMBER and TOTAL   NUMBER   40 and 50   50
35 STRIPED TOMCATS.
TOTAL, EXCLUSIVE OF VAT, IS: 300

Test 3.5

Legal names are:
   NUMBER, MAXVALUE, MAX67, JOHN, PETER, AGENT007
Note. Some versions of COMAL will allow identifier names to hold up to 80 characters
      (CBM and Metanic). In these versions COCKLESANDMUSSELS is also legal.

Test 4.1

?   ARTICLENO
ENTER ARTICLE NUMBER?   ARTICLENO
It is not put in double quotes.

Test 4.2

?   PRINT "HOW MANY EXERCISES",

Test 4.3

107, 210, 12.32, 17, −25.5

Test 4.4

LOAN   1000 in line 40, 0.25 in line 50, 0.30 in line 70
LOAN> 1000
IN ONE YEAR YOU OWE ME 2500 POUNDS

Test 4.5

numeric   truth

Test 5.1

a program file

Test 5.2

GIVE ME 1 MINUTE MORE
GIVE ME 2 MINUTES MORE
GIVE ME 3 MINUTES MORE
GIVE ME 4 MINUTES MORE
NO, I AM NOT WAITING ANY LONGER.

Test 5.3

10, 5, 11, 0

Test 5.4

2, 5, 10, 17, 26

Test 5.5

WHAT TABLE DO YOU WANT TO PRACTICE?   T, FIRST, LAST
4 + 3 = ...
4 + 4 = ...
4 + 5 = ..., etc.

Test 5.6

1

Test 6.1

  5 //SMALL POEM ABOUT GIRLS WITH FRECKLES
110 //END OF POEM WRITING PROGRAM

Test 6.2

```
        FOR N:=1 TO 5 DO
```

```
Y:=N*N+1                    PRINT Y
```

Test 6.3

5, 6, 7, 8, 9, 10   Random numbers

Test 7.1

190   440   NEXT GAME
STAKED:=RND(1,8), OUTCOME:=STAKED MOD 2
COUNTWIN:=COUNTWIN+STAKED; COUNTWIN:=COUNTWIN−STAKED
OUTCOME=0, OUTCOME=GUESS
GAME< MAX

I AM HOLDING 4 PEANUTS
I.E, AN EVEN NUMBER,
SO YOU WIN
CONGRATULATIONS!
NEXT GAME

I AM HOLDING 4 PEANUTS
I.E. AN EVEN NUMBER,
SO YOU LOSE
I AM SORRY!

Test 8.1

A procedure   head   tail   body
[EXEC] PRINTOUT

Test 8.2

TAKEIN, PRINTOUT, KINDLETTER, and RUDELETTER
90, 100   1, 0   300

```
                    PRINTOUT


PRINT "...",DATE$                  LEVEL=1


            RUDELETTER              KINDLETTER
```

Test 8.3

60–70, 170–180, 190–200, 210–220, 280, 380, 400, 410, 420, 440, 450, 120–130,
170–180, 190–200, 210–220, 280, 490, 510, 520, 530, 540, 560, 120–130

Test 9.1

5

NOW T IS EQUAL TO 1
NOW T IS EQUAL TO 2
NOW T IS EQUAL TO 3
NOW T IS EQUAL TO 4
NOW T IS EQUAL TO 5
T TIME IS OUT

0   50, 60   80

Test 9.2

3
P:=1
REPEAT
   PRINT "NO PARKING ON THIS REFUGE."
   P:=P+1
UNTIL P> 3

Test 10.1

5, 25, 125, 625

Test 10.2

10, 20, 25, 18

Test 10.3

5, 10, 15, 20

Test 10.4

2025

Test 11.1

string variables   the number of characters it holds
PETER DAVID JOHN MARMALADE–SP

Test 11.2

"WHAT DATE IS TODAY (MM/DD/YY)"   DATE$ 29
By typing it in from the keyboard
No DIM statement is shown (no declaration is shown)

Test 11.3

declared

Test 12.1

5   10   index   variable   expression
YELLOW, BLUE   RED, BLUE   2

Test 12.2

the empty string   ·   press the RETURN-key

Test 13.1

THIS IS RUN NO. 0

Test 13.2

6

Test 14.1

130   150, 160, and 170   data queue
13   10
"ACE", "TWO", "FIVE", "KNIGHT", "SEVEN", "QUEEN"

Test 14.2

CARD$:=CARD$+" OF "+COLOUR$(RND(1,4))
CARD$ " OF "   COLOUR$

Test 14.3

11, 2   5,2   7, 4   12, 4   5, 1   1, 1
It is used to prevent the same card from being drawn twice.

Test 15.1

"GREEN", 3   "YELLOW", 2   "RED", 1.5
"GREEN", 3   "BLUE", 9

Test 15.2

GREEN   4, 10, 13

Test 15.3

<pre>
                        WHEEL

OUTCOME:=RND(1,15)   CASE OUTCOME OF
    1,3,6,9,12,15   4,10,13   7
COLOR$:="RED"   COLOR$:="GREEN"
FACTOR:=1.5   FACTOR:=3
            2,5,8,11,14
              COLOR$:="YELLOW"   COLOR$:="BLUE"
              FACTOR:=2   FACTOR:=9
</pre>

Test 16.1

I<= 5   6   1, 2, 3, 4, 5

Test 16.2

I>5   6   1, 2, 3, 4, 5

Test 16.3

WE HAVE PACKED 0 EGG TRAY(S),
AND LEFT OVER −8 EGG(S).
20.5   20.5 is a positive number

Test 16.4

330–340, 420–430, 710, 600–610, 640, 330–340, 420–430, 710, 560, 570, 580, 640,
330–340, 370, 380–390, 420–430, 460, 470, 480–490, 710, 560, 570, 580, 640

Test 17.1

110 and 130   NUMERATOR1, NUMERATOR2
DENOMINATOR1, DENOMINATOR2   A, B   actual
5   2, 3, 4, 5   2, 3, 4, 5

Test 17.2

"MARY", "HANNIBAL"   6   True
FOUND AS NUMBER 6
MORE (Y/N)?
8   False
PERSON NOT FOUND
MORE (Y/N)?
102–130, 200, 240–250, 120–130, 220, 240–250, 120–130, 200, 240–250   2, 8, 5

Test 18.1

NAME$, 5, 20   TRADE$, 5, 10   60–100   120, 270
ANSW$="N"   260

Test 18.2

In the two arrays NAME$ and TRADE$
no   180–200, 220   190, 200
PERSON NUMBER 3
IS CALLED ROY MANNING
AND IS A MECHANIC
NO PERSON WITH THAT NUMBER

Test 18.3

140–150, 180, 190, 200, 250–260, 140–150, 220, 250–260
140–150, 180, 190, 200, 250–260

Test 19.1

5, 20   TEL, 5   N$, 20   N$ NAME$
I:=0
REPEAT
   I:=I+1
     FOUND:=N$=NAME$(I)
UNTIL FOUND OR I=5
3
ROY MANNING HAS TELEPHONE NUMBER 346712
5, FALSE
BRIAN MEEK HAS NO TELEPHONE
NO TALK
NO TALK HAS NO TELEPHONE
"NAME: "   a prompt

Test 19.2

180–200   N$=NAME$ OR EOD   no more data
Sets the data-pointer back to first element in the queue

Test 19.3

3, 81, 15, −7, −8, −24
The integer part of X

Test 19.4

```
S I M O N    H A R R I S                    1 7 9
. . . . . . . . . . . . . . . . . . . . . . . . . . . . . .
        5          10         15         20         25         30


        S I M O N    H A R R I S                              1 7 9
. . . . . . . . . . . . . . . . . . . . . . . . . . . . . .
        5          10         15         20         25         30
```

Test 20.1

NAME$, 10, 20   PERSDATA, 10, 3   5   10
hight, weight
"ROY MANNING", 45, 176, 75, "MINNA JACOBS", 43, 172, 0
PERSDATA(4,2), PERSDATA(5,2)
PERSDATA(4,1)
PERSDATA(3,3)

Test 20.2

160, 190
To prevent illegal input
ERROR! ONLY 1 . . 5 MAY BE USED
ENTER NUMBER:

(Use dotted line below as a gauge with the following):

```
P E T E R    B R O W N
A G E :                          3 8
H I G H T :                      1 7 2
W E I G H T :                    6 8


M O R E    R E Q U E S T S    ( Y / N ) ?


1 2 3 4 5
1        2          3          4          5
. . . . . . . . . . . . . . . . . . . . . . . . . . . . . .
        5          10         15         20         25         30
```

Test 20.3

```
READ NAME$, TEL
WHILE NOT (N$=NAME$ OR EOD) DO READ NAME$, TEL
```

Test 20.4

```
FOR I:=1 TO 4 DO
   FOR J:=1 TO 3 DO PRINT TABLE(I,J)
NEXT I
```

Test 21.1

Type in the programs and run them to check your answer

Test 21.2

On the printer, on the printer, on the screen

Test 21.3

```
0030 DIM NAME$(5) OF 20
0040 DIM TRADE$(5) OF 10
0050 DIM ANSW$ OF 3, ENTRY$ OF 10
0060 NAME$(1):="PETER BROWN"; TRADE$(1):="JOINER"
0070 NAME$(2):="JOHN SMITH"; TRADE$(2):="ELECTRICIAN"
0080 NAME$(3):="ROY MANNING"; TRADE$(3):="MECHANIC"
0090 NAME$(4):="ELIZA MOOR"; TRADE$(4):="TEACHER"
0100 NAME$(5):="MINNA JACOBS"; TRADE$(5):="CAB DRIVER"
0110 //
0120 REPEAT   //REQUESTS
0130    PRINT CHR$(147) //CLEAR
0140    PRINT "ENTER TRADE",
0150    INPUT ENTRY$
0160    I:=1
0170    WHILE ENTRY$<>TRADE$(I) AND I<5 DO I:=I+1
0180    IF ENTRY$=TRADE$(I) THEN
0190      PRINT NAME$(I)," IS A(N) ",TRADE$(I)
0200    ELSE
0210      PRINT "WE HAVE NO ",ENTRY$," ON OUR LIST."
0220    ENDIF
0230    PRINT
0240    PRINT "MORE (Y/N)",
0250    INPUT ANSW$
0260 UNTIL ANSW$="N"
```

Test 22.1

BIOLOGY, GERMAN, INFORMATICS, and MUSIC   60, 15, 4

Test 22.2

Biology at basic level, German at advanced level, Music at advanced level.
1, 3   1, 2, 3, 4
1 – Music, 2 – Music, 3 – Informatics, 4 – German and Informatics

Test 22.3

3, True
ANIE BURTON'S OPTION:

BIOLOGY   AT LEVEL 1
GERMAN   AT LEVEL 2
INFORMATICS   AT LEVEL 2

(PRESS RETURN TO CONT.)

Test 22.4

0, 1   A Boolean variable
TRUE, FALSE, FALSE, TRUE, FALSE, FALSE, FALSE, FALSE,
FALSE, TRUE, FALSE, FALSE, FALSE

Test 23.1

"OPTIONS"   2   retrieved
The statement ends with the keyword READ
580, 600, 610   CLOSE

Test 23.2

MAX, NAME$(1), OPTION(1,1), OPTION(1,2), OPTION(1,3)
OPTION(1,4), NAME$(2), OPTION(2,1), OPTION(2,2),
OPTION(2,3), OPTION(2,4)

Test 23.3

NOT EOF(2)
A Boolean function that returns the value TRUE (=1) when the last element in the file
has been retrieved WHILE NOT EOF(3) DO

Test 23.4

OPTIONS   3   stored   730
CLOSE signs off all files that are opened
CLOSE FILE 3 only signs off the file opened as 3
10, PETER HARROW, 1, 2, 2, −1

Test 24.1

NAME$(1), OPTION(1,1), OPTION(1,2), OPTION(1,3), OPTION(1,4)
NAME$(7), OPTION(7,1), OPTION(7,2), OPTION(7,3), OPTION(7,4)
a record   its fields

```
0670 OPEN FILE 3,"ⴰ0:OPTIONS",WRITE
0680 WRITE FILE 3: MAX
0690 FOR I:=1 TO MAX DO WRITE FILE 3: NAME$(I)
0700 FOR I:=1 TO MAX DO
0710   FOR J:=1 TO 4 DO WRITE FILE 3: OPTION(I,J)
0720 NEXT I
0730 CLOSE
```

```
0570 OPEN FILE 3,"OPTIONS",READ
0580 READ FILE 3: MAX
0590 FOR I:=1 TO MAX DO READ FILE 3: NAME$(I)
0600 FOR I:=1 TO MAX DO
0610   FOR J:=1 TO 4 DO READ FILE 3: OPTION(I,J)
0620 NEXT I
0630 CLOSE
```

```
0670 OPEN FILE 2,"ⴰ0:NAMES",WRITE
0675 OPEN FILE 3,"ⴰ0:THE'OPTIONS",WRITE
0680 WRITE FILE 2: MAX
0690 FOR I:=1 TO MAX DO WRITE FILE 2: NAME$(I)
0700 FOR I:=1 TO MAX DO
0710   FOR J:=1 TO 4 DO WRITE FILE 3: OPTION(I,J)
0720 NEXT I
0730 CLOSE
```

```
0570 OPEN FILE 2,"NAMES",READ
0575 OPEN FILE 3,"THE'OPTIONS",READ
0580 READ FILE 2: MAX
0590 FOR I:=1 TO MAX DO READ FILE 2: NAME$(I)
0600 FOR I:=1 TO MAX DO
0610   FOR J:=1 TO 4 DO READ FILE 3: OPTION(I,J)
0620 NEXT I
0630 CLOSE
```

Index